SPREE KILLERS

Devastating Massacres by Unpredictable Gunmen

Nigel Cawthorne

MJF BOOKS
NEW YORK

Published by MJF Books
Fine Communications
322 Eighth Avenue
New York, NY 10001

Spree Killers
LC Control Number: 2011938933
ISBN-13: 978-1-60671-089-0
ISBN-10: 1-60671-089-3

Contents

SPREE KILLERS

Chapter 1

Opening Shots

On 16 October 1991 thirty-five-year-old George Hennard drove his truck through the plate glass window of Luby's restaurant in Killeen, Texas.

It was lunchtime in Killeen and the diner was crowded. 'Texas, this is what you have done for me,' Hennard shouted as he opened fire with two semi-automatic pistols.

The first victim was a man who had been hit by Hennard's truck as it ploughed through the window. He was trying to get up when Hennard advanced on him.

'Today is payday,' said Hennard as he shot him, point-blank. A child cried: 'He's just shot Daddy.'

Then Hennard turned on the lunch queue and started picking off the customers one by one. In his blue T-shirt and dark glasses, Hennard had the blank look of the robot from *The Terminator*, one witness said. It was plain that his intention was to kill everyone. When his guns were empty, he coolly changed the magazines and continued the slaughter. 'Was it worth it, people?' he taunted.

He was heard shouting 'You bitch' at one woman before pumping bullets into her defenceless body. Yet, he showed mercy to another woman. He told Anica McNeil, who was with her four-year-old daughter Lakeichha, to 'get your baby and get out of here'.

'Tell everybody, Bell County was bad today,' he shouted after them as they scuttled to safety. It was the only time he showed compassion. Anica's own mother, Olga Taylor, who was lunching with her daughter and granddaughter, was then coldly gunned down by the killer.

As the massacre continued, seventy-one-year-old retired builder Al Gratia, cowering behind a table, decided that someone had to do something. He got up and walked towards the crazed gunman. A bullet smashed into his chest. Gratia's daughter, Susanna, took the opportunity to escape. But his wife, sixty-seven-year-old Ursula, could not leave her dying husband. She too was killed.

Distraught women were hiding under the tables, screaming and crying. Another, hiding in the toilets with her daughter, dodged bullets ricocheting off the walls.

Some managed to escape, thanks to twenty-three-stone car mechanic Tommy Vaughn. He smashed through a back window and let fifteen people scramble to safety as the gunman bore down on them. But those who stayed behind in Luby's were tracked down and murdered by Hennard, who showed all the coolness of a professional executioner.

Fifty-six-year-old Aden McElveen had found himself trapped under Hennard's jeep as the gunman advanced on him. He was convinced he was going to be next. Then, ten minutes after the shooting had started, he heard sirens wailing outside. The police ordered Hennard to drop his gun. He refused. The police opened fire. In the ensuing gun battle, Hennard was hit twice. He staggered into the back of the restaurant and turned his gun on himself.

More than a hundred spent cartridges were found among the wreckage of the restaurant. It was a ten-minute orgy of killing that left twenty-three people dead, one of the worst mass shootings in America's history.

Rescuers found a scene of appalling horror. Bodies lay scattered among a battlefield of upturned tables. The wounded were helicoptered out to an army hospital at nearby Fort Hood.

'It was worse than anything I saw in Vietnam,' said one medic.

Twelve hours later one of the restaurant's employees, Mark Mathews, was found alive, hiding in a dishwasher.

According to some, the killings may have been motivated by a pathological hatred of women. George Hennard's mother was highly strung and domineering. He had often talked about killing her. According to a friend, he compared her to a snake, picturing her head on a rattlesnake's body. After the carnage and Hennard's death, all she was concerned about was her own tragedy – the death of her beautiful son. In a letter to Jill Fritz and Jana Jernignan – two sisters with whom Hennard was obsessed – he had referred to 'the abundance of evil women' and 'female vipers' in Killeen and his home-town of nearby Belton. Of the twenty-two victims, fourteen were women.

Spree killing at first seems to be a curiously twentieth-century phenomenon, in fact late twentieth century. And yet it can be argued that the great Mongol ruler, Genghis Khan, was a life long spree killer. Between 1206 and 1227 he killed an estimated twenty million people – that is nearly a million people a year and around one-tenth of the world's population at the time.

Born in 1162, he was the son of Yesugei, the chief of a small, impoverished Mongol clan. Orphaned at thirteen, the young

Genghis Khan – his name meant 'universal ruler' – began his career in casual butchery by murdering his brother over a fish. In the spring of 1206, at the age of thirty-three, Khan established his rule over all the Mongol tribes and, in 1211, he began his legendary conquest of imperial China, burning and pillaging every city and village that stood in his way. Three years after his invasion, the Mongol hordes controlled the entire country north of the Yellow River and Khan forced the Kin Tartars to deliver to him 500 young men and women, plus 3,000 livestock, as the price of peace.

To the west lay the kingdom of Khwarizm, the vast territory between the Ganges and the Tigris rivers, covering what today is India and Iran. Khan promised the ruler of Khwarizm, Shah Mohammed, peace and favourable trade agreements. But the Shah's answer was to murder a caravan of one hundred Mongol traders near the border town of Otrar. Khan sent more envoys, but they too were murdered. Khan did not try and make peace again. Between 1218 and 1222 Khan's armies swept through Khwarizm, killing 400,000 enemy troops who stood in their way. The governor of Otrar was executed by having molten metal poured in his eyes and ears. In Bukhara the defeated inhabitants were ordered outside the city walls and forced to watch their women being raped.

In May 1220 the Mongol armies reached as far west as Samarkind, where they defeated a garrison of 50,000 men. Most of the defenders were murdered for refusing to surrender their city. And at Termez every dead body was torn open by Khan's men after one old woman had swallowed her pearls to prevent them falling into the hands of the marauders. Genghis Khan took no prisoners. He would stack the severed heads of his victims in bloody pyramids.

Shah Mohammed retreated farther and farther west. Khan followed. He began killing all the men and taking all the women and children into slavery. While the carnage grew, Shah Mohammed died of pleurisy in a village on the Caspian Sea. But this was not the end of it. Khan continued to pursue the Shah's heir, Jelaleddin, cutting a wide swathe of death through Afghanistan, killing thousands of innocent people along the way. His bloody empire stretched from the China Sea to the Persian Gulf at the time of his death, of natural causes, at the age of sixty, in August 1227. But even death did not stop his killing. He ordered that if anyone gazed on his coffin, the next coffin would be theirs.

Throughout history there have been many other mass murderers. Many, like Khan, have their murderous desires cloaked in political ambitions. Vlad the Impaler – the historical Dracula – was a minor Romanian king who was hardened by the war fighting the Turks. He took tremendous pleasure from the senseless killing of large numbers of people. Woodcuts show the massed ranks of his victims impaled with spears through their stomachs. In fact he had his victims impaled with blunt wooden stakes stuck up their anus or vagina, so that their own weight made them sink slowly down on to it. Impalements were regular entertainment at meals. One Russian boyar who held his nose because the smell of blood put him off his food found himself impaled on a particularly long pole. After a quarrel with a Saxon merchant in 1460, Vlad held another mass impaling and burnt 400 apprentices alive. When Vlad discovered that there were a large number of beggars and sick people in his kingdom, he invited them to a banquet, locked them in and set fire to the building. Imprisoned in Hungary for twelve years and unable to satisfy his lust for killing, Vlad would torture animals to death. He was killed in battle against the Turks, in 1476, probably by his own men.

Gilles de Rais – the legendary Bluebeard – was a contemporary of Vlad the Impaler's. He was also a distinguished soldier who saw battle against the English at the side of Joan of Arc. After she was captured and killed, he returned to his estate, where he kidnapped, tortured and killed perhaps as many as 140 children. He would lure his victims to his castle and sodomise them – both male and female – while strangling them or cutting off their heads. He also enjoyed disembowelling his victims and masturbating over their entrails. Some fifty dismembered bodies were found in a disused tower in his castle when he was arrested.

Other hardened soldiers in history have committed huge and senseless atrocities. Russia's warrior-tsar Ivan the Terrible had 4,000 people tortured and killed when he suspected that the citizens of Novgorod were planning to rebel. However, it was not until the twentieth century that private individuals took up arms in their own war on the world.

Chapter 2

The Outsiders

German-American Carl Panzram dedicated himself to a thirty-year campaign of motiveless mayhem and slaughter in the early years of the twentieth century. Born in 1891 to a family of immigrant Prussian farmers in Warren, Minnesota, Panzram became a criminal as a young boy. His father deserted the family soon after his birth and his mother could not control him. When he was just eight years old, in 1899, Panzram was brought before a juvenile court for being drunk and disorderly. Then, after burgling the house of a well-to-do neighbour, he was sent to Minnesota State Training School in Red Wing. The discipline was rigid, if not sadistic. Panzram burned the place down.

Released in 1906, he began his war against the world in earnest. He started in the American West, committing a series of robberies and assaults. Travelling the country, he was raped by four hoboes. This gave him a new mode of revenge. 'Whenever I met a hobo who wasn't too rusty looking,' he wrote later in his autobiography, 'I would make him raise his hands and drop his pants. I wasn't very particular either. I rode them old and young, tall and short, white and black.' Finding himself in Montana State Reformatory, he quickly escaped. Over the next couple of months he robbed and burnt down several churches. Then he joined the army, only to be court-martialled on 20 April 1907 for insubordination and pilfering US government property. Three years at Fort Leavenworth, breaking rocks under the blistering Kansas sun, honed his meanness to a razor edge.

Later he returned to the States, moving up through California and the Pacific Northwest. He left a trail of murder, robbery, assault and rape. Totting up his score, he claimed to have killed twenty-one people, committed thousands of burglaries, robberies, larcenies and arson, and sodomised more than a thousand men.

Arrested in Chinook, Montana, for burglary, he was sentenced to a year in prison. He escaped after eight months. A year later, Panzram was arrested again, this time under the alias 'Jeff Rhoades', and given a two-year sentence. Paroled in 1914, he went straight back to crime. In Astoria, Oregon, he was arrested for burglary and offered a minimal sentence if he would reveal the whereabouts of the goods he had stolen. He kept his side of the bargain but, in exchange, he was sentenced to seven years. Outraged at this injustice, Panzram escaped from his cell and wrecked the jail. The guards beat him up and sent him to Salem correctional facility, the toughest prison in the state. Almost as soon as he arrived there he threw the contents of a chamber-pot in a guard's face. He was beaten unconscious and chained to the floor of a darkened cell for thirty days. He spent his time screaming defiance. When he was let out into the body of the prison again, he helped another prisoner escape. In the hunt, the warden was shot dead. The new warden was even tougher, but Panzram burned down the prison workshop and a flax mill. He went berserk with an axe and incited a prison revolt – for which he was given another seven years.

The next warden was an idealist who believed that Panzram might respond to kindness. When Panzram was caught trying to escape, the warden told him that, according to reports, he was the 'meanest and most cowardly degenerate' the prison authorities had ever seen. Panzram agreed. But instead of punishing him, the warden let him out of the prison, provided he returned that evening. Panzram left with no intention of going back, but that evening he did return. The liberal regime continued and Panzram responded – until one night he got drunk with a pretty nurse. He absconded, only to be recaptured after a gun-battle. He was returned to a punishment cell, where he was fed on a diet of bread and water, beaten and sprayed with a fire-hose. But, ever resourceful, Panzram constructed his own tools and hacked his way out of the prison in May 1918.

He headed east, stealing $1,200 from a hotel in Maryland, and signed on a merchant ship bound for South America. He jumped ship in Peru, where he worked in a copper mine. In Chile, he became a foreman for an oil company but, for no apparent reason, set fire to an oil rig. Back in the US, he stole $7,000 from a jewellery shop and $40,000 in jewels and liberty bonds from the home of the former president William Howard Taft in New Haven. With the money he bought a yacht and hired sailors to help him refit it. He raped them, shot them and dropped their bodies in the sea, killing ten in all.

Panzram served a six-month jail sentence in Bridgeport for petty theft before being arrested again for inciting a riot during a labour dispute. Jumping bail, he headed for West Africa, where he continued his murder sprees. He was approached by a twelve-year-old boy, begging. 'He was looking for something. He found it too,' wrote Panzram. 'First I committed sodomy on him and then killed him.' He smashed the boy's head in with a rock. 'His brains were coming out of his ears when I left him and he will never be deader.'

Panzram decided to go crocodile hunting. He hired six black porters to guide him through the backwaters. He shot them in the back and fed them to the crocodiles. Back in America, he raped and killed three more boys. In June 1923, while working as night watchman for the New Haven Yacht Club, he stole a boat. He killed a man who clambered aboard and tossed the body into Kingston Bay in New York. Eventually he was caught attempting to rob an express office in Larchmont, New York, and sentenced to five years in Sing Sing But the guards there were unable to handle him and he was sent to Clinton Prison in Dannemora, considered to be the end of the line for hard cases. There he received savage beatings and smashed his leg after falling from a high gallery. He spent his days plotting revenge against the whole human race. He planned to blow up a railway tunnel with a train in it, poison a whole city by putting arsenic in the water supply and start a war between Britain and America by blowing up a British battleship in American waters.

When he tried to escape he was tortured by having his hands tied behind his back then being suspended from a beam with the rope. He could endure this for twelve hours on end, screaming and cursing his mother for bringing him into the world. Despite his horrendous treatment, one of the guards, Henry Lesser, was sympathetic and persuaded Panzram to write his autobiography. In it Panzram makes no excuses for himself. He says that he had broken every law of God and man – and if there had been more laws he would have broken them also.

Released yet again in 1928, Panzram hit the Washington-Baltimore area like a one-man crime wave, committing eleven robberies and one murder, and was soon arrested again. At his trial, he told the jury: 'While you were trying me here, I was trying all of you. I have found you guilty. Some of you I have already executed.

If I live, I'll execute some more of you. I hate the whole human race.' The judge sentenced him to twenty-five years in jail. 'Visit me,' Panzram snapped back.

At Leavenworth Panzram told his guards: 'I'll kill the first man that bothers me.' True to his word, he killed mild-mannered civilian prison laundry supervisor Robert G. Warnke with an iron bar. After a hasty trial Panzram was sentenced to hang. Meanwhile Lesser had been showing Panzram's autobiography around the literary establishment, including legendary newspaperman H. L. Mencken. People were impressed. But when Panzram heard that they might start a movement to get him reprieved, he protested: 'I would not reform if the front gate was opened right now and I was given a million dollars when I stepped out. I have no desire to do good or become good.'

The Society for the Abolition of Capital Punishment also stepped in. He told them to forget it. Hanging would be a 'real pleasure and a big relief,' he said. 'The only thanks you or your kind will ever get from me for your efforts is that I wish you all had one neck and I had my hands on it. I believe that the only way to reform people is to kill them. My motto is: "Rob 'em all, rape 'em all and kill 'em all."' He even turned on Henry Lesser in the end. In his last letter Panzram wrote: 'What gets me is how in the heck any man of your intelligence and ability, knowing as much about me as you do, can still be friendly towards a thing like me when I even despise and detest my own self.'

The end could not come soon enough for Carl Panzram. He raced towards the gallows on 11 September 1930. When the hangman asked him if he had any last words, Panzram said: 'Yes, hurry it up, you Hoosier bastard. I could hang a dozen men while you're fooling around.'

While Panzram was on his lifelong crusade of robbing, raping and murdering, back in Germany a mild-mannered school teacher named Wagner von Degerloch killed fourteen and severely injured twelve more in a single night. Born in 1874, in the village of Eglosheim near Ludwigsburg, Wagner was the son of a peasant – a drunkard and a braggart – who died when Wagner was two. His mother, allegedly a promiscuous woman, married again, but divorced her new husband when Wagner was seven. In the village Wagner, a sensitive boy, was taunted as the 'widow's boy' and began to suffer from nightmares and bouts of suicidal depression.

An intelligent boy, he did well at school. He became a schoolmaster himself, but nursed ambitions to become a playwright. While living and working in a village called Mühlhausen, Wagner found lodgings in an inn. After a brief affair with him, the landlord's daughter fell pregnant. Wagner was horrified. He felt that the girl was socially beneath him, little more than a servant. But when the affair became public, he married her out of honour.

Following the scandal, Wagner was transferred from prosperous middle-class Mühlhausen to a more lowly post in the impoverished district of Radelstetten. There his wife gave birth to four more children, though the last died while still a baby.

Wagner continued to write, but none of his work was ever performed. He had it published at his own expense. No one took any notice. Feeling himself a failure, he toyed with the idea of suicide, but did not have the courage to go through with it. Then in 1906 he began to plot his revenge. In the woods around Radelstetten he practised marksmanship and began drafting a detailed plan of action.

Throughout, he maintained the facade of the model citizen, although in Radelstetten he was considered rather eccentric. He always dressed extremely formally and insisted on speaking High German while those around him, whatever their social background, spoke the local dialect. But his record as a schoolmaster was excellent and in 1912 he was promoted to a position in Stuttgart. There, after a glass or two of beer, he would still boast of his literary prowess. But nothing ever came of it.

On the night of 4 September 1913, the citizens of Mühlhausen were awoken by several large fires. As they ran into the street, they were shot at by a masked man armed with two pistols. He killed eight men and a girl, wounding twelve more, before he was beaten unconscious by a mob. The innkeeper identified him as his brother-in-law, the mild-mannered school teacher Wagner. Earlier he had killed his wife and their four children – out of pity, he said.

When he was overpowered Wagner still had 198 bullets in his possession. His plan was to murder the entire population of Mühlhausen, then go back to Eglosheim, kill his brother and his family, burn down his brother's house and the house he himself had been born in, then go to the royal castle in Ludwigsburg, overpower the guard, set the castle on fire and die by flinging himself from the battlements into the flames below.

Wagner was declared insane and confined to a lunatic asylum. He continued to insist that he was sane and demanded to be executed. In the asylum he admitted to homosexual activities shortly before he was married. He also exhibited feelings of guilt over what he considered excessive masturbation. People, he felt sure, gossiped about his sexual practices. To protect himself from their slander, he had always carried a loaded pistol.

Wagner eventually settled into asylum life and used his time to forward his literary career. However, his plays were never performed and his only readers were psychiatrists who studied them as symptoms rather than as works of art. Wagner was proud of the fact that he was the first inmate of his asylum to join the Nazi Party and he turned his literary talents to producing propaganda. He died of pneumonia in 1938.

Although in his later years Wagner stopped writing plays he did accuse others of stealing his ideas. He even believed that the plot for the 1907 version of *Ben-Hur* was stolen from one of his dramas. But his idea for randomly murdering innocent people was certainly pinched, and, in the cafes and salons of Paris, intellectuals began giving such murderous actions a spurious pretext. Disillusioned by the mass slaughter of World War One, the Dadaists, Surrealists and other artistic movements found themselves cut off from the individual 'bourgeois' morality. Surrealist poet André Breton speculated on the philosophical significance of taking a machine gun and mowing down innocent people. Breton was, perhaps, the intellectual precursor of the modern spree killer; he raised the concept of spree killing as an artistic act.

While Breton was philosophising, Hungarian businessman Sylvestre Matuschka was putting the theory of mass murder into practice. After World War One his company prospered, but Matuschka was accused of fraud. Although he was acquitted, he sold his businesses in Budapest and started afresh in Vienna. It was there that he began to experiment with causing train crashes. His first attempt was on 1 January 1931, when he tried unsuccessfully to derail the Vienna to Passat express near Asbach. Then on 8 August he managed to overturn several coaches at Juelerboy in Hungary. They rolled down an embankment, injuring seventy-five people. But his greatest success came on 12 September 1932. The crowded Budapest to Vienna express was crossing a viaduct at Bia-Torbagy when Matuschka set off an explosion which blew out part of the track. The train plunged from the elevated track, killing twenty-two people – some literally blown to pieces. As the dust settled, Matuschka smeared blood on his face and lay down among the victims.

A journalist covering the train crash grew suspicious, though, when he noticed that Matuschka's clothes seemed well-kempt compared to those of the other victims. None of the other passengers could remember seeing him on the train and his ticket had not been punched. Nevertheless, Matuschka tried to sue Hungarian Railways over his feigned injuries. They grew suspicious and when the police were sent to search his house, they found plans for similar train disasters in France, Italy and Holland. Matuschka was arrested and soon confessed. At his trial it was claimed that train crashes sexually excited Matuschka and that witnessing them was the only way he could achieve orgasm. Matuschka himself blamed a hypnotist whom he had met at a country fair and an invisible spirit named Leo. After a second trail Matuschka was found guilty and sentenced to life imprisonment. During World War Two, though, he was released by the Soviets who used him as a demolition expert. He reappeared in 1953 in the Korean War as head of a unit that specialised in blowing up trains.

While World War Two was still raging, another French intellectual lent new insight into the philosophical stance of the spree killer. Albert Camus, a leading figure in the French resistance, wrote in 1942 a novel called L'Étranger. Published in America as The Stranger and in Britain in 1946 as The Outsider, it was hailed as a brilliant depiction of twentieth-century alienation and as one of the first expositions of the post-war philosophy of existentialism. In the novel the protagonist – this was the age of the anti-hero – kills an Arab for no discernible reason, but is condemned to death more because he refuses to say what he genuinely feels and refuses to conform to society's demands. Existentialism rejected objective reality and the conformity of society, and held that each person must discover values for themselves through action and living each moment to the full.

Chapter 3

Veterans

Although many spree killers have been in the armed forces – or have had delusions about being in them – few of them are actually combat veterans. One such killer was Howard Unruh. A German-American, Howard Unruh was born in 1921 in East Camden, on the Delaware River in New Jersey. The only child of hard-working, religious parents, he shunned the noisy games of his boisterous schoolmates, preferring to sit quietly reading the Bible on his own. He was deeply attached to his mother, Freda, who worked in a local soap factory.

Unruh graduated from high school and planned to go on to college to study pharmacy. But World War Two intervened. He was called up and willingly enlisted in the army. Surprisingly he fitted in well, though he wrote long letters home to his mother every day. When he was given a gun, it became his obsession. Early in training he became a sharpshooter.

While other GIs were out drinking, Unruh would stay in the barracks and sit quietly on his bunk reading the Bible or stripping down his rifle, lovingly cleaning it, greasing it and reassembling it. He would even offer to clean other men's rifles for them. During the Italian campaign, Unruh distinguished himself as a tank gunner. He moved on into France and fought in the Battle of the Bulge. Throughout the war Unruh kept a diary. One day a fellow soldier took a sly look at it. He was horrified. The diary listed every German Unruh had killed, giving date, time, place and how the body looked in death.

At the end of the war Unruh was honourably discharged with several citations for bravery under fire. He resumed his plan to become a pharmacist, took a high-school refresher course and enrolled at Temple University in Philadelphia.

He also enrolled in a Bible class, where he met a girl and began dating her. The relationship led nowhere though. His feelings for his fellow student could not rival his love of guns.

He bought a number of weapons – a 9 mm German Luger pistol with several clips, several other pistols with thousands of rounds of ammunition, a hunting knife with a nine-inch blade and a machete honed to a razor sharp edge. These were kept locked in his bedroom. Not even his parents were allowed to enter. In the basement he set up a firing range, where he practised daily.

After ditching his girlfriend so he could spend more time practising, he became withdrawn, then increasingly paranoid. He began to keep a diary, detailing the slights and imagined slights he had suffered at the hands of others. His next-door neighbours, the Cohen family, were his chief target. When they chided him for taking a short cut through their back garden or their twelve-year-old son made too much noise, Unruh's diary spoke of 'retaliation' against them. His diary used the word 'retaliation' 180 times.

Unruh erected a high wooden fence around the rear of the house to block out the world he hated. His father helped him, thinking it might calm his increasingly disturbed son. When it was finished, Unruh was triumphant. But on the afternoon of 6 September 1949 he returned home to find the gate missing, leaving a gaping hole in the fence. Unruh concluded that it had been taken by one of his neighbours. He lay on his bed fully clothed, staring at the ceiling and plotting his revenge.

At 8 a.m. Unruh went downstairs for breakfast. His mother had prepared cereal and eggs for him. He sat at the breakfast table but would not eat or speak and there was a wild look in his eyes. Suddenly he shot back his chair and ran from the room. His mother followed him to his room, where he threatened her with a heavy wrench. Terrified, she ran to a neighbour's house.

Unruh loaded his Luger and stuffed another pistol into his pocket. He loaded himself up with ammunition and grabbed his hunting knife. At 9.20 a.m., wearing his best tropical worsted suit, the twenty-eight-year-old veteran went out through the gap in the back fence, on to the street.

He walked deliberately to a delivery truck parked two blocks away, thrust his gun through the window and pulled the trigger. The driver, thirty-three year-old Roxy DiMarco, hurled himself backwards from his seat as the bullet whizzed past the steering wheel. Unruh shrugged and moved on.

A little way down the street was a shoe repair shop run by John Pilarchik, who had known Unruh since he was a boy. Pilarchik was on his knees, nailing the heel on a shoe. Unruh walked to within three feet of him. When Pilarchik looked up, Unruh shot him in the chest. Without a word he turned and strode on to Clark Hoover's barber's next door. Orris 'Brux' Smith, a six-year-old boy, was perched on a white, painted carousel horse with a barber's bib around his neck. Clark Hoover was cutting his blonde hair, while Brux's mother, forty-two-year-old Mrs Edwina Smith, and his eleven-year-old sister, Norma, sat watching.

Another patron witnessed the hollow-cheeked Unruh with his brown crew-cut hair, walk into the barber's. 'I've got something for you, Clarkie,' Unruh said to Clark Hoover, who had known him since he was a child. Unruh walked up to the boy, put the Luger to his chest and fired, before he gunned down the thirty-three-year-old barber with a second shot. Ignoring the screams of the child's mother and sister, Unruh then stepped quietly back out on to the sunlit street.

Local restaurant owner Dominick Latela ran to the barber's, picked up the bleeding boy and raced to Cooper Hospital in a futile rescue dash. The child was dead.

In annoyance, Unruh sent a volley of bullets through the door of Dominick Latela's restaurant, just missing Latela's wife, Dora, and six-year-old daughter who were taking cover behind the counter.

Unruh headed on to the drugstore owned by his hated neighbour Maurice Cohen. On the way he bumped into the family insurance agent, forty-five-year-old James Hutton. Hutton said hello. Unruh's savage reply was two 9 mm slugs from his Luger – one in the head, one in the body – killing the insurance agent instantly. Unruh later told the police that he had politely asked Hutton to get out of his way, but Hutton had not moved fast enough.

The shots alerted Maurice Cohen who ran up the stairs into the stockroom above his store to warn his wife Rose, his mother Minnie and his son Charles. Sliding a fresh clip into his Luger, Unruh bounded up the stairs after him. The stock-room was open and Unruh saw thirty-eight-year-old Rose Cohen as she took cover in a cupboard. Unruh put a bullet through the cupboard door. The weight of her body pushed the door open and she fell sprawling across the floor. She was still moaning when Unruh put another shot through her head.

Hiding in another cupboard in the stock-room was the Cohens' son, but Unruh was distracted by a noise from the adjoining office.

In it he found sixty-three-year-old Minnie Cohen, phone in hand, dialling the police. Two shots ended the call, and her life.

As she fell, the receiver dropped from Minnie Cohen's hand with a loud thud. Then there was silence, broken only by a soft scraping sound. It came from above. In an effort to escape, Maurice Cohen was crawling across the pitched porch roof. Unruh climbed out of the window and fired twice, hitting Cohen in the back. Cohen lost his grip and rolled off the roof, crashing to the sidewalk below. Unruh put another bullet through his head, just to make sure. By the time Unruh walked back out on to the pavement, twelve-year-old Charles Cohen was up on the roof, screaming hysterically. Unruh turned and walked away. He had no quarrel with the boy.

He had no quarrel either with TV repairman Alvin Day from nearby Mantua who was driving up the street. But Unruh walked to the car window and shot once with deadly accuracy. Another passing motorist, Charles Petersen, the eighteen-year-old son of a local fire man, stopped. He and two teenage friends got out of the car to tend the dying James Hutton. Unruh fired several times, wounding Petersen in the legs. The other two ran off unharmed.

Unruh reloaded again and started hunting more strangers. At the end of the street a coupé was waiting at a stop light. Unruh walked over to it and leaned in the open window. The driver, a thirty-seven-year-old Mrs Helen Wilson, found herself staring down the barrel of a loaded pistol. Unruh pulled the trigger. Mrs Wilson died instantly. Unruh went on to pick off the passengers one by one. In the back of the car were Mrs Wilson's elderly mother, sixty-eight-year-old Mrs Emma Matlack of Pennsauken, who was killed outright, and her ten-year-old grandson John Wilson, who was fatally wounded.

A long shot wounded a truck driver climbing from his cab in the next block. Unruh then headed for a tavern owned by Frank Engel.

The customers made a concerted rush for the rear as a rain of bullets tore through the panelling of the front door. Engel went upstairs to get his .38 revolver. From a second-storey window he took a pot-shot at Unruh, wounding him in the leg. But Unruh took no notice and continued about his murderous business.

By now the local residents were alerted. Shopkeepers and restaurant owners started barricading their doors. Unruh tried firing a few shots through the door of a supermarket, but the lock held. Next door, though, the tailor's shop was open. The tailor, Thomas Zegrino, was away, but in the kitchen at the back, Unruh found the owner's wife, Mrs Helga Zegrino. The twenty-eight-year-old woman fell to her knees and begged for her life. Unruh shot her twice.

Back on the street Unruh spotted a two-year-old boy, Tommy Hamilton, watching his murderous progress from a window. A single shot smashed the window and hit the child between the eyes, killing him instantly.

Then Unruh saw a small yellow house with its door slightly ajar. Inside he found a woman, Mrs Madeline Harris, and her two sons cowering in a kitchen at the back. The older boy flung himself at the gunman. Unruh loosed off two shots, one hitting the boy in the arm, the other wounding Mrs Harris in the shoulder. The younger child escaped unscathed.

Unruh was now out of ammunition. As he turned to walk back home, he could hear police sirens wailing in the distance. Soon the house was surrounded. Machine-gun rounds came pouring through the window. In the middle of the mayhem the telephone rang. Unruh picked it up. It was local newspaper reporter Philip Buxton.

'I'm a friend,' said Buxton. 'How many have you killed?'

'I don't know yet,' said Unruh in a matter-of-fact voice, 'but it looks like a pretty good score.'

Buxton asked him why he was killing people.

'I don't know,' Unruh replied. 'I can't answer that yet – I'm too busy. I'll have to talk to you later.' He put the phone down.

Tear-gas canisters were then being lobbed through the windows. The choking fumes drove Unruh downstairs. A few minutes later he laid down his weapons, opened the back door and came out with his hands up. The guns of fifty police marksmen were trained on him.

Police officers scrambled forward and handcuffed him. As he was hurried off, one cop asked him: 'What's the matter with you? Are you a psycho?'

'I'm no psycho,' said Unruh, apparently unconcerned. 'I have a good mind.'

Unruh never stood trial. He was declared incurably insane and committed to New Jersey State Mental Hospital. He never expressed the slightest remorse for the victims of his murderous spree. He had only one regret – that there were so few. 'I'd have killed a thousand if I'd had enough bullets,' he said years later. However, his conscience was troubled by the fact that he had threatened his mother with a wrench.

Another veteran of World War Two was Frank Kulak, a big man and a good soldier. He was five foot eleven and weighed fifteen stone. At sixteen he lied about his age to enlist in the Marines. He saw action against the Japanese in the bitter fighting on Okinawa, one of the bloodiest battles of the Pacific war. Later he re-enlisted to fight the Communists in Korea. When he returned to his home in Chicago's South Side in 1952, he had a Purple Heart and a right hand with only two fingers on it. The other three had been lost to enemy artillery. But he was, perhaps, more seriously scarred internally by the violence he had seen.

Kulak's missing fingers made it impossible for him to hold down a regular job. Over the years he soured into the neighbourhood crank who yelled at children and made them cry. Unmarried, he lived with his sister in a seven-room flat on the third floor of a large house. Brooding in the apartment, he constantly relived the nightmares of combat. 'He was always talking about the war,' recalled Susan Kulak, a niece who was nineteen when Frank Kulak finally exploded. 'He was always talking about the Japs.' But Kulak's problem went a lot further than talking.

The beginning of the Vietnam War disturbed Kulak deeply. His ugly memories of war were being made terribly real again. And he could not get away from it. News of the war filled every newspaper and television screen. In 1969, seeking, in his own warped way, to bring the reality of war home to the American public, Kulak began making bombs and setting them off around the neighbourhood. The campaign gathered momentum and culminated with a blast at a local department store.

The Chicago bomb-squad's investigation led them to Kulak. When two officers – Sergeant James Schaffer, forty-eight, and Detective Jerome A. Stubig, forty – arrived at Kulak's apartment, Kulak reacted like he was back in a foxhole. Inside the apartment he had a massive arsenal – two carbines, an M1 rifle, two automatic pistols, two twelve-bore shotguns, 2,000 rounds of ammunition, hand grenades and a launcher, 25 lbs of gunpowder, chemical explosives and an assortment of home-made bombs.

In Kulak's eyes the knock on the door meant the enemy was now massing for attack. The ex-Marine knew how to deal with this situation. He tossed a grenade out of the window at the two officers standing on the wooden stairs that led up to the third floor. The stairs splintered and the two men fell over twenty feet to the ground. Then

Kulak emptied his carbine into their twisted bodies. Satisfied they were dead, he quickly prepared for a fresh assault. He set up weapons at each of the apartment windows and began heaving bombs at the street below. Then he started firing randomly at pedestrians who scrambled for cover.

The five other tenants in the building cowered in the basement and the school children huddled under their desks at Sacred Heart Parochial School across the road. Meanwhile, Kulak traded fire with a force of over one hundred policemen outside. Special sharpshooters were brought in, but ex-Marine Kulak was too good for them. They could not pin him down.

The police used bullhorns to plead with Kulak to come down. Relatives were brought in. Kulak's fifty-one-year-old brother Harold shouted: 'Frank, Frank, this isn't a war zone. The war is over. We have a Marine ambulance here for you.'

Kulak's sister, Mrs Katherine Potts, made the same appeal. But for Frank Kulak the war was still on. His sister's plea was answered with another rifle shot.

The siege continued for another three hours until the cops stopped firing and sent a squad of men creeping into the building. From a sheltered position on the second floor Police Deputy Superintendent James Rochford managed to talk to the gunman. Three hours later, at 8.45 p.m., Kulak appeared at the back window. Instantly a hundred guns were trained on his head and chest. He stood in the window for a while, then sat down on the window-sill. Slowly running his disfigured hand through his Marine-style crew cut, he began to cry. Twenty minutes later he surrendered. Four were dead; twenty wounded.

The next day, his forty-second birthday, Frank Kulak was arraigned on two murder charges. He confessed to the bombings, claiming that his self-appointed mission was to show people 'what the Vietnam War was like'. He had attacked the department store to blow up war toys in the toy department. Kulak also explained that he was trying to alert the American people to the threat of Chinese Communism.

Kulak was found unfit to stand trial. He was remanded to the custody of doctors at the psychiatry facility in the state prison at Chester, Illinois. But Illinois law makes prisoners incarcerated in mental institutions eligible for release after the same period that would make them eligible for parole, if they were serving a regular sentence. In January 1981, after he had served eleven years at Chester, Kulak was brought back to Chicago where he appeared in the criminal court before Judge Frank B. Machala. Machala refused to dismiss the charges against Kulak – and Kulak was returned to the jail at Chester.

The lone figure came running across the leafy square of Harrisonville, Missouri. The M1 carbine in his hands was blazing. Two policemen fell dead in front of the bank. Inside, two clerks were wounded. The gunman raced on down the street, killing the laundry delivery man in his tracks. He put two more shots through the window of the sheriff's office, wounding Sheriff Bill Gough. Then, on the steps of the Harrisonville Retirement Home, the gunman, twenty-four-year-old Charles Simpson stopped. He put the muzzle of the rifle into his mouth and pulled the trigger one last time.

The massacre on the small town square of Harrisonville that spring afternoon was not the work of a brooding loner. Simpson was one of a group of nine long-haired young men who spent their time hanging out in the town square – under the hostile glare of the short-haired farmers who made up much of the town's population of 5,000. But Simpson and his friends were no gypsy band of hippies who had descended on the town from outside. They were local boys, born and raised in the area. They still lived with their parents. But most of them had been away, in the army, in Vietnam. Simpson himself had failed the physical. Chronic asthma had kept him out of the service. It was his greatest disappointment.

By 1972 America's attitude to the Vietnam War had changed radically. Their fighting men were no longer considered heroes. Vietnam veterans could not find jobs. They became outcasts, spat upon, ostracised.

The group now drew unemployment benefit, which was sin enough to the hard-working residents of Harrisonville. And they flaunted their idleness by hanging out in the town square. Although their hair was barely down to their collars, they seemed to be the very personification of the radical youth that the townsfolk had heard so much about.

'The people in this town were scared,' said Police Chief William H. Davis Jr. 'I just can't understand these kids' thinkin' – sittin' on their can, doin' nothin'. If they had just acted decent from the start, and had haircuts and shaves…' Davis's men had the group under surveillance.

'These kids were interfering with the public,' the mayor of Harrisonville, M. O. Raine said. 'They'd stare at the people and scare them to death.'

The town was swept with wild rumours about sexual goings-on in the town square. Complaints mounted, particularly from women. Concerned citizens accused the group of being revolutionaries and threatened them, sometimes with guns. The town council passed a bylaw banning gatherings of more than three people in the town square. Simpson's group complained that this bylaw was enforced only against them.

The night before the shootings, the group were arrested for loitering. Simpson had been out of town, but when he returned in the morning he took his entire life savings – $1,800 – and bailed out his friends. That afternoon he, and three innocent people, lay dead.

Simpson's buddies carried his coffin to the grave three days later and raised a clenched fist salute in tribute to their fallen comrade. But they were at a loss to explain Simpson's crack-up.

'He was no more upset about the arrests than we were,' said group-member John Risner, twenty-three, who had been target shooting with Simpson shortly before he went berserk.

Simpson was a high-school drop-out who lived with his father in a rooming-house twenty miles from town. One friend described him as calm and cool; showing no sign of the violence that plainly lurked inside him. But another friend said that Simpson had been under stress for some months before the fatal incident.

'He was up at the square and he looked like he didn't feel well,' high-school chum Mike Young recalled. 'I asked him how he was, and he said, "I'm sick of the world, but it's nothing serious." Then I noticed he was crying.'

Some in Harrisonville reacted to the killing with renewed anger. But four days after the shootings, half a dozen of the town's more respectable citizens had a meeting with Simpson's long-haired friends in the basement of a local Methodist church. These soon became weekly events and attendance climbed. The town council also called in two specialists in community relations from nearby Kansas City. John Risner later reported that communication between the generations in Harrisonville was improving, making Charlie Simpson one of the only spree killers to leave behind him any positive legacy.

Chapter 4

Rebel Without a Cause

Born on 24 November 1938 in a poor quarter of Lincoln, Nebraska, Charles Starkweather was the third of eight children – seven boys and a girl. His father, Guy Starkweather, was a convivial man who liked a drink. A handyman and a carpenter, he suffered from a weak back and arthritis, and could not always work. His wife, Helen, a slight, stoical woman, worked as a waitress and, after 1946, became practically the sole provider for her large family.

Although the Starkweathers knew little of their roots, the first Starkweather had left the old world in the seventeenth century, sailing from the Isle of Man in 1640. The name was well known across the mid-West. There was even a small town called Starkweather in North Dakota. Somehow the name Starkweather seemed eerily redolent of the wind sweeping the Great Plains.

Charles Starkweather had only happy memories of his first six years, which he spent playing with his two elder brothers, Rodney and Leonard, helping around the house with his mother and going fishing with his dad. But all that changed in 1944 on his first day at school. When they enrolled at Saratoga Elementary School, all the children were supposed to stand up and make a speech. When it came to Charlie's turn, his classmates spotted his slight speech impediment and began to laugh. Starkweather broke down in confusion. He never forgot that humiliation.

Starkweather soon gained the impression that the teacher was picking on him, and he believed that the other children were ridiculing him because of his short bow-legs and distinctive red hair. Later, from his condemned cell, he wrote: 'It seems as though I could see my heart before my eyes, turning dark black with hate of rages.' On his second day at school he got into a fight, which he found relieved his aggression. He claimed to have been in a fight almost every day during his school life, though his teachers remembered little of this.

Despite his high IQ, Starkweather was treated throughout his school career as a slow learner. It was only when his eyes were tested at age fifteen that it was discovered he could barely see the blackboard from his place at the back of the class. He was practically blind beyond twenty feet.

Starkweather felt that life had short-changed him. He was short, short-tempered, short-sighted and short on education. He was forced, by poverty, to wear second-hand clothes. Classmates called him 'Little Red' and he remembered every perceived slight. It made him as hard as nails.

Starkweather's reputation as a fighter spread throughout Lincoln and toughs from all over the city came to take him on. He said later that it was the beginning of his rebellion against the whole world, his only response to being made fun of. At the age of fifteen, he was challenged by Bob von Busch. They fought each other to a standstill. Afterwards they became firm friends. Von Busch was one of the few people who saw the amusing and generous side to Starkweather's nature. The rest of the world saw barely repressed hostility.

Starkweather dropped out of Irving Junior High School in 1954, when he was just sixteen years old. He took a menial job in a newspaper warehouse. His boss treated him as if he was mentally retarded and he hated it.

Although Starkweather continued to love and respect his mother, his relationship with his father sometimes degenerated into open hostility. In 1955 they had a fight and Starkweather went to stay with Bob von Busch and his father. The two teenagers were car fanatics. They spent a lot of their spare time at Capital Beach, the local race-car track. Starkweather raced hot rods there and participated in demolition derbies. The two boys also took to joyriding in stolen cars, occasionally stripping them down for spare parts.

When von Busch started dating Barbara Fugate, Starkweather began to see less of him. Then, in the early summer of 1956, Bob took Charlie to a drive-in movie on a double date with Barbara and her younger sister Caril. Caril Fugate was just thirteen years old, though she could easily pass for eighteen. She and Barbara were the daughters of Velda and William Fugate, a drunkard and a convicted peeping Tom. The couple had divorced in 1951 and Fugate later died in jail. Velda married again and the family lived at 924 Belmont Avenue, an unpaved road in the poor quarter of Lincoln.

Caril Fugate seemed the perfect mate for the moody Charlie Starkweather. Although she was short – five foot one – she was self-confident and most people found her opinionated and rebellious. She often wore a man's shirt with the sleeves rolled up, blue jeans and boots. Like Starkweather, she did badly at school. Considered slow, she had little experience of life. She had left Lincoln only once, for a holiday in Nebraska's Sand Hill.

To the girls of Lincoln, Charles Starkweather did not seem like much of a catch. He had never had a proper girlfriend before. He was just five foot five, with bow legs, a pug face and the reputation of a hoodlum. But Fugate liked him. His tough, rebel image appealed to her. She did not care about his working-class origins or his dead-end job. Far more fascinating were the stories he told, his fantasies about being a cowboy or the fastest hot-rod driver in town. What's more, with his slicked back hair and cigarette dangling from his lips, he thought he looked like the latest teenage idol, James Dean, whom Starkweather consciously modelled himself on.

Starkweather liked Fugate too. He liked the way she wore make-up and swore. After their first date, Fugate went out with another local boy. Starkweather tracked him down and threatened to kill him if he saw Fugate again.

Caril Fugate and Charles Starkweather started going steady. It made Starkweather feel good to be wanted. With Fugate, he forgot about his problems. They lived in a world of their own. He quit his job at the warehouse. He had been working part-time as a garbage collector with his brother Rodney since he was thirteen. Now he worked the garbage trucks full-time. He earned a pittance – just forty-two dollars a week – but he got off work early enough to meet Fugate from school.

Fugate's mother and stepfather were against the match. They thought that eighteen-year-old Starkweather was too old for Fugate – and they thought that he was leading their daughter astray. Starkweather's parents were no more favourable. Starkweather's father, who co-owned Starkweather's pale blue '49 Ford sedan, banned Fugate – whom Starkweather had taught to drive – from taking the wheel. In the late summer of 1957, however, Fugate was involved in a minor accident with the car. Starkweather's father hit his son so hard that he knocked him through a window.

Starkweather left home for good. He moved in with Bob von Busch, who had just married Barbara. Soon he was persuaded to move out of their cramped apartment and took a room of his own in the same apartment block, one of the very few in town at the time.

Starkweather and Fugate went on dates to the movies, sometimes alone, sometimes with Bob and Barbara. Or they would just drive around, listening to distant rock 'n' roll stations on the radio. Starkweather also liked to get out of the small city of Lincoln, which had a population of just 100,000 in 1958. He found Nebraska's capital city claustrophobic and felt contempt for the local people's law-abiding, Christian ways. Lincoln was the scene of just three murders a year before Starkweather went on his spree, and boasted more churches per head than any other city in the world. Out in the huge, flat countryside around Lincoln, Starkweather felt at home. He had craved the solitary life of a backwoodsman since he was a child. 'When the sun was setting in its tender glory,' he later wrote of an early experience of the wilderness, 'it was as though time itself was standing still. The flames still burn deep down inside of me for the love of that enchanted forest.'

Fugate shared that romantic view of the natural world. She would accompany him on hunting trips and, in the evening, they would lie back, holding hands, and stare up into the clear, starry, black Nebraskan sky. There he told her of the deal he had done with death. Death, he said, had come to him in a vision. Half-man, half-bear, it had taken him down to hell, but hell was not as he had always imagined, 'it was more like beautiful flames of gold'. The few other people he had trusted enough to tell his vision to had thought him crazy and had changed the subject. But Fugate said she loved him and that she wanted to go there, to hell, with him. And in his love for her, Starkweather thought, at last he had found 'something worth killing for'. His one great aim in life now was for Fugate to see him 'go down shooting, knowing it was for her'.

Starkweather liked to buy presents for Fugate – soft toys, a record player and a radio, so she could enjoy music at home. He also bought her jewellery, including a locket with 'Caril' and 'Chuck' – her nickname for him – engraved on it. But buying presents on his meagre wages did not come easy, especially when there was rent to pay and a car to keep on the road. Starkweather soon began looking around for an easier way of making money.

Nebraska was on the eastern edge of the old Wild West. Cattle ranchers had wrested it from the Sioux and it had been cowboy country until the cereal farmers fenced it in and forced the cattlemen to move on. Starkweather felt himself very much part of that old tradition. He loved guns and spent hours stripping them down and oiling them. And he loved to shoot. Although he was short-sighted, he was a good shot and practised shooting from the hip like an old time gunfighter. He also loved detective movies and true crime comics, and he began to fantasise about being a criminal. But he was not interested in being a burglar or a sneak thief. To Starkweather, crime meant armed robbery.

Although he had had a few adolescent scrapes, he had never been in any real trouble with the law. Now, to keep Fugate, he started planning a criminal career. Bank robbery was plainly the pinnacle of the profession, but he thought he had better start small – by robbing a gas station. He chose the Crest Service Station on Cornhusker Highway that ran out of Lincoln to the north. He used to hang out there tinkering with his car and knew the gas station pretty well. A couple of times, when he had been locked out of his room for not paying the rent, he had slept there in his car, surviving on chocolate bars and Pepsi from the vending machines. The attendant would wake him at 4.15 a.m. so that he would be on time for work.

On 1 December 1957 a new attendant had just taken over. Robert Colvert was twenty-one and just out of the Navy, where he had been known as 'Little Bob'. He was nine stone, and around five foot five. Earlier that year he had got married. His wife, Charlotte, was expecting and he had taken the night job at the gas station to support his growing family. He was new to the job and barely knew Starkweather, though they had had a row the day before when he refused to give Starkweather credit on a toy dog he wanted to buy Fugate.

It was a freezing night and a bitter Nebraskan wind was blowing in from the plains. Starkweather pulled into the service station around 3 a.m. Colvert was alone. Starkweather was nervous. At first he bought a pack of cigarettes and drove off. A few minutes later he came back. This time he bought some chewing gum and drove off again. The coast was clear. It was now or never.

Starkweather loaded the shotgun he had stolen from Bob von Busch's cousin, Sonny. He pulled a hunting cap down over his red hair and tied a bandanna around his face.

Back at the gas station, Starkweather pointed the shotgun at Colvert and handed him a canvas money bag. Colvert filled the bag with the notes and loose change from the till. But then Starkweather's plan went badly wrong. Although he knew the station's routine and how much money was kept there overnight, the new man did not know the combination of the safe and could not open it. Starkweather forced him into the car at gunpoint. Colvert drove. Starkweather sat in the passenger seat, the shotgun trained on Colvert. They headed for Superior Street, a dirt road a little way north, used by teenagers as a lovers' lane.

The only witness to what happened next was Starkweather. He claimed that, as they got out of the car, Colvert made a grab for the gun. 'I got into a helluva fight and shooting gallery,' he said. 'He shot himself the first time. He had ahold of the gun from the front, and I cocked it and he was messing around and he jerked it and the thing went off.' Colvert was hit and fell, but he was not dead. He tried to stand up. Starkweather reloaded the shotgun. He pressed the barrel to Colvert's head and pulled the trigger. 'He didn't get up any more.' Five months later, Robert Colvert's widow would give birth to a daughter. The robbery had culled Starkweather just $108.

Although Starkweather had been nervous before, the killing filled him with a feeling of serenity he had not experienced since childhood. He felt free, above the law. When he picked up Fugate later that day, he told her about the robbery, but claimed that an unnamed accomplice had done the shooting. That evening he threw the shotgun in a creek. A few days later he fished it out, cleaned it and put the gun back in Sonny's garage. It had not even been missed.

During the police investigation, several of the other service station attendants mentioned Starkweather's name, but no one came to visit him. He paid off his back rent, had his car resprayed black and spent ten dollars on second-hand clothes, paying in loose change. The owner of the store was suspicious and reported the matter to the police. But no effort was made to question him.

The fact that no one seemed even to suspect him of the robbery and murder gave Starkweather a great deal of satisfaction. It was his first taste of success. Until then he had always been the underdog, picked on at school, hauling other people's garbage. Now he had showed that he could outwit authority. 'I learned something, something I already knowed. A man could make money without hauling other people's garbage.'

He stopped turning up for work and was fired. He spent his time going to the movies, reading comics, playing records, working on his car and practising shooting and knife-throwing. The money from the robbery did not last long. He got behind with the rent again and ended up sleeping in his car in a garage he rented. But it did not bother him. He knew he could get cash again as soon as he wanted. And the idea of killing again did not bother him one little bit.

On Sunday 19 January 1958 there was a terrible row. Fugate was putting on weight and her family feared she was pregnant. When Starkweather turned up, Fugate told him that she was sick of his wild ways and that she never wanted to see him again. He did not take her seriously. He had already arranged to go hunting jack-rabbits with Fugate's stepfather, Marion Bartlett, two days later, and he figured that he would see her then.

On the morning of 21 January 1958 Starkweather helped his brother Rodney out on the garbage round, then went to check that his room was still padlocked. It was. His hunting rifle was inside and he had to borrow Rodney's, a cheap, single-shot, .22 bolt action rifle. He took some rugs he had scavenged from his garbage round with him to Belmont Avenue and gave them to Fugate's mother, Velda, as a peace offering. Velda was not appeased. As Starkweather sat cleaning his brother's rifle in the living room, she told him that Marion was not going hunting with him and that he should leave and never come back. When he did not respond, according to Starkweather: 'She didn't say nothing. She just got up and slammed the shit out of me... in the face.' As Starkweather ran from the house, he left the rifle. A few minutes later, he returned to collect it. Fugate's father was waiting. 'The old man started chewing me out. I said to hell with him and was going to walk out through the front room, and he helped me out. Kicked me right in the ass. My tail hurt for three days.'

But that was not the end of it. Starkweather walked down to the local grocery store and phoned the transport company where Marion Bartlett worked. He told them that Mr Bartlett was sick and would not be in for a few days. Then he drove his car over to a friend's house nearby, left it there and walked back to Belmont Avenue. Fugate and her mother were still yelling their heads off when Starkweather returned. Then Velda accused him of making her daughter pregnant. She began slapping him around the face again. This time he hit back, knocking her back a couple of steps. She let out a strange cry – 'a war cry,' Starkweather thought. Marion Bartlett came flying to the rescue. He picked Starkweather up by the neck and dragged him towards the front door. But Starkweather was younger and stronger. He kicked the old man in the groin and wrestled him to the ground. Bartlett managed to slip from Starkweather's grasp and went to look for a weapon. Starkweather thought he had better do the same.

As Starkweather hurriedly slipped a .22 cartridge into his brother's hunting rifle, Marion Bartlett ran at him with a claw hammer. Starkweather fired, shooting the old man in the head. Velda Bartlett grabbed a kitchen knife and threatened to cut Starkweather's head off. Starkweather reloaded the rifle, but Fugate grabbed it from him. She threatened her mother, saying she would blow her to hell. The old woman did not take her daughter's threat seriously and knocked her down. Starkweather grabbed the rifle back and shot the old woman in the face. He hit her with the butt of the gun as she fell, then hit her twice more.

Fugate's two-and-a-half-year-old half-sister Betty Jean was screaming. Starkweather hit her with the rifle butt too. She screamed all the louder, so Starkweather picked up the kitchen knife and threw it at her. He said he aimed for the chest, but the knife pierced her neck, killing her. Fugate then pointed out that her stepfather was still alive in the bedroom. Starkweather went through and finished Marion Bartlett off, stabbing him repeatedly in the throat.

The house fell quiet. Starkweather reloaded his gun and sat down to watch television. 'I don't even remember what was on,' he later told police. 'I just wanted some noise.' That evening he and Fugate wrapped the bodies of her murdered family in rugs and bedclothes and dragged them out into the frozen backyard. They stuffed Velda's body into an outside toilet. Betty Jean's body was placed in a box on top of it. Marion Bartlett's corpse was hidden in a disused chicken coop.

Back in the house the two teenagers tidied up as best they could. They mopped up some of the blood and mess with rags and splashed perfume around to hide the smell. Then they went into the living room to watch television together.

Fugate later claimed that she had not been present during the slaughter of her family. She had come home to find Starkweather there with a gun and her family gone. She said that he had told her that he was planning a big bank robbery. Her parents had found out and the family had been taken hostage by the rest of the gang. He had only to make one phone call and they would be killed, unless she co-operated. Starkweather said that Fugate had participated in the slaughter of her family, egging him on.

The young couple settled down together for what Starkweather would later describe as the best week of his life. They were alone together, with no one to push them around. Certainly he had no conscience troubling him. Later he confessed: 'Shooting people was, I guess, a kind of thrill.'

In Starkweather's eyes they were now living like kings. With money taken from Marion Bartlett's pockets he made the occasional run to the local grocery store to stock up on chewing gum, ice cream, potato chips and Pepsi Cola. Fugate later claimed that he tied her up when he went out. Starkweather denied it.

They lived, for the first time, as husband and wife. The two of them played cards, watched television a lot and tended the family pets: two parakeets, a dog called Nig and a puppy called Kim, which Starkweather had bought for Fugate. Everything would have been idyllic except for the bodies in the backyard.

Visitors were warned off by a sign on the kitchen door saying: 'Stay away Every Body is sick with the Flue'. Brave souls who knocked were told by Fugate that the family was sick and they were in quarantine, while Starkweather hid in a room off the hall with his rifle cocked.

On Saturday 25 January, Fugate's sister, Barbara, came to visit with Bob von Busch and their new-born baby. Fugate spotted her sister before she was halfway up the pathway. She called out that the whole family had the flu and that the doctor had said no one should come near the house. But Barbara, who was concerned that her mother had not been in touch, kept on coming. Fearing the game was up, Fugate screamed: 'Go away! If you know what's best you'll go away so mother won't get hurt.'

Barbara stopped, turned around and went back to Bob's car. Something in her sister's voice scared her. Once the baby was safely home, Bob von Busch and Rodney Starkweather returned to the house to find out what was going on. Again, Fugate sent them away. Her mother's life would be in danger if they did not go, she said.

They reported the matter to the police and a patrol car was sent out to Belmont Avenue that evening. Fugate gave the officers the regular story about the family having the flu. She also mentioned that her family did not get on with Bob von Busch – that was why he had called the police. Noting that Fugate was calm and controlled, the policemen left their inquiries at that.

After the police had left, Starkweather took his brother's rifle to the house of a mutual friend. He called Barbara von Busch to reassure her. He had bought some groceries for Fugate's family, he said, and he left a message for Rodney, saying that he should go and pick up his gun at the friend's house. When Rodney went to collect his rifle, he noticed it was damaged. The butt plate had been knocked off.

The next day, Sunday, Starkweather's sister Laveta arrived at Belmont Avenue. She was not put off by the story of the flu. She was one of Fugate's few friends and, when she would not go away, Fugate pulled her close. Her brother was inside planning a bank robbery, Fugate confided, and that was why she could not come in. Laveta went home and told her father what had happened. He did not believe a word of it. But next day he began to get concerned.

On Monday morning Fugate's grandmother, Pansy Street, was also getting worried. She turned up at Belmont Avenue and shouted until Fugate showed herself. When Mrs Street refused to believe the flu story, Fugate reverted to the story about her mother being in danger. Mrs Street went straight to the police precinct. While she was there, Starkweather's father phoned, relating the story Laveta had told him. The police sent a second squad car out to Belmont Avenue. When they knocked on the door, they got no answer. So they broke in. Charles Starkweather and Caril Fugate had already figured that the game was up. Fugate had packed a bag with some clothes and a few family snapshots. Starkweather had wrapped his hunting knife, Marion Bartlett's shotgun, the barrel of which he had sawn down, and a .32 pistol he had found in the house in a blue blanket. And they slipped out of the house the back way. By the time the police turned up, everything was neat and tidy. With nothing to excite their suspicions, they took Pansy Street home and let the matter rest.

Bob von Busch and Rodney Starkweather were not so easily satisfied. At 4.30 p.m. they went over to Belmont Avenue to check the place out for themselves. Almost immediately they found the Bartletts' bodies. The hunt was now on, but the young lovers had several hours' start.

After picking up two spare tyres from the lock-up garage Starkweather rented in the wealthy part of town, the couple stopped at the Crest Service Station to fill up with petrol and buy maps. Then they turned south, out of Lincoln, on to the open highway. They headed out across the frozen farmlands of the Great Plains. They stopped at the small town of Bennet, where Starkweather bought some ammunition at a service station and they ate a couple of hamburgers. Starkweather often came to Bennet to spend time in the surrounding countryside. An old family friend, seventy-year-old August Meyer, would let him hunt on his land in return for half the kill.

Meyer lived two miles east of Bennet, down a dirt track. Starkweather thought they might be safe there, for the night at least. But there had been a six-inch fall of snow and the track was muddy. Their car got stuck. Nearby was a derelict schoolhouse with a cyclone cellar, where the children would have taken shelter from the tornadoes that tore across the Great Plains every spring. Starkweather and Fugate went down into the cellar to warm up before traipsing up to Meyer's farm on foot, ostensibly to ask the old man's assistance in shifting the car. At the farmhouse Starkweather shot Meyer and his dog. 'Caril got pissed off because we got stuck,' he said. 'She said that we ought to go up and blast the shit out of him because he did not shovel the lane.' He also claimed that he had shot Meyer in self-defence. After a heated argument the old man, Starkweather said, went into the house to get a coat, but came out on the porch firing a rifle. 'I felt a bullet go by my head,' he said. But Meyer's gun had jammed after the first shot. 'Meyer started running back in the house, and I shot him at almost point-blank range with the sawn-off.' Fugate said that Starkweather had simply asked Meyer if he could borrow some horses to drag the car out of the mud, then shot the old man as he went into the barn.

Starkweather dragged Meyer's body into the wash-house and covered it with a blanket. The two of them ransacked his house for money, food and guns. Their total haul was less than a hundred dollars, a pump-action .22 repeating rifle, some socks, gloves, a shirt, a straw hat and some jelly and biscuits. They took a brief nap before trudging back to the car. After an hour or two of digging they managed to shift it. But it slid off the track into a ditch and Starkweather stripped the reverse gear trying to back it out. Eventually they were rescued by a farmer, a neighbour of Meyer's, who towed the car out with his truck. Starkweather insisted on giving the farmer two dollars for his trouble.

They drove up towards Meyer's farmhouse, where Starkweather planned to stay the night. But fearing that the body had been found, Fugate insisted they turn back. The car got stuck in the mud again. It was already dark so they abandoned it and headed back to the derelict school to spend the night in the cyclone cellar. On the way they were offered a lift by seventeen-year-old Robert Jensen, the son of a local store-owner, and his fiancée, sixteen-year-old Carol King. When Starkweather explained his car trouble, Jensen offered to take them to the nearest service station where they could telephone for help. As they got in the back seat, Jensen asked why they were carrying guns. Starkweather had the .22 and Fugate the sawn-off shotgun. Starkweather insisted they were not loaded.

Starkweather later claimed that, at this point, he toyed with the idea of ringing the police and turning himself in. But when they reached the service station, it was closed. On their brief acquaintanceship, Starkweather had already decided that these two high-school kids were exactly the sort of people he hated – clever, popular at school, conservative, middle class. Jensen was a football player. King was a cheerleader, drum majorette and a member of the school choir. They planned to get married once they had graduated. It struck Starkweather that if he turned himself in, Jensen would get the credit. He could not bear the thought of this chubby, all-American boy being feted as a hero.

He put his gun to the back of Jensen's head and told him to hand over his wallet. Fugate emptied it and handed the money to Starkweather, who then ordered Jensen to drive them back to Lincoln. After a couple of miles, he changed his mind and told him to drive back to the derelict school. He said he was going to leave Jensen and King there and take their car – a dark blue, souped-up 1950 Ford with whitewall tyres.

When they got there, Starkweather left Fugate in the car, listening to the radio, while he marched his prisoners off at gunpoint As they walked down the steps into the cellar, Starkweather shot Jensen from behind. Later he claimed that Jensen had tried to grab the gun but, when the body was found, there were six shots in the left ear. Starkweather made several conflicting statements about how King died. He was alone with her for fifteen minutes and claimed to have shot her when she started screaming. Later he claimed that Fugate had killed her.

King was killed with a single shot from behind. When their bodies were found the next day, Jensen was found lying on his stomach in a pool of blood at the bottom of the stairs. King was partly nude and lying on top of him. Her coat had been pulled over her head, her jeans and panties were round her ankles. And her back was scratched and streaked with mud as if she had been dragged across the floor. She had been stabbed viciously, several times, in the groin, The autopsy found internal damage to the vagina, cervix and rectum. It had been caused by a rigid, double-edged blade that could not have been Starkweather's hunting knife. But doctors found no semen and no indication of sexual assault. Starkweather at first said that he had raped King, but later admitted only to having been tempted to rape her and having pulled down her jeans. Fugate, he insisted, had then murdered and mutilated King in a fit of jealousy.

Starkweather closed the heavy storm doors on the cellar and went back to Jensen's car. But it, too, was stuck in the mud. He and Fugate managed to dig it out by about 10.30 p.m. Starkweather claimed that he was now determined to abandon the spree and give himself up to the police, but Fugate talked him out of it. They headed back to Lincoln to see if the Bartletts' bodies had been discovered yet.

Squad cars lined Belmont Avenue and number 924 was crawling with policemen. Starkweather slowly drove by. He headed west out of Lincoln with the vague idea of finding refuge with his brother Leonard who lived in Washington State, over a thousand miles away. But after about three hours driving, before they had even crossed the state line out of Nebraska, they turned back and headed for Lincoln once more. Starkweather was tired, had a streaming cold and the car was not running too well. The idea was to rest up in one of the wealthy mansions in the country club area of town, steal a new car and make a run for it again the following night. Starkweather knew the area well. He had collected garbage there and deeply resented its affluent residents. It was 3.30 a.m. when they arrived back in Lincoln. They parked up in the secluded street and took a nap. When they awoke in the early morning they began cruising the streets, hunting for a suitable property. They settled on the five-bedroom mansion belonging to millionaire industrialist C. Lauer Ward, just down the street from the garage Starkweather rented.

Mr Ward was the forty-seven-year-old president of Lincoln's Capital Bridge Company and Capital Steel Company, and had gone to work before Starkweather rang the doorbell. The fifty-one-year-old maid, Lillian Fencl, answered the door. She had been with the Wards for twenty-six years and may have known Starkweather from his time as a garbage man in the area. Starkweather and Fugate brandished their guns and forced their way into the house.

Mrs Ward, a forty-six-year-old graduate of the University of Nebraska who was active in community affairs, was the only other person at home. The Wards' fourteen-year-old son, Michael was at boarding school in Connecticut. When Mrs Ward came downstairs, Starkweather ordered her to sit down at the table. Mrs Ward readily agreed to co-operate – the Bartlett murders were front-page news.

While Mrs Ward and Lillian Fencl got on with their household chores, Starkweather went wandering about the mansion's elegant rooms, amazed by their opulence. Before noon, he ordered Mrs Ward – not the maid – to serve him pancakes in the library, then petulantly changed his order to waffles.

While Starkweather was enjoying his late breakfast, twenty-five armed policemen were surrounding August Meyer's farm. Starkweather's abandoned car had been found nearby and the police were convinced the two fugitives were holed up there. A bulletin on the radio news said that they would be taken just as soon as the tear gas arrived. But when the gas cleared and the state troopers went in all they found was August Meyer's dead body. The bodies of Robert Jensen and Carol King were found soon after. Within the hour a hundred policemen were combing the frozen countryside.

Around 1 p.m. Starkweather allowed Mrs Ward to go upstairs to change. When he went to check on her, he claimed, she came out of her son's room with a .22 calibre pistol and took a shot at him. She missed and turned to run. Starkweather threw his hunting knife at her. It stuck in her back. He dragged the groaning woman into her bedroom and put her on the bed. The Wards' dog then began to worry him. He broke its neck with a blow from his rifle butt. Later, suspecting that Mrs Ward might try and make a phone call, he bound and gagged her and covered her with a sheet.

Later in the afternoon Starkweather called his father and asked him to tell Bob von Busch that he was going to kill him for coming between him and Fugate. He also wrote a note, addressed to 'the law only', saying that he and Fugate had intended to commit suicide after he had killed the Bartletts but Bob von Busch and others prevented them by coming round to the house.

Around 6 p.m. Mr Ward's Chevrolet came up the drive. That afternoon he had been visiting the state governor, who was a personal friend. When Ward came in through the kitchen door he was confronted by Starkweather brandishing a rifle. Ward made a grab for the gun. In the ensuing fight, the rifle fell down the stairs into the basement; Ward tumbled down after it, and Starkweather followed. Starkweather got to the gun first, and Ward turned and ran back up the stairs. Starkweather shot him in the back. Despite his wounds, Ward kept going. He ran through the kitchen and the living room and was opening the front door when Starkweather caught up with him. He shot Ward again, this time in the side of the head. 'I asked him if he was all right,' Starkweather said later, 'but he did not answer.' Ward was dead.

Starkweather took the maid upstairs, took ten dollars from her and tied her up. He left Fugate to watch her, while he took seven dollars from Mrs Ward and tried to dye his hair black with shoe polish. Fugate packed some clothes while Starkweather loaded up Mrs Ward's blue Packard with tins of food he found in the kitchen. As evening fell they drove down Belmont Avenue one last time, then headed west out of Lincoln on Highway 34.

Next morning a relative of Lauer Ward went to his house to find out why he had not shown up at work. He found Ward shot and stabbed just inside the front door. The two women were dead too. Both had been stabbed repeatedly, with the same double-edged blade that had been used to mutilate Carol King. The knife was never found. Later Starkweather maintained that the two women had been alive when he left them. But Fugate said Starkweather had admitted to her that he had killed Mrs Ward with a kitchen knife and that, after he had tied Lillian Fencl up and stabbed her, she screamed. So he put a pillow over her face and kept on stabbing her every time she hollered.

News of the killings spread quickly. A grinning picture of Starkweather and Fugate was on the front page of the evening paper. Now nine were dead and Starkweather was still in the area. People in Bennet and Lincoln barricaded themselves in their houses. Gun stores were packed. People were buying anything that would shoot. One shop reported selling over forty guns in two hours as parents armed themselves to escort their children to school. Lincoln's mayor posted a $1,000 reward for Starkweather's capture. Soon a hundred strong posse gathered outside the sheriff's department – though some of its members were not entirely sober. The governor called out the National Guard. Soldiers cruised in jeeps with machine guns mounted on them. The city was sealed off and searched block by block. And an aircraft circled the city, looking for the blue Packard. The fugitives pressed on westwards throughout the night. They claimed that, as they went, they wrote notes, boasting of what they had done, and tossed them out of the window. None were ever found.

In the small hours of morning Starkweather fell asleep at the wheel and only just managed to keep the car out of a drainage ditch at the side of the road. He persuaded Fugate that having sex was the only thing that would wake him up enough to keep driving. It did not work. Ten minutes later he pulled off the road again to sleep.

At around 9 a.m. they crossed the state line into Wyoming and found themselves in the Badlands – an area scarred by ravines that provided a safe haven for the outlaws of the Wild West. At midday they stopped in the small town of Douglas where they filled the car with petrol and bought Pepsi and candy bars to keep themselves going. It was there that they heard on the radio that the Wards' bodies had been found and police were looking for Mrs Ward's Packard. Starkweather decided to look for another car.

About twelve miles beyond Douglas, Starkweather saw a Buick parked off the highway. In it, Merle Collison, a thirty-seven-year-old shoe salesman, was asleep. Married with two children, he was on his way home from a sales trip to Grand Falls, Montana. Starkweather woke Collison and told him they were going to swap cars. Collison left the door locked and ignored him. Starkweather got the .22 pump-action rifle from the Packard and shot at Collison twice through the window of the car. Collison agreed to the trade and opened the door. But Starkweather cold-bloodedly blasted him seven times – in the nose, cheek, neck, chest, left arm, right wrist and left leg. The fugitives transferred their belongings – and their booty – into Collison's Buick. With Collison still jammed in the front seat and Fugate in the back, Starkweather tried to drive off. But the handbrake was stuck fast. Fugate said Starkweather turned to Collison's corpse for help. 'Man, are you dead?' Starkweather asked when there was no reply. While

Starkweather struggled with the handbrake, Joe Sprinkle, a twenty-nine-year-old geologist, drove by. Seeing Collison slumped in the front seat of the Buick, he thought there had been some sort of accident. He stopped and walked back to the Buick. 'Can I help?' he asked. Starkweather stuck the rifle in his face and explained that he could. 'Raise your hands. Help me release the emergency brake or I'll kill you,' Starkweather snarled. It was then that Sprinkle noticed the bullet wounds in Collison's dead body. Instinctively he grabbed for the gun. Sprinkle knew that if he did not get the gun away from Starkweather he was a dead man. As the two men grappled in a life-or-death struggle in the middle of the highway, Wyoming Deputy Sheriff William Romer drove by. He pulled up about twenty-five yards down the road. Fugate got out of the Buick and ran down to the patrol car. 'Take me to the police,' she said, pointing at Starkweather. 'He just killed a man.'

Sensing the danger, Starkweather spun round, letting go of the gun, ran back to the Packard and roared off back towards Douglas. The deputy put out an all points bulletin and, with Fugate on board, gave chase. A few miles down the road he was joined by another police car. In it were County Sheriff Earl Heflin and Douglas Chief of Police Robert Ainslie. With the two police cars in hot pursuit Starkweather pushed his speed up to 100 mph. When he hit Douglas, the traffic slowed him and Heflin got off a couple of pot-shots at his tyres with his handgun. For a moment, Ainslie got close enough to lock bumpers, but the bumper tore loose as Starkweather jumped a red light and overtook a lorry on the inside. As he cleared the town, Starkweather put his foot down on the gas pedal again and his speed climbed towards 120 mph. Heflin got out his rifle and started shooting at the Packard. One shot smashed the back window. Then Starkweather screeched to a halt. Bleeding copiously, he thought he had been shot. In fact, a piece of flying glass had nicked his ear.

The police pulled up behind him. Starkweather got out of the car and started to walk towards them. The police shouted for him to put his hands up. As the police shot at the road in front of him, Starkweather put his hands behind him and coolly tucked in his flapping shirt tail. Then he lay face down on the road and surrendered.

'He thought he was bleeding to death. That's why he stopped. That's the kind of yellow son of a bitch he is,' the arresting officer told reporters.

When the prisoners were taken to the state penitentiary they were met by a crowd of newsmen, photographers and newsreel cameramen. Fugate, with her head covered by a scarf, played up to the cameras. But it was Starkweather, ignoring the media, who got all the attention. Wearing tight jeans, a black motorcycle jacket, cowboy boots with a butterfly design on the toe, handcuffed, with a cigarette dangling from his lips, he was the perfect young rebel killer. America had already been rocked by the image of the wayward teenager. They had seen a brooding James Dean in *Rebel Without a Cause* and a cocky and threatening Marlon Brando as the motorcycle gang leader in 1953's *The Wild One*. Elvis Presley had just burst on the scene with wild pelvic gyrations that scared the pants off conservative Middle America. But here, in the person of Charles Starkweather, was the embodiment of their fears. Here was the ultimate juvenile delinquent. FBI Chief J. Edgar Hoover promised a nation-wide crackdown on juvenile crime.

At first Fugate told police that she had been Starkweather's captive and had had no part in the murders. She had only gone along with him because her family were held hostage. But later she undermined her story by saying that she had witnessed their murders. Then she became incoherent and had to be sedated.

Starkweather remained unrepentant. In a note to his parents, ostensibly apologising for the trouble he had caused them, he wrote: 'I'm not real sorry for what I did cause for the first time me and Caril have more fun, she helped me a lot, but if she comes back don't hate her she had not a thing to do with the killing all we wanted to do was get out of town.' He later compared himself to a soldier, killing only when he had to, to achieve an objective.

He quickly confessed to all the murders – except those of Clara Ward and her maid Lillian Fencl. As far as he knew, he maintained, they were alive when he left the house. Despite being charged with the murder of Merle Collison in Wyoming, Starkweather was quickly extradited back to Nebraska. He was ridiculed for being afraid of flying when he refused to go back to Lincoln by plane. In fact he thought that travelling by car he would stand a better chance of escaping.

Caril Fugate and Charles Starkweather were both charged with murder. They pleaded not guilty and were to be tried separately. Starkweather's lawyer tried to get him to enter an insanity plea.

Starkweather refused. 'Nobody remembers a crazy man,' he said, insisting that all the killings had been in self-defence.

Starkweather's trial for the murder of high-school student Robert Jensen began on 5 May 1958. The prosecution quickly established that the six bullets in Jensen's head had all been shot from behind, demolishing Starkweather's self-defence argument. Throughout the prosecution case, Starkweather acted cool, chewing gum and rocking back on his chair. The only time he showed any emotion was when an ex-employer said that Starkweather was the dumbest man who ever worked for him. Starkweather went crazy and had to be restrained.

The ex-employer's testimony was part of the defence lawyer's strategy to show his client was mentally incompetent. In fact, Starkweather had an above-average IQ. The defence attorney also read out some of Starkweather's confessions, hoping to show that his state of mind was abnormal and confused.

When Starkweather took the stand, he was asked why he was mad at Fugate when they were at the derelict school. He replied that it was because of what she had done.

'What did she do?' he was asked.

'Shot Carol King,' said Starkweather.

This was not the first time that Starkweather accused Fugate of killing Carol King. During his time on remand he had begun to fall out of love with her. He had also accused her of finishing off Merle Collison when his gun jammed.

Three psychiatrists appeared for the defence, claiming that Starkweather had a diseased mind. But, under cross examination, they admitted that this did not amount to a recognised mental illness and none of them would be prepared to have Starkweather certified insane. Prosecution psychiatrists agreed that Starkweather had an anti-social personality disorder, but was legally sane. The jury also agreed. They returned a guilty verdict and recommended the electric chair.

During his court appearance, Starkweather became a TV celebrity, appearing on the news each night. Many teenagers identified with the cool and unrepentant Starkweather. Fan mail flooded in, though some urged him to turn to God. Admirers overlooked the fact that one of his first victims was Fugate's half-sister, a two-and-a-half-year-old child.

Five months later Caril Fugate became the youngest woman ever to be tried for first degree murder in the US for being an accomplice in Jensen's murder. Starkweather himself was the prosecution's star witness. Taking the stand, he told the jury that he no longer loved Fugate and did not care if she lived or died. At one time he was even reported as having said: 'If I fry in the electric chair, then Caril should be sitting on my lap.'

He said that she had known he was involved in the murder of the filling-station attendant Robert Colvert and that she had been present when he had killed her family. She had gone with him willingly and had even expressed a desire to be shot down with him when the denouement came.

Fugate's attorney believed that she was innocent, but could not shake Starkweather's story, which was partially corroborated by witnesses to their spree and early statements to the police. She was found guilty and sentenced to life imprisonment.

She continued to protest her innocence, but settled in to become a model prisoner at the state women's reformatory at York, Nebraska. In 1972 she was the subject of a documentary called Growing up in Prison and in 1976 was released on parole. In 1983 she appeared on TV to protest her innocence once more and took a lie detector test on camera. It indicated that she was telling the truth. However, a public opinion poll in Nebraska showed that most people did not believe her.

On death row Starkweather spent his time writing. He also talked for more than eighty hours to James Melvin Reinhardt, professor of criminology at the University of Nebraska, explaining why he had taken to crime. His main motive was to take 'general revenge upon the world and its human race'.

'The people I murdered had murdered me,' he said. 'They murdered me slow, like. I was better to them. I killed them in a hurry.'

Poverty was another reason. 'They had me numbered for the bottom,' he said. He blamed the world and was sure that other people hated him – 'because I was poor and had to live in a goddamned shack'. But there was a way out of this class trap – 'all dead people are on the same level,' he said.

He saw his murderous spree as the only way out of a life of drudgery. 'Better to be left to rot on some high hill, and be remembered,' he wrote, 'than to be buried alive in some stinking place.'

Now Starkweather had everything he wanted. He was going to die – but he was famous. Nothing gave him more pleasure than to see his name in the papers.

Professor Reinhardt published *The Murderous Trail of Charles Starkweather*, which alleged that Starkweather was paranoid and that this problem was self-inflicted. In fact, Starkweather did have something of a change of heart in prison. His murderous rampage seemed to have quenched his hatred. A gentler side took over. One of his prison guards said: 'If somebody had just paid attention to Charlie, bragged on his drawing and writing, all of this might not have happened.'

At the parole board Starkweather spoke of his remorse and his new-found Christian faith. It did no good. The execution was scheduled for 22 May 1959. He wrote to his father, talking of repentance and his hopes of staying alive. The execution was delayed by a federal judge, and then rescheduled for 25 June.

When the prison guards came for him, he asked: 'What's your hurry?' Then, in a new shirt and jeans, he swaggered ahead of them to the electric chair with his hands in his pockets. Outside, gangs of teenagers cruised the streets, playing rock 'n' roll on their car radios.

Fifteen years later the Starkweather story was retold in the 1973 cult movie *Badlands*, starring Martin Sheen and Cissy Spacek, and is seen as the inspiration behind Oliver Stone's *Natural Born Killers* in 1994.

Eight years after Starkweather was executed, two other teenagers went on an eerily similar rampage. On 17 August 1967 stocky six-footer Thomas Eugene Braun and his smaller, leaner best friend Leonard Maine, both eighteen, began a murder spree that spread across three states. Tom Braun left his job as a gas-station attendant in the service depot at Ritzville, Washington that evening and went to pick up Maine. Braun was driving a battered black German-made Borgward open-top sedan.

'Are you still driving that old boneshaker?' said Maine.

'Take your last look,' Braun said. 'We are going to have ourselves a new car.'

'How come?' Maine asked.

'You'll see,' said Braun. He had stashed in the car a Frontier Colt single-action .22 pistol, an automatic .22 Luger and several hundred rounds of ammunition.

The two youths headed for Seattle, Washington's state capital, where they decided to stay for the night. But the landlady of the rooming-house they stopped at took fright when one of them pointed a gun at her. She screamed and fled into an adjoining room. The two teenagers took off at speed. They headed back out of the city and drove aimlessly around the local countryside.

By morning they were driving down Route 202 outside Redmond, Washington, when they saw an attractive woman driving a maroon Skylark up ahead. Braun stepped on the gas. Pulling alongside, the two boys signalled frantically, indicating that something was wrong with one of her wheels. The driver was newlywed Mrs Deanna Buse, twenty-two years old, returning from her job to her mother's house. When she saw the youths' frantic gestures, she pulled to a halt on the grassy verge. The two boys pulled their car up in front of her. Mrs Buse got out of her car and examined each of the wheels in turn.

There was nothing wrong with them. She turned to the boys to ask for an explanation and found a gun pointing at her head.

Braun ordered her back into her Skylark. He got in with her, keeping the gun trained on her. Maine took the wheel of Braun's Borgward and the two cars drove off slowly down the highway. At the next junction they turned off and wound through a series of side roads until they reached a dirt track which came to a dead end in the woods near Echo Lake.

The two cars stopped and Braun forced Mrs Buse at gunpoint into the woods. Maine waited by the cars. A little later he heard five shots. A few days later Mrs Buse's naked body was discovered, her clothes piled neatly beside her. She had been forced to strip at gunpoint, but she had not been raped and no semen was found near the corpse.

Braun and Maine drove the two cars back to Seattle, where they abandoned Braun's Borgward in a sidestreet. In Mrs Buse's Skylark they drove down to Fife, Washington, twenty-two miles south of Seattle, to visit Maine's uncle who lived there. He put them up for the night. During their stay, they asked the quickest way to Portland, Oregon.

Next morning the two teenagers crossed the state line into Oregon. Again they tried to rent a room, but the motel manager, alerted by their dishevelled appearance, demanded identification and quizzed the boys about their car registration. They sped off.

Sports fisherman Samuel Ledgerwood was returning home in his green late-model Buick with an impressive day's catch when he spotted two youths changing a tyre on their car. He stopped to give them a hand. Braun shot him through the head, twice, killing him instantly.

The two youths bundled their gear into Ledgerman's Buick and shot a couple of slugs through the petrol tank of Mrs Buse's Skylark, setting it on fire. They headed south, following the Pacific coast highway until they reached northern California. On deserted, mountainous Route 120 they spotted two young hitchhikers. Timothy Luce and his girlfriend, student Susan Bartolomei were seventeen. They were both at the same teacher-training college and were on a hitchhiking vacation together.

Braun shot Luce out of hand and ran over his chest with the car to make sure he was dead. Bartolomei was then raped repeatedly before she, too, was shot. But she did not die immediately. At 6 a.m. the next morning she was found lying on the road, still alive. Horribly injured, she was still able to give a description of her assailants. They were two eighteen-year-olds who had said they were from Oklahoma. They called each other 'John' and 'Mike'. Bartolomei also gave the police a detailed description of their appearance and of their car. She said it was a Buick, which tied the attack to Ledgerwood's murder, and the burnt-out Skylark by Ledgerwood's body tied that murder to the slaying of Mrs Buse.

Police throughout Oregon, California and Washington started to be on the lookout for Ledgerwood's Buick. It was spotted outside a small hotel in Jamestown, California by a local patrolman. He called in back-up.

Braun and Maine were registered in the hotel under the names John and Mike Ford. Maine was surprised in his room and gave up without a fight. As the police broke down the door of Braun's room, Braun grabbed for a gun. But a policeman leapt on him and pinned him to the floor before he could let off a shot.

Braun and Maine protested their innocence. Even in the face of all the evidence they pleaded not guilty. In court they sat emotionless while still photographs and even a movie film of their victims were shown. Only when the case was proved did they admit their guilt.

Braun was sentenced to death, Maine to life imprisonment. Neither had given police investigators, psychologists or researchers any clue to the motive behind their senseless crimes.

Sixteen-year-old Michael Clark did not tell why he suddenly went on a killing spree in 1965 either. Until the moment he first squeezed the trigger, Michael Clark had been the perfect son. On the morning of 8 May 1965, for example, he put on his starched, neatly pressed whites and went to a Sea Scout inspection. In the afternoon the gangling, soft-spoken youth went shopping with his mother and scrubbed the bathroom floors in the house. That evening he tended the pigeon with a broken wing that he was nursing back to health. Then suddenly, without warning or permission, he took the family's Cadillac and drove off to a rendezvous with mass murder.

Concerned that Michael had taken the car, Michael's mother called her husband, Forrest Clark, who was working late at the Clark Tank and Manufacturing Company in Long Beach, California. Mr Clark sped home to find that his gas-station credit card was also missing. Michael had only a provisional driving licence and, after an hour, when he had not come home, the Clarks called the police. Then, with their younger son Ronnie, they sat down in the spotless living room of their colonial house and waited.

Michael was driving north on the freeway. Bypassing downtown Los Angeles, he continued driving up the coast all night. In the car beside him was his father's Swedish Mauser deer rifle with a four-power telescopic sight and several dozen armour-piercing bullets.

Sometime before dawn he was on Route 101 near Santa Maria when he collided with the crash barrier. He abandoned the car, crawled through a gap in the barbed wire fence that bordered the highway and climbed the hill at the side of the road. At the top he lay prone in the dewy, three-foot-high wild oat grass. From there he had a commanding view over the four-lane highway below. The place where he had decided to play 'king of the hill' was the exact spot where Mexican bandito Solomon Pico had fired on passing stage-coaches a century before.

At around 6 a.m. Michael Clark fired his first shot at a driver of one of the cars below – and missed. When the driver stopped to see what was happening a second bullet hit his front fender. He sped off to alert the police.

Shortly after, William Reida was driving down that section of Route 101. His wife and four small children were in the car. They were on their way back from a funeral in Portland. At a few minutes past six Reida drove into Clark's sights. Two bullets were fired in rapid succession, hitting both Reida and his five-year-old son Kevin in the neck. Their car veered off the road and pulled to a halt on the hard shoulder. Mrs Reida leapt from the car and waved down passing motorists. Two stopped, but both drivers were shot dead before they could get out. Mrs Reida stumbled back to her car and, though a non-driver, managed the next five miles to a highway patrol station. Her husband survived. Her son did not.

Back at the hill, Michael Clark's sniper spree was in full swing. He shot at anything that passed. Two more passing motorists were hit, though not fatally, and six more were wounded by flying glass. The police arrived and tried to encircle the hill. But they could not locate the sniper properly as he slithered around the hill in the long grass. Keeping up a constant stream of fire, he hit one officer in the arm.

For over two hours the sniper managed to hold them off. Then around 8.30 a.m., as police and armed civilians closed in, he stood up, waved, and shouted: 'Come and get me.' Then he turned the muzzle of his rifle to his own forehead and blew his brains out.

The Clarks had sat up all night waiting for news of Michael. It came an hour later – at exactly the time Michael Clark would normally have been going into his Sunday school class at the Fifth Christian Science church a few blocks from home. At 9.30 a.m. that Sunday morning Long Beach Police Department called to say that their model son had killed three people, injured ten and, finally, taken his own young life. The Clarks were aghast. 'He was always full of love,' Michael's mother said. 'We always tried to protect him.'

No one could make out why a young boy, who had never been in trouble in his life, should suddenly turn into a spree killer. Only local psychiatrist Edward Stainbrook, of the University of Southern California School of Medicine, would hazard a guess. 'If feelings dammed up in the heart don't come out the mouth,' he said, 'they will be acted out in some way.'

Chapter 5

Sniper in the Tower

It was a perfect summer day in Austin. The Texan sun was beating down. By mid-morning, the temperature had already soared to thirty-six degrees in the shade and the hot air hung heavy over the downtown campus of the University of Texas. The students had taken the opportunity to linger in the sunshine when classes changed at 11.30. But by 11.45, all was quiet again under the university's thirty-storey limestone tower.

At 11.48, on 1 August 1966, seventeen-year-old Alec Hernandez was cycling across the campus, delivering newspapers, when a .35 rifle bullet ripped through his leg. It slammed into his saddle and catapulted him from his bike. Then, out of the clear blue sky, more bullets came raining down. Three students, late for class, fell in quick succession.

At first, no one could figure out what was happening. There was a distant report, then someone would crumple to the ground. On the fourth floor of the tower building twenty-three-year-old postgraduate student Norma Barger heard what she took to be dynamite exploding. In fact, it was the sound of a deer-hunting rifle echoing from the low buildings that nestled around the tower. When she looked out of her classroom window, she saw six bodies sprawled grotesquely on the mall or public walkway beneath her. At first she thought it was a tasteless joke. She expected them to get up and walk away laughing. Then she saw the pavement stones splashed with blood – and more people falling beneath the sniper's deadly rain of fire.

Eighteen-year-old Mrs Claire Wilson, who was eight months pregnant, was heading across the mall to her anthropology class when a bullet ripped into her belly. She survived, but her unborn child's skull was crushed and the child was later born dead. Eighteen-year-old freshman Thomas Eckman, a classmate and would-be poet, knelt beside the injured mother-to-be when a second bullet shot him dead.

Thirty-three-year-old post-graduate mathematician Robert Boyer was looking forward to his trip to England. He had already secured a teaching post in Liverpool, where his pregnant wife and two children were waiting for him. But when he stepped out on to the mall, heading for an early lunch, he was shot, fatally, in the back. Secretary Charlotte Darehshori ran to help him and found herself under fire. She spent the next hour-and-a-half crouched behind the concrete base of a flagpole, one of the few people to venture on to the mall and survive uninjured.

The sniper took a shot at a small boy. People began to take cover. A woman on the eighteenth floor of the administration block rang a friend in a nearby university building and said: 'Somebody's up there shooting from the tower. There's blood all over the place.' Soon hundreds were pinned down on the campus.

By 11.52, four minutes after the shooting started, the local police received a hysterical phone call. At first, all they knew was that there had been 'some shooting at the university tower'. In seconds, a 'ten-fifty' went out. All units in the vicinity were to head for the university. Soon the quiet of the Texas high noon was torn by the sound of sirens as more than a hundred city policemen, reinforced by some thirty highway patrolmen, state troopers, Texas Rangers and Secret Service men from President Lyndon Johnson's Austin office, converged on the campus – along with a number of ordinary gun-toting Texans.

One of the first policemen on the scene was rookie patrolman Billy Speed. He quickly figured out what was happening. He spotted the killer on the observation deck of the tower. The young patrolman took cover behind the base of a statue of Jefferson Davis and took careful aim. But before he could take a shot, the sniper shot him dead. Speed was just twenty-three and left a wife and baby daughter. The shot alerted the other lawmen. Volleys of small-arms fire cracked around the top of the tower. A few rounds smashed into the huge clock-face above the killer. Most pinged ineffectually off the four-foot-high wall around the observation deck, kicking up puffs of white dust.

Ducking down behind the low wall, the sniper was safe. Narrow drainage slits around the bottom of the wall made perfect gun ports. There the unknown gunman proved impossible to hit. And he kept finding new targets.

A hundred yards beyond Patrolman Speed, twenty-nine-year-old electrical repairman Roy Dell Schmidt was getting out of his truck on a call. He looked up at the tower and saw puffs of smoke coming from the observation gallery. The police told him to get back but, nonchalantly, Schmidt told a man standing next to him that they were out of range. They weren't. Seconds later, a rifle bullet smashed into Schmidt's chest, killing him instantly.

To the west of the campus ran a main thoroughfare called Guadeloupe Street, known to the students as 'The Drag'. Among the window-shoppers on Guadeloupe Street that sunny lunchtime was eighteen-year-old Paul Sonntag. He was a lifeguard at Austin swimming pool and had just picked up his week's pay cheque. With him was eighteen-year-old ballet dancer Claudia Rutt who was on her way to the doctor's for the polio shot she needed before entering Texas Christian University. Suddenly Claudia sank to the ground, clutching her breast 'Help me! Somebody, help me!' she cried. Bewildered, Sonntag bent over her. The next shot took him out. Both were dead before help could get to them.

Further up Guadeloupe Street, visiting professor of government thirty-nine-year-old Harry Walchuk was browsing in the doorway of a news-stand. Father of six and a teacher at Michigan's Alpena Community College, he was hit in the throat and collapsed, dead, among the magazines. In the next block, twenty-four-year-old Thomas Karr, who had ambitions to be a diplomat, was returning to his apartment after staying up all night, revising for a Spanish exam which he had taken at 10 a.m. that morning. Before he reached his own front door, he dropped to the sidewalk, dying. In the third block, basketball coach Billy Snowden of the Texas School for the Deaf stepped into the doorway of the barbershop where he was having his hair cut and was wounded in the shoulder.

Outside the Rae Ann dress shop on Guadeloupe Street, twenty-six-year-old Iraqi chemistry student Abdul Khashab, his fiancée twenty-year-old Janet Paulos – they were to have married the next week – and twenty-one-year-old trainee sales assistant Lana Phillips, fell wounded within seconds of each other. Homer Kelley, manager of Sheftall's jewellery store, saw them fall and ran to help. He was trying to haul them into the cover of his store when the shop window shattered. A bullet gashed the carpeting on the sidewalk outside his shop and two bullet fragments smashed into his leg. The three youths had to wait over an hour, bleeding on

Sheftall's orange carpet, before an ambulance could get to them. In all, along picturesque, shop-lined Guadeloupe Street, there were four dead and eleven wounded.

To the north, two students were wounded on their way to the biology building. Beyond that, to the north of the campus, thirty-six-year-old Associate Press reporter Robert Heard was running full tilt from cover to cover when he was hit in the shoulder. 'What a shot,' he marvelled as he winced with pain.

To the east, twenty-two-year-old Iran-bound Peace Corps trainee Thomas Ashton was sunning himself on the roof of the Computation Centre. A single round ended his life. A girl sitting at the window of the Business Economics Building was nicked by a bullet. But to the south was the worst killing field. The university's main mall had been turned into a no-man's-land. It was strewn with bodies that could not be recovered safely.

One man was responsible – one man, thirty storeys up the university tower, had turned the peaceful campus into a free-fire zone. The Austin Police Department had never had anything like this to deal with before.

The bullet-scarred clock of the Austin tower was booming out its chimes at 12.30 when a local civilian turned up in camouflage fatigues and began chipping large chunks of limestone off the wall of the observation deck with a tripod-mounted, high-calibre M-14. Meanwhile a Cessna light aircraft circled the tower with police marksman Lieutenant Marion Lee on board. He tried to get a clear shot at the gunman but the turbulent air currents around the tower made aiming impossible. The plane was eventually driven away when the sniper put a bullet through the fuselage.

Down below an armoured truck laid down smoke cover and a fleet of ambulances, sirens wailing, began loading up the dead and wounded. Students braved the sniper's fire to haul other victims to shelter.

Austin Police Chief Robert Miles decided that he could not risk using helicopters against the sniper. His accurate fire could easily bring one down. So Police Chief Miles ordered his men to storm the tower. His directive was curt – 'Shoot to kill'.

Patrolmen Houston McCoy and Jerry Day found their way through the underground passageways that connected the university buildings into the foyer of the tower. There they met Patrolman Ramiro Martinez who had been at home cooking steaks when he heard news of the massacre on the radio. A handsome twenty-nine-year-old and veteran of six years with the Austin Police Department, he had driven to within a couple of blocks of the tower, then ran, zigzagging across the open plaza with the sniper's bullets kicking up dust around him. None of the three patrolmen had ever been in a gun fight before.

With them was forty-year-old retired Air Force tailgunner Allen Crum, who was a civilian employee of the university. Although he, too, had never fired a shot in combat, Crum insisted on accompanying the officers. He was given a rifle and deputised on the spot. That day, he was to see more action than during his entire twenty-two years in the Air Force. One of the four men punched the lift button. They were about to make the same twenty-seven-floor elevator ride that the crazed gunman had taken less than two hours before.

Dressed in tennis sneakers, blue jeans and a white sports shirt under a pair of workman's overalls, the gunman had pulled into a parking space reserved for university officials between the administration building and the library, at the base of the tower, at around 11 a.m. He unloaded a trolley and placed a heavy footlocker on it. Then he wheeled the trolley into the foyer of the building. The ground-floor receptionist thought he was a maintenance man.

When the elevator door opened he wheeled the trolley into the lift and pushed the button for the top floor. During the 30-second ride, he pulled a rifle from the locker. On the twenty-seventh floor, he unloaded his heavy cargo, then climbed the four short flights of stairs from the lifts to the observation deck. The observation gallery was open to visitors and the gunman approached the receptionist, forty-seven-year-old Edna Townsley, a spirited divorcee and mother of two young sons, who was working on what was normally her day off. He clubbed her with the butt of his rifle with such force that part of her skull was torn away, and dragged her behind the sofa.

At that moment, a young couple came in from the observation gallery. The girl smiled at the gunman, who smiled back. She steered her date around the dark stain that was slowly spreading across the carpet in front of the receptionist's desk. The gunman followed them back down to the lift. As they travelled innocently down in the elevator car, he lugged his heavy locker up the stairs and out on to the observation gallery which ran all the way around the tower, 231 feet above ground level. From that height he could see clean across the shimmering terracotta roofs of old Austin's Spanish-style buildings. Below him were the handsome white university buildings separated by broad lawns and malls. This gave the gunman a clear field of fire across the campus below and the surrounding streets. He assembled his equipment for what he plainly imagined would be a long siege, the lift began to climb from the ground floor up to the twenty-seventh storey again. In it were Marguerite Lamport and her husband, together with Mrs Lamport's brother, M. J. Gabour, his wife Mary and his two teenage sons, sixteen-year-old Mark and nineteen-year-old Mike, who were visiting from Texerkana, Texas.

The two boys led the way up the stairs from the lift, followed by the two women. The men dawdled behind. As Mark opened the door on to the observation deck, he was met with three shotgun blasts in quick succession. The gunman slammed the door shut. The two boys and the women spilled back down the stairs. Gabour rushed to his younger son Mark and turned him over. He saw immediately that Mark was dead. He had been shot in the head at point-blank range. Gabour's sister Marguerite was dead too. His wife and his older son were critically injured. They were bleeding profusely from head wounds. Gabour and his brother-in-law dragged their dead and wounded back down into the lifts.

The gunman quickly barricaded the top of the stairs with furniture and jammed the door shut with the trolley. He went over to the receptionist Mrs Townley and finished her off with a bullet through the head. Then he went out on to the gallery, which was surrounded by a chest-high parapet of limestone eighteen inches thick. He positioned himself under the 'VI' of the gold-edged clock's south face and began shooting the tiny figures in the campus below.

As the elevator reached the twenty-seventh floor again, two hours later, Officer Martinez said a little prayer and offered his life up to God. Immediately the lift doors opened, the officers were faced with a distraught Mr Gabour, whose wife, sister and two sons lay face up on the concrete floor.

'They've killed my family,' he cried.

Mad for revenge, he tried to wrest a gun from the officers.

As officer Day led the weeping man away, Crum, Martinez and McCoy stepped around the bodies and pools of blood on the floor, and began to climb the stairs up to the observation deck. The door at the top of the stairs was all that stood between them and the mad killer they were about to confront.

Although he had already killed 15 innocent people and injured 31 more, the sniper was nothing like the crazed psychopath who rampaged through their adrenaline-charged imaginations. Until the night before, Charles Whitman Jr had seemed the model citizen. Ex-altar boy and US Marine, he was a broad-shouldered, blonde-haired, all-American boy who was known to one and all as a loving husband and son.

Born in 1941 at Lake Worth, Florida, Charles Whitman Jr was the eldest of three brothers. He had been an exemplary son. Pitcher on the school's baseball team, manager of the football team and an adept pianist, he brought home good grades and earned his pocket money doing a paper round. At twelve, he became an Eagle Scout, one of the youngest ever.

His father was a fanatic about guns and raised his boys knowing how to handle them. By the time Whitman enlisted in the US Marines in 1959, he was an expert marksman, scoring 215 out of a possible 250, which won him the rating of sharpshooter. He was also a keen sportsman, enjoying hunting, scuba diving and karate.

However, in the Marines, things began to go wrong. Whitman got busted from corporal to private for the illegal possession of a pistol and was reprimanded for threatening to knock a fellow Marine's teeth out. Meanwhile the facade of his perfect, all-American family began to crack.

Charles Whitman Sr was a prominent civic leader in Lake Worth and one-time chairman of the chamber of commerce. But he was an authoritarian, a perfectionist and an unyielding disciplinarian who demanded the highest of standards from his sons. Nothing Charles Jr did was ever good enough for his father. He resigned himself to regular beatings. But what the young Whitman could not resign himself to was that his father was also a wife-beater. Whitman could not stand the sight of his mother's suffering. He withdrew into himself for long periods and bit his nails down to the quick.

After winning a Marine Corps scholarship Whitman moved to Austin and enrolled at the University of Texas to study architectural engineering. It was in Austin that he met and married his wife, Kathy Leissner, the daughter of a rice-grower and Queen of the Fair of her home town, Needville. They seemed to be the perfect couple, she a teacher, he the local scoutmaster. But life did not go as smoothly as the young couple had hoped. Whitman began to take his growing hostility out on his wife. He became a compulsive gambler and soon faced court martial for gambling and loan sharking. His academic work suffered and his scholarship was withdrawn. He dropped out of college and went back to finish his tour with the Marines. Then in December 1964 suddenly he quit the Corps and went back to university, determined to be a better student and a better husband. He overloaded himself with courses in an attempt to get his degree more quickly. He tried studying real estate sales part-time in case his degree course did not work out and he took on casual jobs to earn cash. Under the pressure of work, he began to lose control of his temper. Fearing that he might lash out at his wife Kathy, he packed, ready to leave her – only to be talked out of it by a friend.

In March 1966, just five months before Whitman's murder spree, the long-suffering Margaret Whitman left her violent husband. Whitman was summoned home in March to help his mother make the break. While she packed, a Lake Worth patrol car sat outside the house. Charles Jr had called it in case his father resorted to violence. To be near to her devoted son Charles Jr, Mrs Whitman moved to Austin. Her youngest son, seventeen-year-old John, moved out at about the same time. Later, he was arrested for throwing a rock through a shop window. A judge ordered him to pay a $25 fine or move back in with his father. He paid the fine. Only twenty-one-year-old Patrick, who worked in Whitman Sr's lucrative plumbing contractors' firm, stayed on with his father in the family home.

After the separation, Whitman's father kept calling Charles Jr, trying to persuade him to bring his mother home. By the end of March, this constant hassle was troubling Charles so much that he sought help from the university's resident psychiatrist, Dr Maurice Heatly. In a two-hour interview, Whitman told Dr Heatly that, like his father, he had beaten his wife a few times. He felt that something was wrong, that he did not feel himself. He said he was making an intense effort to control his temper but he feared that he might explode. He did not mention the blinding headaches that he was suffering with increasing frequency. In his notes, Dr Heatly characterised the crew-cut Whitman as a 'massive, muscular youth who seemed to be oozing with hostility'. Heatly took down only one direct quote from Whitman. He had kept on saying that he was 'thinking about going up on the tower with a deer rifle and to start shooting people'.

At the time, these ominous words did not cause the psychiatrist any concern. Students often came to his clinic talking of the tower as a site for some desperate action. Usually they threatened to throw themselves off it. Three students had killed themselves by jumping off the tower since its completion in 1937. Two others had died in accidental falls. But others said that they felt the tower loomed over them like a mystical symbol. Psychiatrists say that there is generally nothing unusual about threats of violence either. Dr Heatly was not unduly concerned, but recommended that the twenty-five-year-old student come back the following week for another session. Whitman never went back. He decided to fight his problems in his own way. The result was that he declared war on the whole world.

Whatever plans Whitman made over the next four months we cannot know. But those who knew him said that in his last days his anxiety seemed to pass and he became strangely serene. On the night before the massacre, Whitman began a long, rambling letter which gives us a glimpse of some of the things going through his fast-disintegrating mind. Shortly before sunset on the evening of 31 July 1966, Whitman sat down at his battered portable typewriter in his modest yellow brick cottage at 906 Jewell Street.

'I don't quite understand what is compelling me to type this note,' he wrote. 'I have been having fears and violent impulses. I've had some tremendous headaches. I am prepared to die. After my death, I wish an autopsy on me to be performed to see if there's any mental disorders.' Then he launched into a merciless attack on his father whom he hated 'with a mortal passion'. His mother, he regretted, had given 'the best twenty-five years of her life to that man'. Then he wrote: 'I intend to kill my wife after I pick her up from work. I don't want her to have to face the embarrassment that my actions will surely cause her.'

At around 7.30, he had to break off because a friend, fellow engineering student Larry Fuess, and his wife dropped round unexpectedly. They talked for a couple of hours. Fuess said later that Whitman seemed relaxed and perfectly at ease. He exhibited few of his usual signs of nervousness. 'It was almost as if he had been relieved of a tremendous problem,' Fuess said.

After they left, Whitman went back to the typewriter, noted the interruption and wrote simply: 'Life is not worth living.'

It was time to go and pick up his wife. Whitman fed the dog then climbed into his new black '66 Chevrolet Impala and drove over to the Southwestern Bell Telephone Company where Kathy had taken a job as a telephonist during her summer vacation from teaching, to augment the family income. After driving his wife back to the house, he apparently decided not to kill her immediately. Instead, he picked up a pistol and sped across the Colorado River to his mother's fifth-floor flat at Austin's Penthouse Apartments at 1515 Guadeloupe Street. There was a brief struggle. Mrs Whitman's fingers were broken when they were slammed in a door with such force that the band of her engagement ring was driven into the flesh of her finger and the diamond was broken from its setting. Then Whitman stabbed his mother in the chest and shot her in the back of the head, killing her.

He picked up her body, put it on the bed and pulled the covers up so it looked like she was sleeping. He left a handwritten note by the body addressed 'To whom it may concern'. It read: 'I have just killed my mother. If there's a heaven she is going there. If there is not a heaven, she is out of her pain and misery. I love my mother with all my heart. The intense hatred I feel for my father is beyond all description.'

Before leaving, Whitman rearranged the rugs in his mother's apartment to cover the bloodstains on the carpet. And he pinned a note on the front door saying that his mother was ill and would not be going to work that day.

Back at Jewell Street, he typed another line to his letter: '12.30 a.m. Mother already dead.' Some time after that he walked through into the room where his wife was sleeping. He stabbed her three times in the chest with a hunting knife, then pulled the bed sheet up to cover her naked body. He added to his letter, this time in longhand: '3.00 a.m. Wife and mother both dead.' Then he began making preparations for the day ahead.

He got out his old green Marine Corps kitbag which had his name, 'Lance Cpl. C. J. Whitman', stencilled on the side. Into it, he stuffed enough provisions to sustain him during a long siege: twelve tins of Spam, Planters peanuts, fruit cocktail, sandwiches, six boxes of raisins and a vacuum flask of coffee, along with jerry cans containing water and petrol, lighter fuel, matches, earplugs, a compass, rope, binoculars, a hammer, a spanner, a screwdriver, canteens, a snake-bite kit, a transistor radio, toilet paper and, in a bizarre allegiance to the cult of cleanliness, a plastic bottle of Mennen spray deodorant. He also stowed a private armoury that was enough to hold off a small army – a machete, a Bowie knife, a hatchet, a 9 mm Luger pistol, a Galesi-Brescia pistol, a .357 calibre Smith & Wesson revolver, a 35 mm Remington rifle and a 6 mm Remington bolt-action rifle with a four-power Leupold telescopic sight. With this, experts say, a halfway decent shot can consistently hit a six-and-a-half inch circle at 300 yards. He left three more rifles and two derringers at home.

It is not known whether Whitman slept that night. But at 7.15 a.m. he turned up at the Austin Rental Equipment Service and rented a three-wheeled trolley. At 9 a.m. he called his wife's supervisor at the telephone company and said that she was too ill to work that day. Then he drove to a Davis hardware store where he bought a second-hand .30 M1 carbine, which was standard issue in the US Army at that time. At Chuck's Gun Shop he bought some thirty-shot magazines for his new carbine and several hundred rounds of ammunition. And at 9.30 a.m. he walked into Sears Roebuck's department store in Austin and bought a twelve-bore shotgun, on credit.

Back at Jewell Street, he took the shotgun into the garage and began cutting down the barrel and stock. The postman, Chester Arrington, stopped by and chatted to Whitman for about twenty-five minutes. He was probably the last person to speak to Whitman before the massacre. Years later he recalled: 'I saw him sawing off the shotgun. I knew it was illegal. All I had to do was pick up the telephone and report him. It could have stopped him. I've always blamed myself.'

At last everything was ready. Whitman loaded his kitbag and the last of his guns into a metal truck and loaded the locker into the boot of his car. He covered it with a blanket, zipped a pair of grey nylon overalls over his blue jeans and white shirt and, around 10.30 a.m., set off for the university.

Nearly three hours later, Whitman was still fulfilling his deadly mission. Dead bodies were strewn across the streets and plazas below him and hundreds cowered from his bullets. But it could not last for ever. Outside the door to the observation deck, just a few feet away, two policemen and a veteran Air Force tailgunner were determined to put an end to his psychopathic spree.

Crum, the civilian, took charge.

'Let's do this service style,' he whispered. 'I'll cover you and you cover me.'

They cleared away the barricade at the top of the stairs and, while the police on the ground intensified their fire to distract the killer, Martinez slowly pushed away the trolley that was propped against the door. Using an overturned desk as a shield, they crawled towards the observation gallery. Crum, carrying a rifle, headed west, while Martinez, with a .38 service revolver, headed eastwards around the gallery, followed by McCoy who was carrying a shotgun.

Martinez rounded one corner then, more slowly, turned on to the north side of the walkway. About fifty feet away, he saw Whitman crouched down and edging towards the corner Crum was about to come round.

But Crum heard Whitman coming and loosed off a shot. It tore a great chunk out of the parapet. Whitman turned and ran back, into the sights of Officer Martinez. Martinez, who had never fired a gun in anger before, shot – and missed. Whitman raised his carbine and fired, but he was trembling and could not keep the gun level. As he squeezed the trigger the gun jerked and the bullet screamed harmlessly over the officer's head. Martinez then emptied his remaining five rounds into the gunman. But still he would not go down. McCoy stepped forward and blasted him twice with the shotgun. Whitman hit the concrete still holding his weapon. Martinez saw that he was still moving. Grabbing the shotgun from McCoy, he ran forward, blasting Whitman at point-blank range in the head. Crum then took Whitman's green towel from his footlocker and waved it above the parapet. At last the gunman was dead.

At 1.40 p.m. two ambulance men carried Whitman's blanket-shrouded body from the tower on a canvas stretcher. The police quickly established his identity and his name was broadcast on the radio. His father rang the police department in Austin and asked them to check his son's and estranged wife's apartments. Along with the bodies of the two women and the notes he had written, Whitman left two rolls of film with the instruction to have them developed. The photographs had been taken over the previous few weeks, but only showed the killer in various ordinary domestic poses, such as snoozing on the sofa with his dog at his feet.

Interviewed later by the press, Whitman's father announced proudly that his son 'always was a crack shot'. In fact, he said, all of his sons were good with guns.

'I am a fanatic about guns,' he admitted. 'My boys knew all about them. I believe in that.'

Whitman had learned the lesson well. In his house, guns had hung in every room.

An autopsy later revealed that there was, as Whitman himself had suspected, something wrong with his brain. He had a tumour the size of a pecan nut in the hypothalamus, but the pathologist, Dr Coleman de Chenar, said that it was certainly not the cause of Whitman's headaches and could not have had any influence on his behaviour. The state pathologist agreed that it was benign and could not have caused Whitman any pain, but a report by the Governor of Texas said that it was malignant and would have killed Whitman within a year. The report also concluded that the tumour could have contributed to Whitman's loss of control.

A number of Dexedrine tablets – known at the time as goofballs – were also found in Whitman's possession, but physicians were not able to detect that he had taken any before he died. He may simply have laid in the stimulants to keep him alert during a long siege.

As it is, he had claimed the lives of fourteen people during his murderous rampage, not including his own, plus his wife and mother. Thirty-one others had been injured; some were permanently scarred or disabled.

The bodies of Charles Whitman and his mother were returned together to Florida, his in a grey metal casket, hers in a green and white one. With hundreds of curiosity seekers gawking and jostling in the rolling, palm-fringed cemetery in West Palm Beach, mother and son were interred with full Catholic rites. The priest said that Whitman had obviously been deranged which meant he was not responsible for the sin of murder and was therefore eligible for burial in hallowed ground. The grand jury also found that Whitman was insane.

Flags were flown at half-mast on the Austin campus of the University of Texas for a week. The tower was closed to the public for a year, but re-opened in July 1967. Following a number of suicide attempts, it was closed for good in 1975.

Charles Whitman's tower-top massacre threw America into a fit of self-examination. What disturbed America so much was that the lives of so many innocent passers-by had been snuffed out randomly, for no reason. In almost every case they were unknown to their killer, the incidental and impersonal casualties of the uncharted battlefields that existed only in his demented mind. With the massacre coming just two-and-a-half years after the assassination of President Kennedy, which had also taken place in Texas, Americans were concerned that something was going badly wrong in the land of the free.

Charles Whitman may have been unusual in having a dozen guns at his disposal, but he was by no means unique. Americans – especially Texans – have always been gun-toting people. Guns had been used by the first settlers to protect and feed themselves and to subdue the hostile land. Later the colonists became a nation of riflemen who used the gun to win their freedom from the British in the War of Independence. Guns tamed the West and became synonymous with frontier justice. And by the 1960s, there was a massive market for guns among collectors and sportsmen. America had the largest cache of civilian hand guns in the world with over 100 million in private hands. Sales were running at over a million a year by mail order alone. Another million or so were imported. But, following the assassination of President Kennedy, Americans became very conscious that there were very few legal controls over the possession of firearms. In Texas, the gun laws were practically non-existent, and in Dallas, the scene of Kennedy's murder, some 72 per cent of all murders in 1965 were committed with guns. This compared with but 25 per cent in New York City, where New York State's fifty-five-year-old Sullivan Law required police permits for the possession of handguns. Veteran FBI chief J. Edgar Hoover said:

'Those who claim that the availability of firearms is not a factor in the murders in this country are not facing reality.'

American legislators were very conscious that most other countries had much stricter gun-control laws. But given America's passion for firearms, trying to ban them would be unthinkable – especially as it would curb such legitimate activities as hunting, target shooting and, in some cases, possessing a gun for self-defence. Nevertheless, in the wake of the Austin slaughter, the US Justice Department, the American Bar Association and most American police forces felt that much tighter gun controls were called for. This prompted Connecticut Senator Thomas Dodd to propose a federal bill limiting the inter-state shipment of mail-order handguns, curbing the importing of military surplus firearms, banning over-the-counter handgun sales to out-of-state buyers and anyone under twenty-one, and prohibiting long-arm sales to anyone under eighteen.

Several individual states backed Dodd's bill, as they felt it would help them enforce their own gun laws. Some proposed statutory cooling-off periods, so that buyers would have to wait a few days before they could obtain guns, and prohibiting sales to known criminals and psychotics. Yet opposing even these trivial proposals was the influential National Rifle Association, whose 750,000 members vigorously lobbied against any gun-control legislation. Some right-wingers even claimed that gun control was a Communist plot to disarm Americans. Even ordinary citizens claimed the constitutional right to bear arms – even though, at that time, the Supreme Court denied that there was such a right. True, the Second Amendment to the United States Constitution mentioned the 'right of the people to keep and bear arms' but it actually read, in full: 'A well-regulated Militia being necessary to the security of a free state, the right of the people to keep and bear arms shall not be infringed.' What the

Founding Fathers had in mind, the Supreme Court argued, was the collective right to bear arms, not the individual right. Since Americans already needed licences to marry, drive, run a shop or, in some states, own a dog, it was difficult to see why making them take out a licence to own a lethal weapon was any particular infringement of their liberty.

But, even under Dodd's bill, Charles Whitman would still have been able to amass his sizeable arsenal, as none of the bill's provisions applied to him.

Reacting to what he called the 'shocking tragedy' in Austin, President Johnson urged the speedy passage of the bill 'to help prevent the wrong persons from obtaining firearms'. However, no one was sure how you could recognise the 'wrong persons'.

Austin's police chief said that 'this kind of thing could have happened anywhere'. But that was no comfort. Psychiatrists began to speculate that there was something intrinsic to modern American society that created crazed killers like Whitman. *Time* magazine reported that nearly 2.5 million Americans had been treated for mental illness in hospitals and clinics that year. Almost a third of them were classified as psychotic – people who, by the minimum definition, had lost touch with reality. They lived in a world of fantasy, haunted by fears and delusions of persecution. An accidental bump on a crowded sidewalk or a passing criticism from an employer or relative could set any of these psychotics off.

The menace of the psychotic killer was all the more frightening because they may seem like the model citizen – until they go berserk. Many of these people have a feeling that there is a demon within themselves, Los Angeles clinical psychiatrist Martin Grotjahn told *Time* magazine. They try to kill the demon by model behaviour. They live the opposite of what they feel. Like Whitman, they become gentle, very mild, extremely nice people who often show the need to be perfectionists.

Some psychiatrists estimated at the time that the percentage of potential mass killers in the US ranged as high as one in every thousand, or 200,000 people across the country. Most of these, of course, would never carry out their murderous desires. But Houston psychiatrist C. A. Dwyer warned the American public: 'Potential killers are everywhere these days. They are driving cars, going to church with you, working with you. And you never know it until they snap.' Perhaps he was overreacting, but the history of the last thirty years has shown that there is some truth in what he said.

Americans were warned to stay alert. They were to watch for sudden personality changes in friends and loved ones and that special attention should be paid to habitually shy and quiet people who suddenly become aggressive and talkative – or the reverse. Other danger signs were depression and seclusion, hypersensitivity to tiny slights and insults, changes in normal patterns of eating or sleeping, uncontrolled outbursts of temper, disorganised thinking and a morbid interest in guns, knives or other instruments of destruction.

Psychiatrists were quick to point out that the appearance of any of these symptoms does not necessarily mean that someone is about to turn killer. However, those exhibiting them were in need of psychiatric help. Unfortunately, even if a dangerous psychotic – like Charles Whitman – did reach the examining room, it was by no means certain that they could be headed off. Most doctors agreed that the University of Texas psychiatrist who took no action, even after Whitman confessed his urge to climb the Austin tower and kill people several months before the actual incident took place, was not at fault. University of Chicago psychiatrist Robert S. Daniels said that 'thousands – and I mean literally thousands – talk to doctors about having such feelings. Nearly all of them are just talking.'

Deciding who was, and who wasn't, going to follow their murderous impulses was more of an art than a science. It was also a matter of practicality. The practice of psychiatry depended on trust between patient and doctor. Psychiatrists could hardly be expected to report every threatening remark. Besides, as the New York deputy police commissioner pointed out, 'We can't arrest people because they are ill'. New Jersey psychiatrist Henry A. Davidson added: 'We are in a situation now where there is enormous pressure for civil rights. The idea of locking someone up on the basis of a psychiatrist's opinion that he might in future be violent could be repugnant.'

However, some American states had already empowered doctors to forcibly commit any patient they thought dangerous – at least for long enough for a thorough psychiatric examination. But most states insisted that the individual commit themselves voluntarily or that their family or the courts place them in hospital care. Usually the doctor could only try and persuade the patient that voluntary commitment was in their own best interest. Unfortunately, most psychotics were not amenable to having themselves locked up and, in the 1960s, most families regarded mental illness as a shameful thing and resisted formal commitment to a mental institution until it was too late.

Whitman's murderous spree had also been seen to be associated with the Vietnam War, which was bringing true-life violence directly into America's living rooms every night at the time. The first televised war, network coverage of Vietnam became the backdrop to the late 1960s and early 1970s. It brought with it an unprecedented tide of assassinations, urban violence and spree killings. This attitude was made explicit in the 1976 film *Taxi Driver*. Made just one year after the end of the war, it showed Robert De Niro as brooding ex-Marine and Vietnam veteran Travis Bickle. The film follows the insomniac psychopath as he meticulously prepares himself to declare war on the world. It ends, predictably, in a violent bloodbath.

However, although Charles Whitman was a Marine, he was honourably discharged in 1964, a year before President Johnson committed ground troops to Vietnam. Whitman experienced none of the alienation that the veterans of that unpopular war suffered.

Two films were made about him. In *Targets*, made in 1968, director Peter Bogdanovich switched the action to a drive-in cinema, where a psychotic sniper picks off the innocent viewers of a horror film. *The Deadly Tower*, in 1975, gave a literal version of events. However, these films were not entirely without precedent in America. In 1952, a film called *The Sniper* had been released, about a youth who shot blondes. And in 1962, Ford Clark published a novel called *The Open Space*. In it, the protagonist climbs a tower in a Midwestern university and begins picking off people. As far as the police could ascertain, Whitman had neither seen the film nor read the book. The material Whitman had assembled for his murder spree remained in police custody until 1972. Then it was auctioned off to augment the fund set up to help the victims of his crimes. Whitman's guns fetched $1,500 from a dealer in Kansas, proving that the image of Charles Whitman had found a place deep in the American psyche, a chilling legacy that lasted beyond his crime and his death.

Chapter 6

All in the Family

On the evening of 13 November 1974 the Suffolk County Police Department received a phone call from a man who identified himself as Joe Yeswit.

'A kid came running into the bar,' the caller said. 'He says everybody in his family had been killed, and we came down to look.'

The location was Ocean Avenue in the affluent suburb of Amityville, Long Island.

The first policeman on the scene was Patrolman Kenneth Greguski. He found a group of young men milling around the driveway of a large suburban house. One of them was crying. 'My mother, my father are dead,' he sobbed. He gave his name as Ronald DeFeo Jr, aged twenty-three.

Inside the house, Greguski was quite unprepared for what he found. Until then the only crime in the sleepy suburb some thirty-five miles east of New York City was that of vandals ripping boats from their moorings around Great South Bay. The bloodstained bodies of a man and a woman lay face down on the bed in the master bedroom. In a smaller room, Greguski found two young boys who had also been shot. In a third bedroom, a young girl had been shot in the face. Greguski then climbed the stairs into the attic, where he found the body of an older girl face down on the bed.

The victims had been Ronald DeFeo Sr, a wealthy car dealer aged forty-three, his wife Louise, forty-two, their two daughters Dawn, eighteen and Allison, thirteen, and their sons Mark, twelve and John, nine. Ronald DeFeo Jr, sobbing in the driveway, was the family's sole survivor.

DeFeo told the detectives that the murders were the work of Louis Falini, a friend of his father. DeFeo Jr had fallen out with Falini over a botched paint job for the DeFeo family firm, a Brooklyn Buick dealership, and cursed him. DeFeo Sr had then reprimanded him for insulting Falini. 'He's a Mafia hitman,' DeFeo Jr claimed his father had said.

DeFeo also claimed that, on another occasion, his father had had a run-in with Falini and had yelled: 'If anything happens to my son, I'll kill you and your whole family.'

Ronald Joseph DeFeo had been born on 26 September 1951 in Brooklyn, New York. His father was then a twenty-year-old textile worker. His mother, Louise, was nineteen. Her father owned a car showroom in Brooklyn. He offered DeFeo Sr a well-paid job there as service manager.

The family moved out into the bayside village of Amityville to a large house they named 'High Hopes'. They had enough money to spoil their children, but their eldest, Ronald Jr, responded only with sulks and tantrums. At school his classmates called him 'Butch' and the nickname stuck. His classwork was poor and he dropped out at sixteen without graduating.

Drifting through a number of lowly paid manual jobs, he began to get a taste for girls, drink and drugs – all bankrolled by handouts from his father. His drug habit started with pills, marijuana and LSD, but soon he moved on to heroin and amphetamines. He also got into trouble with the police and was on probation for stealing an outboard motor.

In an effort to bring his son under control, DeFeo Sr gave Ronald a job in the family firm – as a mechanic and general dogsbody at just $80 a week. This again was topped up by his father's generous handouts of up to $500 a week.

Neighbours speculated about how a service manager could live so well. There was some speculation at the trial that DeFeo Sr had been swindling his father-in-law, and that DeFeo Jr had attempted a bogus heist of the company payroll.

Although the DeFeos had left Brooklyn for the suburbs, they had brought its aggressive ways with them. Neighbours complained of their shouting matches. In 1973, during a fight between his parents, DeFeo had pulled a gun. He pointed it at his father and pulled the trigger. It misfired. The effect on DeFeo Sr was salutary. He became a devout Catholic and built several shrines in the garden of his home. DeFeo Jr got on no better with his mother, whom he described as a 'lousy cook'. His brothers were 'a couple of pigs'. He liked his sisters no better.

In 1974 DeFeo discovered that, when he stopped taking drugs, he became violent. Then he had problems with girls. He found that they turned him off and he turned to heroin for succour.

In the rambling eight-page statement he gave to the police after the massacre, he said that he had spent the afternoon drinking with friends in a bar, then shot up some heroin. He returned to the bar later – he had arranged to meet a friend named Bobby Kelske there. DeFeo was detained at Suffolk County's Fourth Precinct overnight. When Bobby Kelske was interviewed he said that when he had arrived at the bar, DeFeo was complaining to four or five others that was locked out. He had not got his own keys, he said, and he was 'going to have to break a window to get in'.

DeFeo sped off in his Buick, but within minutes he was back. He stood in the doorway screaming: 'You gotta help me. Someone shot my mum and dad.'

Kelske also told the police that DeFeo was a gun fanatic and that, a couple of weeks before, he had been trying to buy a silencer.

Suffolk County's ballistic expert said that all the victims had been slain with a .35 calibre Marlin rifle. But no such weapon had been found on the scene. Then, in an alcove in DeFeo's bedroom, the police found two cardboard boxes. Their labels showed that they had contained Marlin rifles – a .22 and a .35.

At 9 a.m. three homicide detectives pushed open the door to the room where DeFeo was sleeping.

'Did you find Falini yet?' DeFeo asked when they woke him.

The detectives explained that they had people out on the streets looking for him. Then Detective Harrison said: 'But to tell you the truth, I think you're the guy we want.'

During questioning that morning DeFeo gave several different versions of the killing. But each time, Falini was the culprit.

'That Falini loved it,' DeFeo claimed. 'He was like a mad dog. The gun was smoking and the barrel was hot.'

In one version, Falini had an unnamed accomplice. DeFeo claimed that he had been awoken with a gun to his head. 'You're gonna live with this for the rest of your life,' Falini had told him. 'This is for what you did to me.'

DeFeo claimed that he was then forced at pistol-point from room to room while Falini murdered four of his family. Then DeFeo himself had been forced to shoot his father and his brother Mark.

The detectives patiently pointed out the inconsistencies in his story. Then Detective Dennis Rafferty said to DeFeo: 'It didn't happen that way, did it?' DeFeo cradled his head in his hands and Rafferty said quietly: 'Butch, tell me what happened.'

After a moment, DeFeo confessed.

'It all started so fast,' he said. 'Once I started, I just could not stop.'

At 6 p.m. DeFeo was charged and gave a full confession. He said that he had fallen asleep in front of the TV set on the night of 12 November. When he awoke, he went to his room, loaded his .35 rifle and shot his father and mother in their bed. He shot Allison in the head, then moved on to his brothers' room and shot them where they lay.

Dawn had been woken by the noise. He assured her that everything was all right. When she went back into her room, he followed and shot her.

Carefully, he collected the spent cartridge cases. Back in his room, DeFeo changed. He stuffed the clothes he had been wearing, the rifle, spare ammunition and the cartridge cases into some pillowcases, and he carried the pillowcases out to the car. The rifle he dumped in the bay. Everything else was dropped down a drain in Brooklyn. Then he had breakfast in a diner before reporting for work.

The police found the ammunition and clothes in a sewer on the corner of East 19th Street, in Brooklyn. And a police scuba diver retrieved the rifle from the small village dock at the end of Ocean Avenue.

The case took a year to come to trial. DeFeo planned to plead insanity. He began to act up in prison, setting fire to his cell, ripping up his mail and threatening to commit suicide. But he boasted to a cellmate that, once he had beaten the rap, he would have an inheritance of over $100,000 to spend.

DeFeo also tried to plea-bargain. He told the prosecution that he had had accomplices and named them – Bobby Kelske, his girlfriend Sherry Klein and another couple. They had been ransacking the DeFeo home when Mr DeFeo Sr had disturbed them. DeFeo himself had not actually pulled the trigger, he said, and one of the other gang-members had gone on to kill his mother, sisters and brothers.

In another version of this story, DeFeo had been doing the ransacking himself when his father discovered the hiding place for his loot.

DeFeo had killed his father to silence him, then gone 'berserk' and killed the rest of the family.

The first witness at DeFeo's trial was Patrolman Greguski, whose eyes streamed with tears when he described what he had found in DeFeo's home that night. DeFeo smirked. Later he played the bewildered madman.

The defence psychiatrist said that DeFeo was mentally ill, a paranoid schizophrenic who believed that people were out to kill him and that his only recourse was to kill them first. He did not know what he was doing on the night of the crime, the doctor said.

When DeFeo took the stand he was shown a picture of his mother lying murdered in her bed. DeFeo claimed not to know 'this person'. He had never seen her before, he said.

He recognised a similar picture of his father and admitted killing him, in self-defence. He denied having any accomplices, then said that his evil sister Dawn had made him do it. She had decided to kill everyone in the house and had put the rifle in his hands. 'Very, very calmly' he had gone to his parents' room and had shot them. Then he had dropped the gun, but Dawn had picked it up. He heard shots and realised that she had killed the other children, he said. This made him mad. He grabbed the gun and shot her. On top of that, he said,

Dawn had had an accomplice. He even claimed that he was not sure that his family were all dead. 'One of them might come walking in here any minute,' he said. 'Then we'll see who the laugh is on.'

The jury were not impressed. They found him sane and guilty on all six counts of murder in the second degree. He was sentenced to twenty-five years to life on each count. All his appeals to the parole board have been turned down.

After sentencing, when the clerk of the court took down DeFeo's details – 'Name?', 'Date of birth?', 'Citizenship status?' – he asked: 'Are your parents living or dead?'

'Dead,' came the chilling reply.

Once DeFeo was safely in the state penitentiary, the DeFeo's family home, 'High Hopes', was sold to a family who lived there for less than a month. They fled, claiming that the house was possessed by evil forces. This story led to the book *The Amityville Horror* and a series of films. However, people have lived there since and say that the house is perfectly normal.

Less than six months after Butch DeFeo's Amityville massacre, another killer wiped out his entire family – the largest mass murder of a single family in American history. It was Easter Sunday 1975, the day after James Ruppert's forty-first birthday. Ruppert had never married and shared his mother's small wood-frame house in a leafy, middle-class neighbourhood of Hamilton, Ohio. Short, bookish with thick spectacles, Ruppert had trained as a draughtsman but, at that time, he was out of work and short of money. He stayed in bed, hung-over and depressed.

His mother, sixty-five-year-old Charity Ruppert, was downstairs at 635 Minor Avenue: preparing a big family dinner. Her elder son Leonard, his wife Alma and their eight children – aged between seventeen and four – were driving over from nearby Fairfield after they had been to morning mass.

At 4 p.m. James Ruppert came downstairs and chatted with his brother Leonard. The children were in the garden, hunting for Easter eggs. Ruppert said that he was going to go target shooting and went upstairs to get his gun. When he came down again carrying a rifle and three pistols, the whole family was gathered in the kitchen. His mother was cutting sandwiches. Leonard and Alma were sitting together at the kitchen table.

'How's your Volkswagen?' Leonard asked his brother.

Ruppert answered with his gun, One shot sent Leonard tumbling back from his seat. Alma was the next to die. Ruppert's mother lunged at him in a desperate effort to save her family. She died next. Then the eight children were killed one after the other. James Ruppert fired thirty-one times in all. One child was shot just once in the chest. The others were shot three times each, to make sure they were dead. It was all over quickly. Eleven were dead in all. Nobody ran. Nobody screamed. The neighbours heard nothing.

Three hours later Ruppert picked up the phone and called the police. 'There's been a shooting here,' he said.

When the police arrived they found six blood-stained bodies in the kitchen and five in the lounge. The only sign of a struggle was one overturned wastepaper bin.

Ruppert put up no resistance, but he refused to talk, indicating that he intended to plead insanity. This left the police baffled.

'We can't seem to find a motive for this,' Hamilton Police Chief George McNally told reporters.

Neighbours knew little of Ruppert, except that he was intelligent, an avid reader and a bit of a loner. His uncle, Rufus Skinner, claimed that the two brothers had been very close and that they had done everything for their mother since their father died in 1947. Ruppert's only friend, Arthur Bauer, said: 'He's not violent at all. I can't believe he did it.'

At his trial Ruppert entered a plea of insanity. His attorney claimed that he had been insane for ten years. Psychiatrists said he was in a 'paranoid psychotic state' which loosened his hold on reality. Ruppert, it was said, believed that his family, the police and the FBI were involved in a long-term conspiracy against him. This delusion led him, suddenly, to strike back against his persecutors.

The prosecution disagreed. They said that the motive was simple – the $300,000 in property, life insurance, investments and other savings that he stood to inherit from the death of his entire family. Hence, the prosecution said, the plea of temporary insanity. If found not guilty due to insanity, Ruppert would be sent to a mental hospital. But, eventually, he would walk – with $300,000 in his pocket. Found guilty, he would be in for life and Ohio State law would deprive him of his inheritance. Psychiatrists for the prosecution maintained that Ruppert was sane – and in control – when he slaughtered the rest of his family.

In court James Ruppert was painted as a sickly child, whose widowed mother lavished her love on her elder son Leonard. James began to feel like an outcast in his own family. He was shorter than Leonard, less bright, less adept at school. While Leonard had a successful career with General Electric and a hugely successful family life, James – on the threshold of middle age – found himself a failure by comparison. He became a heavy drinker and was threatened with eviction by his own mother because, while he could pay for alcohol, he had no money for rent.

James Ruppert claimed that his brother had beaten him when they were children and had taunted him for his weediness – taunts which had found a deadly echo in an innocent enquiry about his broken-down Volkswagen. By the mid-1960s, when James was thirty, he began to believe that Leonard was a major figure in the conspiracy against him: his brother and his mother had begun whispering to the FBI that Ruppert was a Communist and a homosexual.

Ruppert took comfort in his small collection of guns. He would sit on the banks of the Great Miami River and take pot-shots at floating tin cans with his .357 Magnum. People had seen him doing this two days before the massacre. A gun-store assistant also remembered Ruppert asking about buying a silencer.

Twenty-eight-year-old Wanda Bishop said that she had met Ruppert in a cocktail lounge the night before the shootings. He had complained about being unemployed and his lack of money. His mother, he said, was planning to evict him from his rent-free room at home. She had told him that if he could afford to buy beer seven days a week, he could afford to pay rent.

Ruppert claimed that Leonard's casual enquiry about his VW was the breaking point. Leonard had been trying to sabotage it, he was convinced, and he had asked the question with 'a mocking smile'. This was the final straw. He killed Leonard and his family so that Leonard would never hurt him again.

The three-judge panel found Ruppert guilty on all eleven counts of murder and sentenced him to life imprisonment. Later he was granted a new trial on a technicality. This time he was found guilty of the murders of his brother and mother, but not guilty on the nine other counts due to insanity. Even so, Ruppert's inheritance was lost.

DeFeo and Ruppert were both, in the words of Hamilton Police Chief George McNally, 'gun freaks'. But another family killer, Harry De La Roche Jr, had more conventional associations for a spree killer. He was a cadet at a military academy, and was home for the Thanksgiving holiday when he suddenly went berserk.

Thanksgiving is celebrated in America every year on the third Thursday in November. As a national holiday it is more important than Christmas. Families get together and eat turkey, cranberry sauce, baked yams and pumpkin pie.

On the Sunday of 21 November 1976, eighteen-year-old Harry De La Roche Jr flew home to New Jersey for the holiday. For three months he had been an unwilling student at The Citadel, a military college in South Carolina. He was not happy there.

De La Roche was an introverted and sickly child. He had problems with his ears that made them so sensitive that certain sounds made him scream in agony. At four he underwent a major operation on his ears and throat. He was short-sighted and weedy – the smallest boy in his class at high school. To compensate he wore an army jacket and combat boots. But still he was bullied. Too small to defend himself, he nursed grudges. He was never able to forgive and forget.

His father had a hot temper and would hit his sons over any minor infraction. But De La Roche formed a close relationship with his younger brother, Ronald, and the two boys would cover up for each other's drinking, cigarette- and marijuana-smoking, and late-night excursions.

De La Roche loved animals and the countryside. He also joined the Civil Air Patrol and enjoyed it. The family thought that he would pursue a military career. De La Roche went along with this, probably to please his father. He had already decided never to let anyone know how he felt inside on his own and never let anyone know how he felt inside.

He was disappointed when he was turned down by grander military establishments, including West Point. But the family were

99

proud that he was accepted by The Citadel. De La Roche hated it, however. It was far from home and too much like being back in school. He was picked on, teased and mocked.

Thanksgiving was De La Roche's first trip home since enrolling. He was determined to tell his parents that he was never going back to The Citadel, but he dreaded his father's reaction.

De La Roche Sr had been in the heart of the American dream in Montvale. His own father was illegitimate and fatherless. He had began work as a sewing-machine repairman and worked his way up to a senior position in the export sales division of the Ford Motor Company in Newark. Although his wife's family never accepted him – the source of numerous rows – Harry De La Roche Sr was a model citizen: a church-goer, an organiser of the local Boy Scouts troop and coach to a number of local sports teams.

He also had great ambitions for his sons. Instead, in Harry Jr, he had raised a spotty, myopic dullard.

The whole family drove to New York's Kennedy Airport to meet him. His father, Harry De La Roche Sr, took the wheel of the family's green Ford station wagon for the drive home to 23 East Grand Avenue, Montvale, fifteen miles across the state line in New Jersey.

Harry's mother, Mary Jane, admired her son's new dress uniform and his two young brothers, Ronnie and Eric, teased him about the weight he had put on. But the family were proud of him and happy to see him again.

They asked him about his life at college, but he refused to answer. 'I'll tell you later,' he said. In a letter posted the previous week he had said that he would tell them all about it on Thanksgiving night, and not before.

De La Roche had tried his hardest at The Citadel. He had changed his name to 'Bill' and was determined to make a new start. Craving a life full of friends, he found himself excluded, the object of derision. Seething with pent-up rage, he found it hard to buckle down to the strict discipline expected of raw recruits. Before leaving The Citadel for Thanksgiving, De La Roche had told his tutors that his mother had contracted terminal cancer and he was needed at home. He would not be back.

There were only two things he had ever done right in his life. One was to be accepted at The Citadel; the other, against all the odds and after years of diligent practice, was to become a first-class shot.

It was Harry Sr who had taught his sons to shoot. The $50,000 family home was littered with guns. De La Roche's father even kept a .22 pistol next to his bed. Harry Jr loved to touch them.

He spent the time in the run-up to Thanksgiving smoking pot. Over the Thanksgiving meal questions about his life at The Citadel came up, but De La Roche was evasive. He kept telling his family that he would tell them later.

He was scheduled to fly back to South Carolina on Sunday. By Saturday evening, when the time came to pack, he still had not got around to telling his parents how he felt. Instead he went out for a drive with a friend in his mother's white Falcon. They went for a meal at a Burger King in Rockland County, then De La Roche dropped his friend off and headed for New York City on his own. He sat in a bar until 2 a.m. nursing a beer, then drove home through a thick fog.

In the still Autumn night the fog lay thick across New Jersey.

Montvale slumbered under its blanket. It swirled down East Grand Avenue as De La Roche drove by.

Two hours later it had still barely lifted when, at 4.10 a.m., Patrolman Carl Olsen saw a white Falcon run a stop sign. The car slowed to a halt outside a bar on Park Avenue. Olsen pulled alongside. The driver, a young man with glasses, leapt out and ran over to the patrol car.

'Quick,' yelled the young man. 'Quick, come up to my house. I've just found my parents and my younger brother dead and my middle brother missing.'

Patrolman Olsen went back to 23 East Grand Avenue with De La Roche and while the young man slumped on the sofa in the living room Olsen searched the house. Upstairs he found Harry De La Roche Sr's body lying face down on one of the two twin beds. Mrs De La Roche was also dead, her head on a bloody pillow. Olsen also found the blood-soaked body of twelve-year-old Eric. There were signs that a life-or-death struggle had taken place. All three had been shot. Back downstairs, Patrolman Olsen had just one question for De La Roche: 'What the hell happened here?'

De La Roche lit a cigarette from the butt he had just finished. He told Patrolman Olsen that he had returned home after an evening out with an old high-school friend to find the porch-light out. Normally it was left burning. Upstairs he found his youngest brother and his parents dead. His other brother, Ronald, was missing. Numb with shock, he had driven off to find a cop.

Downtown at police headquarters, De La Roche explained that his father had caught Ronald smoking pot. There had been a fight about it. De La Roche Sr had threatened to turn Ronald in to the police. In protest, Harry Jr said he had planned to refuse to return to The Citadel – wasting his father's money – but he never got the chance. By the time he could make his announcement, his family were dead.

Later that day Ronald's body was found stuffed in a trunk in the attic at East Grand Avenue. He had been shot. There was no sign of a gun. The trunk lid was closed and boxes of Christmas decorations had been piled on top. All this ruled out suicide.

Confronted with this new evidence, De La Roche confessed to massacring his family. In a second sworn statement he described how he had crept into his father's bedroom and picked up the .22 pistol his father kept by his bed. De La Roche could not make up his mind whether to kill his father – and end a life-time of oppression – or not. He claimed to have held the pistol to the old man's head for fifteen minutes before screaming 'I can't go back' and pulling the trigger.

The noise woke his mother. De La Roche shot her. Then he fired again into his father's body. In the next bedroom his two brothers were now awake. Fifteen-year-old Ronald cowered in his bed, where he was shot. But his younger brother Eric fought for his life. He ran at De La Roche, who shot him twice in the face and once more in the chest. Even then Eric did not stop screaming, so De La Roche battered him around the head with the pistol butt until he was silent.

That afternoon, when De La Roche was formally charged with four counts of murder, Bergen County prosecutor Joseph C. Woodcock found him 'extraordinarily calm'. But a few weeks later De La Roche told the family priest, Pastor Roy Nilsen, that he had not killed his family alone. In fact, he claimed his brother Ronald had shot his parents and brother Eric after their father had caught him taking drugs. De La Roche admitted then shooting his brother in rage. Nevertheless, Harry De La Roche Jr was arraigned for all four murders.

After thorough psychiatric examination, both prosecution and defence agreed that De La Roche was not insane. But by the time the case came to trial, the defence team had little option but to plead 'general insanity'. The prosecution agreed that he was sick, perhaps even needed hospitalisation. But legally, he was sane and the four murders were premeditated. The jury found him guilty on all four counts of murder in the first degree. He was sentenced to life imprisonment on each count, the sentences to run concurrently.

The day after the verdict, at De La Roche's request, he was taken in handcuffs to the cemetery where his family had been buried. It was twelve degrees below zero. As a prison officer brushed the snow from the grave stone to reveal the family name, De La Roche began to cry.

Chapter 7

The Age of Innocence

1965 was still an age of innocence and people believed that motiveless multiple murders like Unruh's, Starkweather's and Clark's were isolated incidents. But a year later, just a month before Charles Whitman climbed Austin Tower, a mass murder in Chicago started an epidemic. The senseless spree shocked America. It even sickened the man who had done it. The morning after the hideous crime the killer woke up to hear a radio report of the multiple slaying. He had no idea that he had committed it.

In 1966 there was a long, hot summer in Chicago. On 12 July the police arrested a black youth who had turned on a fire hydrant so the local children could play in its cool spray. Soon the West Side of Chicago was up in arms and the city exploded in a full-scale race riot. Hundreds of stores were looted. The National Guard was called in. Two black people were killed by stray sniper fire and the police arrested over 200 people. The violence only subsided after Martin Luther King had stepped in and the authorities conceded that sprinklers would be fitted to some hydrants.

But on the evening of 13 July the disturbances were still at their height. The authorities were praying for a break in the weather to cool things off. Thunder clouds began rolling in off Lake Michigan, and the temperature dropped a few degrees. But the humidity climbed. In the peaceful suburb of Jeffery Manor the houses had their windows thrown open to catch any breeze in the sultry night air.

On East 100th Street, in the block between Crandon Avenue and Luella, there were six identical two-storey town houses. Three of them belonged to the local hospital, used as hostels for student nurses. In the house at 2319 East 100th Street, three of the eight occupants were qualified nurses from the Philippines who had come to Chicago for post-graduate studies. One of them, Corazon Amurao, had just settled down to sleep in the upstairs front room she shared with Merlita Gargullo when she heard four soft knocks on the bedroom door. It was 11 p.m. Thinking it was one of the other nurses, Corazon unlocked the door. A young man pushed his way into the room. He smelt strongly of alcohol and swayed slightly. His eyes were soft and gentle, but in his hand there was a gun.

'I am not going to hurt you,' he assured her. 'I need your money to go to New Orleans.'

The six nurses in the house at the time were ushered into the master bedroom at the back at gunpoint. The gunman made them sit on the floor in the darkened room and asked them for their money. One by one they were sent to get it. The haul came to less than a hundred dollars. At 11.30 p.m. Gloria Davy, another of the nurses resident in the house, returned from a date. Unsuspecting, she walked into the back bedroom to be confronted by the gunman. He took two dollars from her and she was made to join the others. The gunman then cut a bed sheet into strips with a small pocket knife and, again insisting that he had no intention of harming anyone, tied all the women up.

Instead of leaving, the gunman sat down on the floor with them. For a while he chatted to them amiably, though he tapped the barrel of his gun nervously on the floor and frequently peered anxiously out of the window. Then he untied the ankles of one of the girls, twenty-year-old Pamela Wilkening from Lansing, Illinois and led her out of the room. The six girls left behind let out a sigh of relief. They quickly discussed what to do. The American girls counselled caution. The man was probably just a burglar. It was best to go along with him and not to antagonise him. From outside the room there was silence.

The last of the eight nurses who lived in the house, twenty-one-year-old Suzanne Farris, got home about midnight. With her was the sister of her fiancé, another student nurse, Mary Ann Jordan. When the two of them came into the master bedroom, the gunman appeared behind them. He ordered them out at gunpoint. There was a commotion outside and the women in the bedroom heard muffled shouts. Silence followed, then they heard water running in the bathroom.

About twenty minutes later the gunman came back. This time he picked twenty-four-year-old former Sunday-school teacher Nina Schmale. By now the young women were terrified. The intruder, they figured, was a rapist. They tried to hide. Corazon Amurao rolled across the floor and managed to wriggle under a bed.

When the gunman came back again he took Merlita Gargullo – a twenty-two-year-old Filipina from Santa Cruz who had been in Chicago less than a month – and twenty-three-year-old Valentina Pasion from Jones City in the Philippines who was a devoted Catholic. From her hiding place under the bed, Corazon Amurao heard both girls sigh or grunt and Merlita Gargullo call out 'It hurts' in her native tongue.

After a long period of silence the man returned to the master bedroom once more. He bent down and picked up twenty-year-old Patricia Matusek, the daughter of a liquor salesman. 'Will you please untie my ankles first?' she asked as he carried her away. By this time only Corazon Amurao and twenty-two-year-old Gloria Davy, daughter of a steel mill worker from Dyer, Indiana were left.

After another twenty-five minutes the gunman came back once again. From her vantage point under the bed Corazon Amurao saw him remove Gloria Davy's jeans. He then unzipped his own black trousers and climbed on top of her. Corazon looked away, but the creaking of the bedsprings left her in no doubt about what was going on. At one point she heard the intruder ask, in his disconcertingly gentle voice: 'Will you please put your legs around my back?'

When the bed springs eventually fell silent, Corazon Amurao found a safer hiding place under the other bed, where she was hidden by the bedclothes. Some forty-five minutes later she heard footsteps coming towards the bedroom. She lay absolutely still and held her breath. The man came in and switched on the light and looked around. There were eight beds in the house, and eight girls had been taken from the master bedroom. He did not know that one of the student nurses, Mary Ann Jordan, did not live there. Apparently satisfied, he switched off the light and went out.

Corazon Amurao lay still in her cramped hiding place, afraid to move or make a sound. There was complete silence in the house until 5 a.m., when an alarm clock went off in one of the other bedrooms. Normally the girls left the house at 6.30 a.m. to start their hospital shifts.

At around 6 a.m. Corazon Amurao plucked up the courage to squeeze out from under the bed. She managed to wriggle out of the strips of sheet that bound her hands and feet. Fearfully she crept out of the master bedroom and down the landing to her own bedroom.

There she found the bodies of Pamela Wilkening, Mary Ann Jordan and Suzanne Farris. Blood was everywhere.

Still too frightened to go downstairs in case the killer was still there, she smashed the screen on the bedroom window and crawled out on to the two-foot-wide ledge outside. She crouched there, ten foot above the ground, and started screaming uncontrollably and shouting: 'Help me, help me. Everybody is dead. I am the only one alive.'

Robert Hill, who was out walking his dog, heard her cries. So did Betty Windmiller, a neighbour, who had come out to see what all the noise was. They called the police.

Patrolman Daniel Kelly was the first policeman on the scene. He found the rear door swinging open. One panel had been shoved in. Inside, in the living room, he found the body of a young woman, naked, with a piece of cloth tied tightly around her neck. He turned her over. It was Gloria Davy. He recognised her immediately. Gloria's sister, Charlene Davy, had once been his girlfriend.

He found seven more dead bodies upstairs. In the bathroom was Patricia Matusek. After being kicked in the stomach she had been strangled. Nina Schmale was found on one of the beds in the westernmost of the two front bedrooms.

Suzanne Farris and Mary Ann Jordan had also been stabbed several times, then strangled. They were lying on the floor of the other front bedroom. Suzanne Farris must have put up some sort of a fight. She had been stabbed eighteen times. Pamela Wilkening had been stabbed just once, in the breast, then strangled with a piece of sheet wound around her neck.

Even the Cook County coroner Andrew Toman was shocked by what he saw. 'There has never been anything like it that I have heard of,' he told the reporters who flocked to the house. 'It is the crime of the century. It is the worst crime I have ever seen.' And this was in Chicago, the home of Al Capone and organised crime. But even the infamous St Valentine's Day Massacre in 1929 had only claimed the lives of six people. In East Street, eight young nurses lay dead. That year there were seventy-two murders, in total, in Chicago.

At 11 a.m. a drifter named Richard Speck woke up in his room at the Shipyard Inn, a sleazy hotel on Chicago's South Side. He was fully clothed, still in the dark shirt and trousers he had worn the day before. When he got up to splash his face with water, he noticed a blood stain on his right hand, though his clothes were clean. He did not know how it had got there. He assumed he had cut himself. He also found that he had a gun. He had no idea how he had come by it.

Richard Franklin Speck had been born on 6 December 1947 in Kirkwood, Illinois. He was the seventh of eight children, three boys and five girls. His father, Benjamin Speck, a potter, died in 1947. But in 1950 his mother, Mary, married again. The two youngest children took the name of their stepfather, an insurance salesman called Carl Lindberg, and the four of them moved to Dallas, Texas.

Lindberg was a heavy drinker. Domestic rows often ended up in fist-fights and Richard hated him. To everyone's relief, Lindberg walked out on his wife and stepchildren while Richard was still a teenager. But already the problems with his home life were putting him behind at school. 'He seemed sort of lost,' one of his junior high-school teachers reported. 'It didn't seem like he knew what was going on. I wasn't able to teach him anything. I don't think I ever saw him smile. No one could get through to him. He was a loner. He seemed to be in a fog, sort of sulky. He did not have any friends in class.'

He had been drinking from the age of twelve and began to take drugs. 'When I got to seventeen,' he later confessed, 'I just went wild.' Soon he was getting in trouble with the police. His early arrests were mainly for drunkenness and brawling.

Leaving school with no diploma and a developing police record, he seemed set for a lifetime of dead-end jobs. He worked as a truck driver, a carpenter, a labourer and a dustman. He also graduated into trespass and petty burglary. In 1962 he reverted to the name Speck and married fifteen-year-old Shirley Malone. On 2 July 1962 Shirley had a daughter named Robbie. Speck was fond of Robbie and treated her well, although he claimed that the child was not his.

The following year Speck was sentenced to three years in prison for forgery after signing another man's name to cash a stolen pay cheque. He was sent to Huntsville Penitentiary where the discipline was tough. The able-bodied prisoners spent all summer picking cotton on the prison farm. Speck ended up in hospital, suffering from sunstroke.

In 1965 he was released from prison and returned to his wife. Soon they were fighting all the time and in January 1966 Shirley divorced him. Speck hit the bottle hard and became involved in a series of drunken brawls. He was arrested but skipped bail. He found work on a boat on Lake Superior, but after a week he had appendicitis. While convalescing, he dated a nurse, Judy Laakaniemi, who was impressed by his gentle manner. When he was better, Speck drifted on to Chicago to stay with his married sister, Martha Thornton, and her husband.

Arriving in late June, Speck set about searching for a job. But it was not to be easy. The city was sweltering, with temperatures soaring to over thirty-two degrees. Like many Chicagoans, Speck found a haven from the baking streets in the city's air-conditioned bars. Soon his pale, pock-marked face became a familiar sight in Chicago's shadier haunts. He started taking barbiturates too, and would take any drug that was handed to him.

He moved out of his sister's and checked into a series of seedy, skid-row dosshouses. Every day, though, he would go to the seamen's union on East Street to see if there were any jobs going. Speck's plan was to work his passage to New Orleans. On Tuesday 12 July 1966 he was told that there was a job on an ore ship in Indiana. He quit his rented room and headed off, but when he arrived at the dock he was told that there had been a mix up. Someone else had got the job. Dejected, he returned to Chicago. He arrived penniless, left his bags at a petrol station across the road from 2319 East 100th Street, just a few yards from the National Maritime Union at 2335, and took shelter in a half-finished house for the night.

The next day, though, his luck changed. He found a job on an ocean-going ship that was sailing the following Monday. Speck phoned his brother-in-law, borrowed twenty-five dollars and checked in to the Shipyard Inn, a sleazy hotel on Chicago's South Side. Later he went to play pool. A good player, he won some money. Things were looking up. He took six 'redbirds' – barbiturate tablets – and went for a walk by Lake Michigan.

At 3 p.m., still stoned, Speck returned to the local bars to continue his day-long drinking spree. He fell into conversation with three men who said they were sailors. Around 6 p.m., he left with them. In a discreet spot, the men produced a bottle of clear liquid and began injecting themselves. Speck neither knew nor cared what the clear liquid was. When it came to his turn, he tied off his arm and stuck the syringe into one of his bulging veins. He remembered nothing from that moment until the next morning.

Speck was a hardened drinker. There were plenty of black holes in his life, nights that were surrounded by an alcoholic haze and nights when he could remember nothing at all. So when he woke up on the morning of 14 July 1966 with no recollection of what had happened the night before, it did not worry him. He left his room and went downstairs to buy a bottle of cheap liquor. On the radio in the bar he heard a report about the murder of the eight nurses.

'I hope they catch the son of a bitch,' Speck said to the bartender. What the radio did not say was that the police were already closing in.

Once Corazon Amurao had been coaxed from the ledge, she had been taken to South Chicago Community Hospital, where she was sedated. However, she was still able to give a detailed account of what had happened the night before. By 8.30 a.m. the police had a full description of the suspect. Police artist Otis Rathel drew this up and a picture was circulated to the newspapers.

Forensic experts scouring the house found an abundance of clues. Fingerprints were lifted from the furniture, walls and doors. A sweat-soaked man's T-shirt was found in the living room. Another was wrapped up in Gloria Davy's jeans.

A man answering the suspect's description had left his bags in the gas station across the road the night before the murders. He had told the attendant that he was looking for a job on a ship. The police checked with the National Maritime Union down the block. They said that someone had called by looking to work his passage to New Orleans. His name was Speck.

The police then set a trap. They asked the branch office of the seamen's union to offer Speck a job on a ship bound for Louisiana. Speck phoned in around 3.10 that afternoon and was told that there was a job waiting for him. He said he would come down to the seamen's union. The call was traced to the Shipyard Inn, which was about a mile away. Police raced there, but when they arrived they were told Speck had left a few minutes after making the call.

The US Coast Guard found that they had a record of Speck. They sent a photograph of him to the police, who took it to the hospital. But Corazon Amurao had lapsed into a state of shock and her doctors refused to let the police show it to her.

Speck did not turn up at the Maritime Union. Instead he went bar-hopping with his friend Robert 'Red' Gerrald. In a bar called the Ebb Tide, the murder of the nurses came up in conversation. 'Whoever did it must have been a maniac,' said Speck.

Speck saw his own picture in the newspaper, but did not recognise it. Rathel, the police artist, had made the skin too smooth. Speck's face was pock-marked.

That evening Speck said he was heading off to check out some action. He wanted to get out of the area. All police leave had been cancelled and the South Side was swarming with cops. Speck still had an outstanding warrant in Texas. He jumped into a cab and headed for the North Side. There he hustled some bar-room pool, found himself a hooker and went with her to a cheap hotel.

The next morning around 8.15 a.m., the hotel manager phoned the local precinct. The hooker told him that the man she had been with had a gun. The police arrived to find Speck still in bed. He insisted that the gun belonged to the prostitute. The cops confiscated it, and left it at that. The name Speck had still not been circulated as that of the murder suspect. As soon as the patrolman's report was filed, the police realised their mistake. They went rushing back, only to find that Speck had checked out fifteen minutes earlier.

After she had had a good night's sleep, the doctors decided that Corazon Amurao was well enough to be interviewed again. She picked Speck's picture out from a hundred photographs of convicted rapists. The police checked with the FBI. He had a considerable rap sheet in Texas. By 7.30 p.m. the Chicago murder squad had a new description of Speck from the Texas police. It detailed Speck's tattoos. These included a snake coiled round a dagger on his right forearm, a skull in a pilot's helmet above his left elbow, a crude jail yard drawing of a penis on his left shin, and the words 'BORN TO RAISE HELL' emblazoned across his left arm. In jail, in Texas, he had tried to burn it off with a cigarette butt. That earned him thirty days solitary confinement for destroying state property. He had also tried to destroy tattoos that said 'R. L.' (Richard Lindberg) and 'Richard and Shirley'.

The FBI also supplied Speck's fingerprint card. By 4.30 a.m. the next morning the Chicago police labs were certain that they had found a match for three of the prints lifted from the house on East 100th Street. Speck was definitely their man. That afternoon, at 2.40 p.m., Superintendent Orlando Wilson announced: 'The killer of the eight nurses from South Chicago Community Hospital on Thursday, July 14, 1966, has been named as Richard Speck, white male, twenty-four, a seaman. Latent fingerprints taken at the scene of the mass killings identified Speck as the killer.'

Speck was sitting in a bar when he heard his name on the radio. He was stunned. The police must have made some mistake. He thought of making a run for it, but could think of nowhere to go. Perhaps he should give himself up – but, even if he proved himself innocent, there was still the outstanding warrant from Texas. So, instead, he bought a bottle of cheap wine.

He realised that there was only one way out of his present predicament. He took a room in sleazy doss-house called the Starr Hotel, lay on the bed and drank the wine. And with the broken bottle he hacked open his wrists.

Around midnight Speck's courage failed him. Weakly he called out to anyone who might hear: 'Come and see me. You got to come and see me. I done something bad.'

The man in the next room, George Gregorich, a drifter, heard him, but did not care. 'Leave me alone,' he yelled back.

Speck shouted out again. But Gregorich would take no notice. He yelled back 'You're a hillbilly, you just want to get at me. I don't trust no hillbilly.'

Speck dragged himself to his feet, staggered to Gregorich's door and started pounding and kicking it. Another resident spotted Speck standing there with blood streaming from his wrists. He told the desk clerk, who called the police. There are other reports that indicate another man, Claude Lunsford, called the police identifying Speck before he was taken to the hospital.

Suicides are ten-a-penny in skid-row dosshouse like the Starr Hotel, where Speck was registered as B. Brian. That was the name the cops gave at the Cook County Hospital, little realising that the man they had just delivered to the emergency room was the subject of a city-wide manhunt.

Dr LeRoy Smith, the duty intern, thought he recognised the attempted suicide he examined at 12.30 a.m. And when he cleaned up the man's wounds, he spotted the word 'BORN' tattooed on his left arm. Dr Smith bent over the patient and asked him his name.

'Richard,' the man whispered. 'Richard Speck.'

Dr Smith called the police, then stitched Speck's wrists and gave him a blood transfusion. When Speck came out of surgery, the police were there to arrest him. They clamped him to his bed with leg-irons and took him, bed and all, by ambulance to Bridewell Prison's hospital.

When the police told him of his horrific crimes, Speck lay on his bed in apathetic resignation. His answer to all their questions was the same: 'I don't know any more about it than you do.'

He did not deny that he had killed the eight nurses. He simply said that he could not remember doing it. He could not remember anything at all between injecting himself with an unknown drug on the evening of 13 July and waking up in his room in the Shipyard Inn on the morning of the fourteenth.

'I woke up with a pistol and with blood on my hands,' he told a doctor. 'Where did I get the gun, doc?'

His amnesia, feigned or real, was of no consequence. Corazon Amurao picked him out of a line-up and there was more than enough evidence against him. On 26 July 1966 he was indicted on eight counts of first degree murder. And on 1 August he was formally arraigned. Feelings in the city were still running high and security in the courtroom was tight. Speck was pale and haggard. His suicide attempt had brought on inflammation of the heart, and he was suffering withdrawal from alcohol and barbiturates.

Speck had no money, so the public defender Gerald Getty was appointed to represent him. Getty entered a formal plea of not guilty. Prison psychiatrist Marvin Ziporyn was also assigned to the case, to check Speck's suicidal intentions. Ziporyn found Speck depressed and resigned to his fate.

'If they say I did it, I did it,' Speck told Ziporyn. And he fully realised the consequences. 'If I burn, I burn,' he said.

When Speck's physical health improved, he was transferred to a maximum security prison. Ziporyn continued to examine him and came up with the theory that Speck was suffering from brain damage, caused by drug abuse and head injuries he had sustained as a youth. For years he had been suffering from excruciating headaches and a white haze would form in front of his eyes, as if he had been staring too long at the sun. Drugs and alcohol aggravated the condition. Ziporyn came to believe that Speck was insane at the time of the crime.

A panel of eight psychiatrists declared Speck fit to stand trial. But Speck did not tell them about his use of drugs, or the head injuries he had sustained. When Ziporyn asked why not, Speck simply replied: 'They didn't ask me.'

Speck was equally unhelpful with his defence attorney, Gerald Getty. When it was suggested that he may have gone on a date with one of the girls – which would explain fingerprints in the house – Speck vehemently denied it. Getty had to build a defence without his client's help and entered no less than 35 pre-trial motions which made evidence like the pocket knife the police had found in the Calumet River and the gun confiscated from Speck by North Side police inadmissible.

The police radio announcement that Speck had killed the nurses made any trial in Chicago impossible. So on the night of 14 February 1967 Speck was transferred to the small town of Peoria, 150 miles south-west of Chicago, in a convoy of three unmarked cars full of armed deputies.

The trial started on 20 February. It took more than a month to pick a jury. More than 610 people were cross-examined before twelve jurors were picked. Getty was keen to find people who knew nothing of the case. The prosecutor, thirty-year-old Assistant State Attorney William Martin, was determined that no one on the jury would shrink from recommending the death penalty.

Speck watched the whole proceedings with studied indifference. He wore a blue suit, chewed gum nervously and stared blindly into the distance.

The prosecution case was rock solid. The gas-station attendant and two sailors established that Speck was in the neighbourhood. Patrons of the Shipyard Inn testified that they had seen Speck with a gun and a knife two hours before the first murder. And fingerprints put Speck at the scene of the crime. Then came the testimony of the eyewitness, twenty-three-year-old Corazon Amurao. At just four foot ten, she was a formidable witness. When Martin asked her whether she could point out the man she had seen in the house on East 100th Street that night, she stepped out of the witness box and, without a word, walked across to Speck. Slowly she raised her right hand until it was within inches of Speck's cheek.

'This is the man,' she said without flinching. Speck's eyes momentarily flickered up at her, then he resumed his distant pose.

Martin then unveiled his star witness – a doll's house. It was an exact model of the two-storey house at 2319 East 100th Street. It was five foot wide, three foot high and three foot deep, and it took four bailiffs to carry it into the courtroom. Getty objected strenuously. The wooden figures with the victims' names printed on them resembled tiny coffins, he maintained. When Speck heard that the State of Illinois had spent $5,609 to have it built, he said: 'Boy, they sure love me.'

As Martin took Corazon Amurao through her story, he moved the wooden figures from room to room in the doll's house. She broke down three times during her testimony. The effect on the jury was devastating.

The defence's only quibble was with her identification. Based on her description, police artist Otis Rathel had drawn the suspect with smooth skin and short hair. Speck had unmistakably pock-marked skin and wore his hair long. But Miss Amurao insisted that she had told the police about the pock marks and had never mentioned a crew cut. She had been in shock at the time she had given the description and her command of English was poor. No matter how Getty pressed, she never wavered in her identification of Speck.

Speck did not take the stand in his own defence. He had a phobia about being the centre of attention and talking in front of strangers. Besides, he would have had little to say.

His mother, brother and five sisters loyally spoke up for him as character witnesses. But the main thrust of the defence was an alibi that Getty had established. Gerdena Farmer, a short-order cook at Kay's Pilot House on Chicago's South Side, and her husband, Murrill Farmer, the bartender there, claimed that Speck had come into the bar around 11.30 p.m. on 13 July. He had been wearing a short-sleeved black shirt that showed his tattoos. He drank bourbon and Coke and ate a hamburger and left around 12.30. They remembered the time because a crowd of night-shift workers turned up at midnight. At 11.30, according to Corazon Amurao, Speck had already begun his butchery.

Although the Farmers' story remained unshaken by Martin's savage cross-examination, the jury were not impressed. They found Speck guilty in less than fifty minutes and recommended the electric chair.

Even though an insanity plea had not been entered by Getty, as Speck had not admitted the murders, Getty had a second chance to raise the psychiatric evidence in a plea for mitigation. Psychiatrist Marvin Ziporyn testified that he firmly believed Speck was not faking his amnesia. Nor was he a psychopath as the psychiatric board had contended. Psychopaths would lie and cheat to any extent to gain their own advantage. Speck refused to help himself. Psychopaths felt no guilt. Speck had tried to kill himself when he heard what he was accused of. And psychopaths severed all emotional bonds with their family. Speck felt the same loyalty towards his family that they exhibited towards him.

Ziporyn's alternative theory was that Speck was suffering from brain damage. At the age of three he had contracted pneumonia which had restricted the blood flow to his brain. At five, playing in a sandbox, he had hit himself on the head with a claw hammer. At ten he had fallen from a tree and landed on his head, remaining unconscious for an hour and a half. Aged eleven he ran into the steel support of a shop awning. And at fourteen he had been knocked out again by a bicycle accident and by another fall from a tree. He had sustained more injuries in numerous drunken fist-fights. His headaches had begun a year after he was clubbed by a Dallas policeman and he had been hit over the head seven or eight times with a tyre lever during a bungled burglary. The sunstroke he had suffered picking cotton on the prison farm at Huntsville had not helped, nor had years of alcohol and drug abuse.

Speck exhibited all the classic symptoms of brain damage – impulsiveness, irritability, poor memory, headaches and a reduced tolerance for drink and drugs. Added to that he had a deep-seated hostility towards women. This derived both from the fact that his mother had replaced his beloved father with a man he hated and from his feelings about his ex-wife Shirley.

'She used to say she wanted me to love her more than I did my mom,' Speck told Ziporyn. He told her that that would never be and he would get angry.

Speck told Ziporyn: 'I like girls – I wouldn't hurt women.' But he had attacked his mother when he was eighteen. He had beaten his wife Shirley in a jealous rage. Early in 1966 he hit a Dallas prostitute. Other reports indicate he was the suspect in a rape and the disappearance of three other women in Indiana. And a month or so before the killings he had shown a drinking buddy a picture of his wife and vowed to kill her 'if it was the last thing he ever did'.

There was one single clue as to how this hostility towards his wife could have turned into murder. When Speck was shown a picture of murder victim Gloria Davy he said: 'You know what? This is a dead ringer for Shirley.'

Gloria Davy was the last of Speck's victims. She was the only one who had been stripped and sexually assaulted. After leaving the bedroom, she had been taken downstairs where she was sodomised and murdered. Speck claimed he was revolted by anal sex. Perhaps in assaulting Gloria Davy in this manner he was showing the disgust he felt for his ex-wife.

When Speck was sober, Dr Ziporyn found him witty and charming. But when he was drunk, the demons took over. 'Speck's motor is like everyone else's,' Ziporyn said. 'It is his brakes that fail him.' On 13 July, Ziporyn concluded, a day-long binge of drink and drugs had turned a simple, befuddled burglary into an orgy of murder.

Judge Paschen was not impressed by these arguments and sentenced Speck to death. The execution was scheduled for September. Getty blitzed the courts with new petitions, which delayed the execution long enough for the United States Supreme Court to declare a moratorium. Speck was then sentenced to eight consecutive terms of fifty to 150 years – giving him a total term of imprisonment of between 400 and 1,200 years. This was the longest sentence ever given in United States legal history.

That, sadly, was not the end of it. An intelligent, handsome, shy, eighteen-year-old high-school senior called Robert Benjamin Smith followed the Speck case with obsessive interest. The son of a retired US Air Force major in Mesa, Arizona, he had idolised the gunfighter Jesse James and Emperor Napoleon. But when he read about Speck's horrendous crimes, he found a new hero. Smith's dreams were of full of sadistic torture and mass murder.

On 12 November 1966 Smith walked the two miles from his home in Mesa to the Rose-Mar College of Beauty. He was armed with a revolver his father had thoughtfully given him for his birthday, a knife, lengths of nylon cord and 200 plastic bags. He fired one shot into a mirror and ordered the five women and two children who were in the salon to lie on the floor. He tried to put the plastic bags over the heads of the women, but the bags were too small. So instead he began shooting the women, at point-blank range. He killed eighteen-year-old Glenda Carter, nineteen-year-old Carol Farmer, twenty-seven-year-old Joyce Sellers, her three-year-old daughter Debbie, and Mary Olsen, eighteen. Three-month-old Tamara Sellers was saved when her mother cradled the baby as she, herself, was being shot. One other, Bonita Sue Harris, was shot, but pretended to be dead and survived the attack. When the police turned up, they found a smiling Smith about to leave. He offered no resistance. 'I've just killed all the women in there,' he said, as he was taken away in handcuffs.

In May 1975, twenty-year-old Russell Lee Smith – on probation for a murder he had been convicted of four years before – ended an argument with his girlfriend by shooting her in the head. He shot and wounded two other men who had been involved in the argument, then drove his dead girlfriend's body to a hospital in Dayton, Ohio. On the hospital ramp he shot and wounded one person before driving away. He shot and wounded the driver of another car on the highway and in the parking lot of a movie theatre he shot a family of four, critically injuring their six-year-old daughter.

Smith then moved his rampage to a residential area, where he knocked on doors and shot at anyone who answered. He kidnapped a girl at gunpoint from a restaurant. While making his getaway, he stopped a car with a young couple in it and kidnapped a second girl. He killed the first, and then drove the second to a wooded area where he raped her. The police turned up and Smith turned the gun on himself.

In another mass murder with a sexual motive, on 18 October 1975 twenty-nine-year-old Erwin Charles Simants broke into the house of the Kellie family in Sutherland, Nebraska. He raped ten-year-old Florence Kellie, shot her, then shot the other five members of the Kellie family who came running when they heard Florence's screams. Simants was arrested the next day and confessed to sexually violating Florence again after she was dead and attempting to violate the dead body of fifty-seven-year-old Audrey Marie Kellie. In January 1976, Simants was found guilty on six counts of murder and sentenced to the electric chair. The execution was delayed twice, then the verdict was overturned because the local sheriff had visited members of the jury. At a retrial, Simants was found to be not guilty by reason of insanity and sent to a mental institution where he remained three decades later.

In 1980, twenty-three-year-old Andrew Weiss killed four people with a rifle, handgun and a butcher's knife in a house in Augusa, Maine. Weiss left a note at the scene of the massacre explaining the crime. It read: 'By the time you get this I will be out of the county. I killed Greg' – Greg York, thirty-one, who had been stabbed in the back five times and shot in the head with a handgun three times – 'for getting me addicted to coke. I shot Lynn' – Weiss's twenty-four-year-old fiancée Lynn Girouard who had to be identified from dental records – 'because she too was addicted and was having an affair with Bobby' – Bobby Lizotte, shot once in the head and stabbed four times in the back. 'I shot Jerry' – Jerry Nelson, shot twice in the head with a high-powered rifle – 'because she saw me do it.' Weiss was found in a room in a Holiday Inn in Massachusetts, dead from a drug overdose.

On 22 December 1987, retired Air Force Sergeant Ronald Gene Simmons, bought a .22 calibre handgun from Walmart and shot his wife, seven children, four grandchildren, and his son-in-law and a daughter-in-law. He also strangled another grandchild with fishing line and put the body in the boot of his car. He buried his family in a mass grave, having soaked them in kerosene. He covered the grave with coils of barbed wire – to keep animals and people away, he said.

Like Alvin Lee King (see Chapter 11), Simmons had been accused of incest with his daughter. Unlike King, Simmons was not an upstanding citizen. His daughter Loretta's classmates remember him always with a beer in his hand. They also remember that he stayed in one room all the time – it was dark, spooky and it stank.

In 1981, his sixteen-year-old daughter Sheila's teachers suspected Simmons was carrying on an incestuous affair with her. They were seen kissing at the school gates in a suggestive manner. Then Sheila became pregnant with her father's child. Charges were brought by his wife, forty-six-year-old Rebecca, who described Simmons as a violent and abusive father. But the charges were dropped because the Simmons family had moved from New Mexico to Russell, Arkansas. Left behind in a New Mexico safety deposit box was a long letter addressed to Sheila. In it Simmons accused her of abusing his trust and threatened to see her 'in hell'.

In Simmons' 'fortress-like' house he ruled his family with an iron fist. His wife long considered divorcing him, but never had the courage.

Whatever his family did was not good enough – and he decided to kill all fourteen of them.

On 28 December, Simmons drove to Russellville where he shot and killed James Chaffin, a thirty-three-year-old employee of an oil company where Simmons had worked, and twenty-four-year-old Kathy Kendrick, who had not responded to his amorous advances. He also shot Joyce Butts, who had worked with him in a car salesroom, and Roberta Woodley. Both survived and testified against him at his trial for the murder of Chaffin and Kendrick. He was found guilty and sentenced to death – 'anything short of death would be cruel and unusual punishment,' Simmons said.

Next, he was tried for the mass murder of his family. While the jury were out, Simmons attacked the prosecutor and tried to grab a deputy's pistol. After four hours, the jury returned and found him guilty. Again he was sentenced to death.

Chapter 8

Across the Border

Spree killing could not long be contained within the borders of the USA. Although Canada shares much with its more populous neighbour, it has a much more peaceful and law-abiding ethos and the laws on possession of guns are generally tighter. Its capital, Ottawa, differs particularly from most American cities in having virtually no dirt and no poverty. It has a high proportion of bureaucrats, little night-life and could justly be described as boring. But this has at least one major advantage: compared to other major cities, its crime rate is low, with half a dozen or so murders a year. So Ottawans were completely unprepared for the events of 27 October 1975.

The morning passed normally enough. Then, at 1 p.m., the Ottawa fire department received a call to investigate what seemed like a fairly routine domestic fire. A woman reported that clouds of smoke were pouring from a second-storey window of her home. Ten minutes later two fire trucks halted outside 5 Warrington Drive in a quiet suburban area of Ottawa, and were met by the housewife who had called them, Mrs Mary Poulin. Black smoke was now issuing from the back door of the house, but there were no flames. The fire, it seemed, was in the basement, where her teenage son Robert lived. Two firemen, Lawrence Bowes and Raymond Flavel, donned oxygen masks and made their way down the stairs. The smoke was so thick that they had to feel their way. But even through the breathing gear they noticed an unpleasant smell, like burning meat.

As the firemen entered the basement bedroom, they saw the charred body of a girl spread-eagled on what remained of the bed. She was naked except for a blood-stained blouse. Her head was covered with a plastic bag.

The intense heat quickly forced the two firemen to retreat into the fresh air. Visibly shaken, they asked another officer to call the police department – and report a murder.

The rest of the crew put the fire out, leaving the basement flooded with several inches of water. When the police waded back into the bedroom, they found the dead girl had been handcuffed to the bedpost by her left wrist. Handcuffs hung from the other bedpost, suggesting that her right wrist had also been fastened at one time. There were ski bindings around the posts at the foot of the bed. These seemed to indicate that her feet had also been tied. In fact she had been tied down and raped. The bloodstains on the remains of her plaid blouse quickly led investigators to believe that the girl had then been stabbed to death.

There was a trail of half-charred porn magazines running up the stairs. They had been doused with three gallons of camping fuel and set alight. The arsonist had plainly intended to burn the whole house, not just the bedroom. However, the instigator had forgotten to open the tiny bedroom window. Starved of oxygen, the fire had effectively snuffed itself out.

Suspicions quickly turned to eighteen-year-old Robert Poulin. Mrs Poulin said she had last seen him that morning before she left for her job as a lunch supervisor at a local elementary school. He had come upstairs at about eleven o'clock and asked her to make him a peanut butter sandwich, then sat watching a quiz show on TV. She noticed nothing strange about him. Nor had she any idea of his plans for the day, although she knew he was due to attend a theology class at the St Pius X High School.

In classroom seventy-one, students were listening to Father Robert Bedard. The lesson that day was about Jesus Christ and the problems of modern society. At 2.30 p.m. the door of the classroom creaked slowly open. The students at the back glanced around and saw a foot edge around the door, followed by the barrel of a shotgun. Carrying it was a young man who, from his smiling face, seemed to be in a kind of a trance.

He raised the weapon and started to fire. The noise of his pump-action shotgun was no louder than the popping of a balloon – then the air was filled with screams. Father Bedard flung himself to the floor, shouting at his students to do the same. For some, it was already too late. The firing continued for about two minutes. Then it stopped. The deathly silence that followed was punctuated by the sound of just one more shot, this time outside the classroom.

Then panic erupted. Students were smashing the windows with chairs and hurling themselves out. But Father Bedard remained calm. He got up and walked cautiously to the classroom door. Outside, the gunman lay sprawled on the floor. Half his face was blown away. A sawn-off Winchester shotgun lay beside him. The dead man was little more than a teenager. Despite the boy's appalling self-inflicted disfigurement, Father Bedard recognised him as one of his students – Robert Poulin.

Apart from Poulin, who died instantly when the final cartridge blew off the top of his head, only one person died as a result of the murderous classroom assault. Seventeen-year-old Mark Hough suffered critical wounds to the back of the head and neck. He died four days later.

Six other students were wounded, three of them seriously. They were rushed to hospital. Barclay Holbrook was wounded in the lung area. Two others, Mark Potvin and Terry Handenberg, also had neck wounds. The other three were released almost immediately. Soon after the firemen had extinguished the blaze, Mrs Poulin learned of her son's death. When her husband Stuart, a teacher in the local primary school, was called home, his immediate fear was that the body in the basement was one of their three daughters. In fact all three were safe.

Robert Poulin did not have a girlfriend, so investigators were baffled. However, Poulin's sister said that he had been interested in a seventeen-year-old Sri-Lankan girl named Kim Rabot, who lived a few doors away. Poulin's sister had once invited Kim over to the house at Robert's request.

The last person to have seen Kim alive was her thirteen-year-old brother John. He had been with her at the bus stop on their way to school at 8.30 a.m. that morning when Robert Poulin had approached them. Poulin had told Kim that he had something to show her. A gentle girl who disliked hurting anyone's feelings, Kim had agreed to go with him.

Poulin had taken Kim to his basement room where he threatened her with the shotgun. He forced her to undress and handcuffed her to the bed. Then he raped her. At one point he untied her feet and unhandcuffed one wrist to turn her over. A post-mortem showed that she had been raped and sodomised. Finally he had stabbed her fourteen times with a hunting knife.

When Mrs Poulin had gone downstairs to the basement at around ten o'clock that morning a bizarre incident had occurred. The curtains that closed off Poulin's bedroom were drawn. So she called out: 'Knock, knock, can I talk to you for a minute?'

Poulin said: 'Yeah, but don't come in.' His mother respected his privacy.

Poulin came upstairs an hour later for his peanut butter sandwiches. Then he had returned to the basement, spread the magazines up the stairs and set the room alight. He strapped his hunting knife across his chest, put his twelve-bore shotgun in a blue duffle bag and cycled across town on his ten-speed bicycle to his 2 p.m. theology class.

At St Pius X High School, instead of going straight into class, he went to the school cafeteria, carrying the blue duffle bag. The school's physical education teacher saw him there. Poulin, he said, looked 'scared'. Indeed, with one rape and murder already behind him, Poulin had already burnt his bridges. Shortly before 2.30 he crossed the hall, pulled the gun from the duffle bag and dropped the bag to the floor. Then, like a sleepwalker, he turned the handle of a classroom door and slowly pushed it open with his foot.

Robert Poulin, born in 1957, was described as a 'strange, quiet boy'. At school he was conscientious and hardworking. When he was twelve his third sister, Jody, was born, and Poulin moved into the basement to make room for the new baby. He lived there alone. It was only after his death that his secret life was discovered. He had a passion for war games and played out heroic battles on the basement floor, manoeuvring huge numbers of troops and artillery. His other obsession was sex. The walls of the basement were plastered with pictures of naked girls, and there were piles of soft-porn magazines stacked on the floor. His diaries and notebooks revealed that he was also a desperately lonely boy, yearning for sexual contact and deeply tormented by his inability to talk to girls. One entry read: 'Today is September 5, 1972, a Tuesday... There are some girls at school that

I would love to be good friends with but I know that I am still too shy to go up and talk to any of them. I wish I could overcome this fear of women.'

There were also fragments of essays entitled 'Chance to be a Hero' and 'Inquiry Not Under Arrest'. These described Poulin's shyness and inability to deal with women.

Among his possessions the police found a box containing women's bras, panties and negligees, and a pink blow-up sex doll with a pouting mouth and artificial vagina. There was a condom-type vibrator device, and no fewer than four pairs of handcuffs. The police also found a collection of pornographic books, some of which showed women tied up and handcuffed to bedposts.

One notebook contained the names, addresses and telephone numbers of eighteen girls. Police checked with the girls to see if any of them knew Poulin well. None of them did. But several had received 'heavy breather' phone calls. Plainly Poulin's tormented sex dreams were not entirely a matter of lurid fantasy.

In a neatly typed diary entry, dated 7 April 1975, Poulin spelt out his intentions. He had just flunked a biology test.

For the last couple of weeks I have been fairly depressed… [and] thought of committing suicide, but I don't want to die before I have had the pleasure of fucking some girl. So I decided to order a model gun from an ad in Gallery magazine (April 1975). With this I was going to threaten a girl in one of the dark streets around here and rape her. I planned to carry my father's scout knife strapped to the inside of my right leg. If the girl caused me any trouble I would kill her, for I was planning to kill myself anyhow, and I have nothing to lose. After that, I would wait for a reason for killing myself. The day I would kill myself would be a Sunday, for if I was going to die, the people that made up my family were going to suffer.

Plainly Poulin's mind was becoming rambling and unhinged. At first he thought of taking his father's rifle and killing his whole family, but then decided that 'death is pure bliss and I would not want them to be happy'. Instead he planned to douse the contents of the house with petrol and set it alight before shooting himself. He even planned to burn the place down soon after his parents' payday so that they would lose the largest possible amount of money.

Then Poulin was brought back from the brink. His diary went on to relate that he had found an ad for 'Everything' Dolls in *Playboy* magazine and sent off $29.95 for what he hoped would be a lifelike doll of a girl. With his hopes high, he wrote: 'Now I no longer think that I will have to rape a girl, and I am unsure whether or not I will still commit suicide.' Then on 5 May 1975, he noted: '"Everything" Doll arrived – a big disappointment.' Clearly, sex with a plastic blow-up woman was not everything he had hoped for.

In the months immediately before Poulin's rampage there were a number of sexual assaults and attempted rapes in the area of Poulin's house. The perpetrator was a man wearing a balaclava. According to Poulin's diary, in his planned rape he would use a balaclava to disguise his identity. The attacker was the same general height and build as Poulin.

In early October, in desperation, Poulin ran a small ad in the *Ottawa Journal* for a week. It read: 'Male, 18, looking for companionship. PO Box 4021.'

This did not work out as he expected either. He had received three replies – all from homosexuals. Poulin had replied to one, but had left the letter unposted. He wrote:

I have never had a homosexual experience, though the thought has crossed my mind before. However, I'm not only interested in sex but in sharing other pastimes and hobbies. My favourite hobbies are, in order: war-gaming, reading (science fiction) and collecting (a variety of things, including stamps and models). I hope you have the same sort of hobbies, especially war-gaming.

It is a measure of Poulin's utter loneliness that, with his strong heterosexual orientation, he was even prepared to experiment with homosexuality in order to find a friend.

Poulin came from a military family. His father had been an air force pilot. Poulin's goal was to make a career in the army. Earlier that year he had applied for officer training in the Campbell Highlanders militia and, after an hour-long interview, had every reason to believe he had been accepted. But the three-man board had decided that he was too immature. Instead, he joined the militia as a private. Two weeks before the murders, he dropped out of training. He had lied about his interest in school sports and had been found out by the authorities. This was the final blow. He went to a local store with the remains of his savings and paid $109 for a Winchester shotgun. Then, in his lonely basement, he sawed off the barrel.

Poulin's rampage was not the only killing spree that had hit Canadian schools. Five months before, sixteen-year-old Michael Slobodian went on a shooting frenzy in Brampton, Ontario. On 28 May 1975, Slobodian went to school with two rifles concealed in a guitar case. He left a suicide note in which he wrote that he intended to kill two teachers who had told him off for poor attendance, and 'anyone who got in his way'. He shot seventeen-year-old John Singer in the washroom. Thirteen people were injured as he sprayed bullets around the building. Twenty-five-year-old Margaret Wright, the art teacher, was killed. Then Slobodian shot himself.

Immediately after Poulin's killing spree, a spate of violence erupted in the schools of Ottawa. One student attacked a teacher with a razor. Another beat up a counsellor with an iron bar. And six months later a bomb went off in a high school.

On 6 December 1989, one of the worst mass murders in Canada's history happened at the University of Montreal which stands on the slopes of Mont Royal, overlooking the city.

It was the last day of the Autumn term and the atmosphere was festive. In room 230 on the first floor, sixty engineering students were just about to finish their last class. Just before 5.10 p.m. the door flew open. A young man marched into the room carrying a green bin liner. 'OK,' he shouted in French, 'Everybody stop what they're doing.'

As he spoke, he reached into the bin liner and pulled out an automatic rifle. Nobody moved. The young man was bearded and wore blue jeans, an anorak and a red baseball cap. He looked like a student and everyone suspected this was some kind of end-of-term practical joke.

A moment later they discovered it was anything but. The young man raised the rifle and fired into the ceiling. 'Move!' he yelled. 'Split into two – the girls on the left, the guys on the right.'

The students did as they were told. The girls – there were just nine of them – moved to the far side of the classroom away from the door. 'All right,' said the gunman. 'The guys can leave.' The girls were told to stay exactly where they were. The men filed out. The gunman kicked the door closed behind them.

'Do any of you know why I'm here?' he asked. Someone said no.

'I'm here to fight against feminism,' he said.

'But we are not feminists,' protested twenty-three-year-old Natalie Provost 'We're just engineering students.'

No sooner were the words out of her mouth than the gunman started to spray the girls with bullets, raking the weapon back and forth. The girls' screams were barely audible above the sounds of automatic fire. Six fell dead. The other three were badly wounded.

When he thought he had finished them off, the gunman lowered his rifle and marched out into the corridor. Some of the male students were still there. He fired. They scattered. He did not seem to want to kill the men: 'I want the women,' he yelled.

With his back to the corridor wall, he slipped another clip of ammunition into his gun. Then he moved forward cautiously down the corridor. At the slightest sound, he turned and fired. Every so often he said: 'I want the women.' When one appeared, his action was swift and a moment later, she too fell dead by a photocopier.

One eyewitness to the carnage was twenty-four-year-old student Daniel Depuis. He had been on the third floor when he heard about the gunman. Someone warned frantically: 'Don't go down. He's shooting at everything that moves.' But curiosity drove Depuis to make his way down the stairs to the first floor. He caught a glimpse of the killer who was descending to the foyer.

Depuis went into room 230. One girl was sitting at a desk, bleeding profusely from a gaping shoulder wound and crying hysterically. Depuis made a tourniquet in an attempt to staunch the blood. Another girl was lying on the floor nearby. Half her head had been blown away. He knelt beside her and took her hand.

'If you can hear me, squeeze my hand,' he said. To his surprise she gave a small squeeze. Outside in the corridor, Depuis tended two girls who were lying together, groaning. One of them died in Depuis' arms. The other girl was dead by the time the ambulancemen came.

Downstairs in the cafeteria the gunman began shooting again. Three more women were cut down under the Christmas decorations. Other students ran for the exit. The gunman turned and marched back upstairs.

On the second floor, in room 311, two female students were presenting a project on metallurgy. As soon as the gunman entered the room, he started firing. Both women fell, shot, followed by two women in the audience. Some students dived under their desks. Others ran for the door.

The gunman walked towards the front of the class, where one of the girls who had been addressing the class was moaning and crying for help. A bullet was embedded in her lung. The gunman put down his rifle and pulled a hunting knife from his belt. He stabbed her three times, until she gasped and stopped moving.

The gunman then removed his anorak and carefully wrapped it round the end of the gun barrel. In the eerie silence, some fearless students peered out from beneath their desks. They saw the gunman put the gun to his head and pull the trigger. His baseball cap – with the top of his skull in it – flew across the room.

Students rushed to help those who had been hit. The last victim, Maud Haviernick, was dead from a stab to the heart. So was her co-presenter, twenty-one-year-old Michele Richard. Several other students in room 311 were seriously wounded.

Photographer Claude Rivest, who managed to slip past security guards, found two wounded girls lying at the top of the stairs. He also discovered the body of a female student under a table in the cafeteria.

The dead and wounded were already being lifted on to stretchers when the police arrived. A telephone call had alerted them at 5.17 p.m., just three minutes before the gunman ended his life. At 5.26

p.m. Lieutenant Claude Lachapelle of the homicide squad arrived. He ordered that the university guards were to admit no one else. There could be another gunman inside. Even ambulance crews were not allowed to move the wounded until the police were sure that the killer was dead.

Lachapelle made his way up to classroom 311, where the gunman lay spread-eagled, his brains exposed. His red baseball cap and the top of his skull, still covered with curly black hair, lay on the other side of the room. The rifle, a .223 calibre Ruger semi-automatic, lay beside him. Lachapelle could not figure out why the killer had gone to the trouble of placing his anorak over the end of the barrel to prevent the blast burning his flesh when he intended to blow his brains out.

The dead man appeared to be a typical student. He was slightly built and about five foot six inches tall. A three-page letter, handwritten in French, was found in his pocket. It started: 'Forgive the mistakes – I had only fifteen minutes to write this.' He went on to explain his actions.

Please note that if I am committing suicide today… it is not for economic reasons… but for political reasons. For I have decided to send to their forefathers the feminists who have always ruined my life. It has been seven years since that life ceased to bring me any joy, and being totally bored, I have decided to put an end to those viragos…

Even if a mad-killer label is stuck on me by the media, I regard myself as a rational and intelligent person who has been forced into taking extreme action… Being rather backward-looking by nature (except for science), the feminists always have a talent for enraging me. They want to keep the advantages of women… while grabbing those of the men.

More rambling anti-feminist rhetoric was followed by a list of fifteen local women. 'These nearly died today,' the note ended. 'Lack of time (because I started too late) has allowed these radical feminists to survive.'

At the bottom of the letter, there was a signature. It read 'Marc Lépine'

Within an hour of the shooting, a news flash about the massacre was carried on the radio and TV, though early reports put the death toll at only two or three. Immediately the engineering building was besieged by reporters and frantic parents. The director of public relations for Montreal police, Pierre Leclair, stood on the steps of the building, doing his best to answer the questions. Then someone came out of the building and whispered in his ear. Leclair went pale. He apologised to the crowd, turned and went slowly into the university building. He had been asked to identify the body of his own daughter, twenty-three-year-old Maryse.

At the City Hall, Councillor Therese Daviau was attending a meeting when news of the deaths at Montreal University began to come through. Her twenty-one-year-old daughter, Geneviève Bergeron, was an engineering student there. At first Therese was not too concerned – Geneviève was most probably at choir practice. However, during an adjournment, Councillor Daviau learned that more than two or three had been killed. There had been a massacre.

She rushed to police headquarters to try to find out more – but most of the victims had still not been identified. By 11 that night, she was in a state of terrible anxiety. She sent a male friend over to the university where the grim task of identifying the bodies had begun in earnest. An hour later he rang back. He had just seen Geneviève's body among the dead.

Families all over Canada soon had the same story to tell. At first, they had believed it to be a hundred-to-one chance that their daughter was one of the victims, and then they learned the worst. Even the citizens of Montreal who had lost no one in the tragedy exhibited all the symptoms of people in a state of deep shock. They could not believe that their university had been the scene of the worst mass murder in Canadian history. A local politician asked simply: 'How could such a thing happen in our society?'

It was not until the following day that the full death toll became known. Marc Lépine had killed fourteen women. Thirteen other students, several male, had been wounded, some seriously. All the victims were engineering students except for Maryse Laganière, a twenty-five-year-old office worker. Still nobody understood why he had done it.

Newspaper reporters soon found that Lépine rented a five-room apartment at 2175 Rue Bordeaux, a few miles away from the university. A woman who lived in the flat below remembered how Lépine played his music so loudly at night that the police had been called on three occasions. Lépine himself had always avoided her. He ran up the stairs to his second-floor apartment if he saw her come into the building. The other tenants simply described him as an eccentric loner who seldom spoke.

Chantal Dumais, a girl who rented a flat across the street from Lépine, had even more disturbing memories. She described how she could see into Lépine's dining-room from one of her windows. He kept a human skull on the bookcase, she said. She often sensed that someone was watching her. One evening she had forgotten to close the curtains while undressing when she realised that she could be seen from Lépine's flat. She quickly closed the bedroom curtains. As she did so, she heard a sound from Lépine's apartment like someone blowing his nose loudly. Then she heard someone laughing. The eerie sound was repeated every night for weeks after.

A girl who knew Lépine said that he was bored, lonely and sex-starved, completely unable to attract a steady girlfriend. Former schoolmate Jean Belanger, Lépine's closest and probably only friend, said that Lépine was extremely shy and had never had any girlfriends.

'It's not that he wasn't interested,' Belanger said. 'But the way he approached women wasn't exactly the way women like.' Lépine had not had any friends of either sex after he and Belanger parted company for reasons unknown.

When journalists tracked down Lépine's mother, forty-three-year-old nurse Monique Lépine, they found a broken woman. She had survived a disastrous seven-year marriage to Marc's father, a brutal Algerian named Raschid Liass Gharbi.

Gharbi was convinced that women were fundamentally inferior to men. Their true role was as servants. His mood changes were sudden and violent.

'He would speak of love… then, out of nowhere, I would receive a blow in the face,' Monique Lépine recalled. He also hit his two children in the face, often making their noses bleed. Afterwards, he would not allow his wife to comfort them.

Gamil Gharbi – who later changed his name to Marc Lépine – suffered more than his elder sister Nadia and was terrified of his father. The fear did not go away even after his parents were separated. If he realised that his mother was driving him over to see his father, he would grab the steering wheel. Once he almost caused a crash.

Raschid Gharbi vehemently denied any responsibility. He had never beaten anyone, he said. The worst punishment he had ever meted out was to make the children stand to attention for ten minutes with their arms by their sides. But other relatives said they had seen Gharbi repeatedly slam his young wife against the wall in front of the children.

After their divorce Monique began to use her maiden name, Lépine. Her son started using it too, and called himself Marc instead of Gamil. Even though they were free of the violent Gharbi, the family was not happy. Monique had to work long hours to support Marc and his sister. The children were alone together a great deal and Nadia treated her shy younger brother with open contempt.

Early on at school Lépine had shown great promise, but gradually he lost interest in his studies. An obsession with war films took over and he dreamed of joining the army. But when he applied, he was turned down. He also failed to get a place to study engineering at the polytechnic.

With no close friends and no girlfriend, Lépine lived completely alone. At the age of just twenty-five, he was slowly overtaken by an overwhelming sense of madness and defeat. But no one ever discovered why he believed feminists had ruined his life.

Chapter 9

Women Who Kill

Brenda Spencer was one of the few women to turn to spree killing. Her stated reason for killing two and wounding nine in a senseless shoot-out was made world famous by The Boomtown Rats in their song 'I Don't Like Mondays'. Sixteen-year-old Brenda must have been thrilled. The Monday before the shootings she had said that she was going to do 'something big to get on TV'. She succeeded beyond her wildest dreams.

In 1978, the year before she resolved her inner conflicts with a gun, Brenda's parents had divorced. Brenda lived with her father in San Diego, California, and soon showed signs of severe disturbance. She played truant from school, committed petty thefts and was caught taking drugs. She watched violent videos and enjoyed shooting birds. She also shot out the windows of the Cleveland Elementary School across the road from her father's house with an airgun. Nevertheless, for Christmas, her father bought her a .22 semi-automatic rifle and 500 rounds of ammunition.

Early in the New Year Brenda began to make plans. She moved her weapons into the garage and dug a hideout in the garden. Then on Monday 29 January she got Burton Wragg, the principal of Cleveland Elementary, in her sights as he walked across the playground. When he opened the school gates to allow the waiting children in, she opened fire. Wragg and the school janitor, Michael Suchar, were killed. The first policeman to arrive on the scene, thirty-year-old Robert Robb, found eight children aged from six to twelve wounded. He was wounded in the neck as he tried to tend a victim.

After a twenty-minute spree, Brenda Spencer blithely chatted on the phone to the police. Who was she trying to kill in Cleveland Elementary? they asked. 'No one in particular. I kinda like the red and blue jackets.'

She told reporters: 'I just started shooting. That's it. I just did it for the fun of it.' Then she uttered the immortal line: 'I don't like Mondays. I did this because it's a way to cheer up the day. Nobody likes Mondays.'

While Brenda was chatting, kids in the bullet-torn school across the road were huddling on the floor. She held the police off for six hours, then meekly gave herself up. She walked calmly out of the house and put her gun on the ground. Then she turned and went back in. When she re-emerged she handed 150 rounds of .22 ammunition over to the waiting police.

The next day teachers at Cleveland Elementary encouraged their students to talk about the tragedy. 'Why did she do it?' asked one bewildered eight-year-old. No one had an answer.

In Illinois in 1988, thirty-year-old divorcee Laurie Dann shot seven people, one fatally, and attempted to kill hundreds of others.

Laurie Dann, née Wasserman, was the daughter of a respectable accountant and was brought up in the exclusive North Shore area of Chicago. Although she was unattractive as a child, Laurie's parents lavished the attention of America's plastic surgeons upon her. And by the time she graduated from high school, Laurie was as cute as a Barbie doll. However, she did not have the academic ability or social skills to match her looks. She failed to cut it as a cheerleader. Even the boys were not fooled.

At college in Arizona, where she studied to be a primary school teacher, she pursued men with a passion. Most did not want to know. They found her slavish and possessive. And when her relationship with a pre-med student broke up, she fled home to Illinois. Enrolling in psychology at nearby Northwestern University, she supported herself by working as a waitress at Green Acres Country Club. There she met young, dynamic sales executive Russell Dann. They fell in love and married in 1982.

Even during their honeymoon in the Virgin Islands, Russell Dann began to notice that something was very wrong. Though she had held herself together during their courtship, suddenly Laurie seemed totally devoid of self-confidence. Back in Chicago she felt herself totally outclassed by the other women in the Dann family. They were all successful in business and accomplished sportswomen. Laurie dropped out of college and soon found that she was unable to hold down a job. She killed her days sleeping, shopping, watching TV and having lunch with her mother.

When the marriage began to come apart at the seams, Laurie sought psychiatric help, but soon dropped out of therapy. In desperation her husband found her a new house, full of the latest gadgets, in the hope that it would help. Laurie found herself more than ever out of her depth, storing money in the microwave and canned food in the dishwasher. She also did the unthinkable. In a social gaffe that would reverberate around North Shore for years, she served frozen vegetables instead of fresh at a dinner party – unforgivable in those circles.

The couple separated. Laurie went back to her parents, but Russell paid for her to go back to teacher-training college, this time at the National College of Education in Evanston. Nevertheless the divorce became messy, with petitions and counter-petitions mounting up in the courts. She complained that Russell was harassing her, even accusing him of breaking into her parents' home. Meanwhile, Russell, and other acquaintances, were pestered by phone calls, usually in the middle of the night, where the mysterious caller hung up as soon as the phone was answered.

In May 1986 Laurie bought a gun – a .357 calibre Magnum – and one hundred rounds of ammunition. When Russell got to hear of it, he called the police. They persuaded Laurie to lodge the gun in her father's bank deposit box – but they were not allowed to inspect it there.

Laurie found a new boyfriend, a little younger than herself. But he was disturbed by the fact that she compulsively washed her hands all the time. Meanwhile, allegations continued to fly between Russell and Laurie. He claimed that she had broken into his home and stabbed him with an ice-pick one night, while she alleged that he had tried to petrol-bomb her parents' home and had sexually assaulted her one night while she was having a bath. According to her statement, she had heard a noise in the house, had put on a dress and some underwear and gone to investigate. Russell had grabbed her, she said, dragged her into the bedroom and tore her dress and her panties off with one yank. Then he stuck a steak knife into her vagina and threatened to 'cut her all the way up' unless she signed the divorce papers. But there was no evidence to support either side and no charges were filed.

After her divorce Laurie moved on to campus at Evanston. She lied her way into several baby-sitting jobs, but her clients found her reliable and had no hesitation recommending her to their friends. However, she was forced to move out of the college dormitory after she was suspected of being behind a wave of petty pilfering.

Back home again, she kept up the baby-sitting. But complaints started rolling in of bizarre thefts from the homes of her employers. Those who complained suffered the same pestering phone calls.

In November 1987 Laurie bought her second handgun – a .32 calibre Smith & Wesson revolver. And in December 1987 she bought her third – a .22 calibre semi-automatic Beretta. Her phone campaign became more serious. She threatened Russell's family and friends with death. And former employers were told: 'Your children are going to die.'

Laurie's father arranged treatment for her with the experimental drug clomipramine at the University of Wisconsin Hospital in Madison. She was also treated with lithium carbonate and swallowed birth control pills, antibiotics and aspirins in large quantities. Other drugs were prescribed for depression.

Laurie continued stealing. Her thefts included poisons from the university hospitals and a book on their effects. She was arrested for shoplifting and released on bail. She put on more than thirty pounds, but still managed to find herself a boyfriend – a weedy student who wore combat fatigues and read *Soldier of Fortune* magazine. Laurie's own reading included true-crime books and soft-porn magazines like *Penthouse*. But soon her telephone-threat campaign reached such a pitch that the FBI were called in. They recorded Laurie making hysterical death threats to Russell's sister and Laurie was indicted.

The day before the grand jury hearing Laurie took the Greyhound bus home to Chicago. There she called two local primary schools, where acquaintances including Russell Dann's sister had their children. Pretending to be calling from a modelling agency, she invited cheerleaders she had known from high school to bring their children over to those schools for auditions that Friday. Laurie herself arranged to take the two youngest children of a former employer.

That Friday morning Laurie spiked a pack of Rice Krispies with arsenic and sent it to a former roommate at college. She injected lead into orange juice cartons and sent them to other people she knew – including both her therapist and her ex-husband – as 'free samples'. She also drove around delivering poisoned foods through people's letterboxes. Fraternity and sorority houses at Northwestern University got similar deliveries.

Then Laurie went to pick up the two kids she had arranged to take to school, leaving behind in the kitchen more poisoned cookies. She even managed to slip a few drops of arsenic into a jug of milk.

Laurie and the two kids arrived at the Ravinia Elementary School at around 9 a.m. There were some 300 children inside. Laurie left the two boys in the back of the car, and walked into the school unchallenged. With her she had a bag which contained highly flammable liquid, acids and other toxic chemicals. She hid in the playhouse and lit the draw-string as an elementary fuse. Fortunately the bag was spotted and the staff extinguished the flames before the contents went up.

Outside the nearby Kennedy School Laurie tried to murder the two children in the car with poisoned milk – but they refused to take more than a tiny sip because the arsenic made it taste so bitter. So Laurie took a can of petrol from the boot of the car and, with the two boys, walked over to the school entrance. But they would not let her in with the can.

Frustrated, Laurie took the two children back to their mother. There she poured petrol on the basement carpet, threw a lighted match at it, and locked the mother and two children in. They managed to escape through a tiny window, suffering some nasty cuts and bruises.

At nearby Hubbard Woods Elementary School Laurie gained admission by giving the impression she was still a teacher-training college student, and was allowed to sit in on the class of teacher Amy Moses. However, Laurie could not sit still. She went out into the corridor, grabbed six-year-old Robert Trossman from the drinking fountain, bundled him into the boys' toilets and shot him point-blank with a pistol she had concealed in her shorts.

Back in Amy Moses' elementary class, Laurie ordered the children into one corner. Amy Moses tried to grab her gun and shout for help, but Laurie broke free. She shot eight-year-old Mark Teborek in the neck. Then, coolly and deliberately and at point-blank range, she shot seven-year-old Kathryn Miller, and eight-year-olds Peter Munro, Lindsay Fisher and Nicholas Corwin. Blazing with two guns, Laurie made her escape. But the police spotted her speeding car. She lost them in a suburban area and screeched to a halt in the driveway of a mock-Tudor mansion. There she took off her shorts and tied a bin liner around her as if it were a Superman cape.

She entered 2 Kent Road by the back door, claiming that she had been raped. She had shot her assailant and the police were after her, she said. Twenty-year-old Philip Andrew and his parents Ruth and Raymond were half-believing her when she waved her pistols in their direction and took them hostage.

Laurie called her mother a few times, but their conversation did not calm her. Meanwhile the police were combing the area. Philip Andrew managed to persuade her to release his parents and to hand over one of her guns, the Beretta. He unclipped the magazine. Then, for no apparent reason, Laurie shot him in the chest. Critically wounded, Philip managed to edge his way out of the back door and was almost shot by the patrolmen – who were now surrounding the house – because he was carrying a gun.

Laurie's parents were brought in to make an appeal to her through a police bullhorn. There was no reply from the house. Laurie had already put her .32 calibre Smith & Wesson in her mouth and pulled the trigger. Later that day an assault team cautiously worked their way through the twenty-two-room mansion to find Laurie in the top-floor bedroom with her brains blown out.

The only other fatality from her murderous rampage was eight-year-old Nicholas Corwin who died in his classroom at Hubbard Woods Elementary. But if Laurie Dann had succeeded in all her plans her death toll would have been one of the highest in the bloody history of spree killing. But, thankfully, female spree killers are still mercifully rare.

Chapter 10

The Race Card

On the morning of 8 January 1973, in the comfort of their own living rooms, American TV viewers watched as a marine helicopter attacked Howard Johnson's hotel in downtown New Orleans which was surrounded by more than two hundred uniformed policemen, detectives and sharpshooters. They called it the Battle of New Orleans and it was the first spree killing to be carried out live on national television.

Two dozen heavily armed policemen stormed the roof of the high-rise building which they believed was being held by a militant black guerrilla unit, which had held them at bay for thirty-two hours and already killed seven people and wounded twenty-one in a spree of arson and gun play. The police erupted from the stairwells on to the pebbled roof in a blaze of shotgun- and rifle-fire. Several fell wounded. As it turned out, the police were shooting each other. The man who had held them off for more than a day lay dead, his corpse riddled with more than a hundred sharpshooters' bullets and machine-gun rounds from the helicopter. Even then, with the siege over, the police were loath to admit that they had been held off for so long by a single man. Rumours circulated that one, possibly two, accomplices had escaped through the police cordon. But as the investigation continued it became clear that twenty-three-year-old Mark James Essex had acted alone. And Essex had felt he had the most powerful of motive. He was a black man in a white world.

He had not always felt that way. Essex was brought up in the quiet Midwestern town of Emporia, Kansas, where racism, if not unknown, did not reach the vilest excesses of that in the southern states or the urban ghettos. His father worked as a meat packer and his mother, who had a master's degree in education, worked at the local Head Start programme. They were a God-fearing family and Essex tithed part of his part-time earnings to the local Baptist Church.

However, the spectre of the Vietnam War haunted every young man at that time. And in 1969, after a poor semester at Kansas State College, Essex joined the Navy to avoid the draft and almost certain assignment to Vietnam. He finished boot camp with an outstanding performance rating and was encouraged by superior officers to take advanced training in a speciality. He enrolled for a three-month course in X-ray procedures and oral surgery at the Naval Dental Center. Again he passed with flying colours and was posted to the Naval Air Station at Imperial Beach as a dental assistant. He got on with everyone he worked with there, though he gradually became aware of the undertow of racism. No one called him 'nigger' to his face but he was constantly harassed by petty regulations that did not seem to apply to white seamen. He wrote to his parents, complaining that the Navy was 'not like Emporia. Blacks have trouble getting along here.' He spoke of other black friends on the base who told him to wise up. This was the real world. Racism was as deeply entrenched in the Navy as it was in the rest of America. He was just going to have to learn to live with it. A friend said: 'Essex came to the Navy expecting to be treated in the same decent way he always had been treated back in Emporia, and he found it wasn't like that at all.'

Essex and three of his black bunk mates were put on report for playing their stereo too loud – although whites played their music just as loud without punishment. Essex's boss, a white dentist, spoke up for him at his hearing, claiming that the charge was racially motivated. The proceedings were halted, but Essex and his buddies were separated and assigned to different barracks. This was not the sort of justice Essex expected.

The case had made him notorious among the white seamen at the base. He was reported for the tiniest infraction of Navy regulations and subjected to endless bed-checks, extra guard-duty and regularly told to turn his stereo down, even though the volume was so low that he could hardly hear it. Racial slurs were half-whispered behind his back. Friends said that he had been singled out as a 'cocky nigger'. The harassment took its toll on his work and he began to take sedatives.

In August 1970 a white petty officer made a remark about Essex 'smiling and shuffling'. For Essex, this mild racial taunt was the straw that broke the camel's back. He leapt on the officer and began beating him with his fists. It was the first time he had hit a white man. And for Essex, it was a liberation.

However, it did not improve his situation. Now every white man on the base was on his case. Unable to sleep, he went absent without leave for self-preservation. He went home to his parents to think his situation through. The local minister in Emporia persuaded him to return to the base and give himself up. At his court martial, Essex explained that he 'had begun to hate all white people: I was tired of going to white people and telling them my problems and not getting anything done about it.' He was found guilty, fined, demoted and confined to barracks for thirty days. A few weeks later, he was discharged from the service for a 'character disorder'.

Essex returned home to Emporia, but having experienced the intolerable racism of the outside world he could not settle. He made several mysterious trips to New York, ostensibly to visit friends from the Navy, but he may have been in contact with various Black Muslim and Black Power organisations that were rife in the US at that time. A lot of their literature was found in his possession and he certainly had some weapons training after he left the Navy.

In the summer of 1972 he went to New Orleans to see a Navy buddy called Rodney Frank, who was a Black Muslim. He joined a vocational training course for the hard-core unemployed where he was described as 'probably the best student in the class'. In his spare time he began studying his African heritage. He took the nickname 'Mata', the Swahili for 'bow'.

The murder of two black students during a campus demonstration on 16 November 1972 seemed to push Essex over the edge. 'I have now decided that the white man is my enemy,' he wrote to his mother. 'I will fight to regain my manhood or die trying.' And he began giving his possessions away.

Essex began his war against the white world with an attack on a police station on New Year's Eve 1972. His first victim, ironically, was a nineteen-year-old black police cadet. Two white officers were also injured. Essex was pursued by the police through a disused hemp factory. He had suffered a flesh wound in the shoot-out. If the police had trouble following the trail of blood, Essex dropped a trail of bullets. The police followed him to a nearby Methodist church. They surrounded it, but the church was in a black area and they were afraid of sparking a full-scale race riot. During an agreed cooling-off period, Essex escaped.

Throughout the afternoon of New Year's Day, several fires were set in the area which took 200 firemen to extinguish. Essex seems to have been responsible. Local grocery store owner Joseph Perniciaro reported seeing him return to the church, and more blood and bullets were found there.

On 7 January Essex walked into Perniciaro's shop and shot him in the chest. Out in the street, Essex stuck his rifle in through the window of a car and forced the driver to get out. He took the 1968 Chevrolet and made his getaway. Later the stolen car was found in the garage of the Howard Johnson's hotel.

Within an hour a black maid in the hotel bumped into a man with a rifle on the eighth floor. She screamed. 'Don't worry,' he said. 'We're not going to shoot any blacks, just whites. The revolution's here.'

The scream brought a twenty-seven-year-old doctor, Robert Steagall, from his room. Essex shot him in the chest. Steagall's wife Betty rushed from the room and fell to her knees by her husband's body. Essex shot her in the head. The couple had come to New Orleans on their honeymoon.

Essex began to set fire to curtains and mattresses. Forty-three-year-old San Francisco broadcast executive Robert Bemish smelt smoke. He opened the door to his room and noticed 'light bulbs popping all over the place' with the heat. He was standing facing the hotel's swimming pool when a black youth with a rifle jumped out from some bushes, stared at him for a full second, took aim and fired. Shot in the stomach, Bemish fell into the pool, pretending to be dead. Air trapped inside his coat kept Bemish afloat as he lay still for two-and-a-half hours. Bemish said that his assailant had a goatee beard and was carrying a bolt-action rifle. Essex was clean-shaven and was carrying a .44 Ruger semi-automatic.

Police converged on the hotel while frightened guests huddled in the corridors and the lobby. Told that a sniper was on the eighth floor, Deputy Sheriff Dave Munch raced up the stairs of the Rault Center across the street for a better look. On the eighth-floor pool deck he saw an armed black man with a companion who looked like a woman. This was the only other indication that Essex had accomplices. The sniper spotted Munch and fired at him. Twenty-three shards of shrapnel cut into Munch's flesh.

The hotel's assistant manager Frank Scheider went up from the lobby to investigate reports of a fire on the eleventh floor. He was later found dead, shot in the face at point-black range. A fireman climbing a ladder to the tenth floor was also shot.

Policeman Paul Persigo was shot in the head by the sniper as he moved across Duncan Plaza, opposite the hotel. Deputy Police Superintendent Louis Sirgo personally guided a search party through the hotel. On the fifteenth floor the gunman shot him in the back. Both Persigo and Sirgo were declared dead on arrival when they reached hospital.

Downtown New Orleans became a city under siege. Smoke billowed from the damaged hotel while firemen crouched behind their fire engines. One policeman lay wounded on the grassy mall, another under a tree. Patrolman Phil Coleman was shot in the head and killed as he scrambled to the aid of a wounded comrade. The police had had two tense confrontations with local black militants in the past two years. Now they assumed that they were facing a well equipped band of urban guerrillas.

The gunfire was coming from a concrete structure on the roof which covered the top of the stairwell. The police returned fire using grenades, mortars, rockets and even 20 mm canons. They tried using tear gas but it drifted away in the wind. It was then that a Sea King armour-plated helicopter was called in. Carrying a squad of police sharpshooters, the helicopters swooped past the hotel ten times, sometimes coming in as close as thirty feet. The marksmen fired hundreds of glowing tracer bullets into the shadows on the roof – to no avail. As the helicopter veered away, police and newsmen in adjacent buildings heard cries from the roof: 'I'm still here. Come and get me, you motherfucking pigs. Power to the people.'

At 9.25 p.m. the helicopter lumbered past again. This time a slight figure, armed with a rifle, bolted into the open. The crossfire from the helicopter and marksmen on the two adjacent buildings tore the sniper's body apart. Bullets still ripped into him even when he went down, his body twitching as each fresh bullet hit.

The police radio crackled: 'We've got one of them.' But in the dark it was impossible to tell whether he was alone. Reports of fresh shots and taunts from the roof spread. Cold and exhausted, the police waited out the long hours of the night. It was not until the following afternoon that the police staged their assault on the roof.

There were rumours that a black couple – the other man and woman witnesses had seen – had checked into the hotel before the shooting. This would imply a premeditated terrorist plot. But a five-hour search uncovered nothing but three suitcases of .44 Magnum ammunition. Police Superintendent Clarence Giarrusso said: 'Either there was only one, or another got away. The speculation might run the gamut all the way from negligence on the part of the police to a super-brain on the part of the sniper.'

Louisiana Attorney General William Guste maintained that the shooting was part of a black conspiracy. Essex's mother maintained that he had acted alone from private motivation. 'It all started in the Navy,' she said. 'He was all right when he left.'

At Essex's run-down apartment, the police found the walls daubed with revolutionary slogans – 'My destiny lies in the bloody death of racist pigs', 'Political power comes from the barrel of a gun', 'Black war', and 'The quest for freedom is death, then by death I shall escape to freedom'. And on the ceiling, he had written for the police to read: 'Only a pig would read shit on the ceiling.'

'White Power', not Black Power, was the slogan behind a racist spree in 1977. Frederick Cowan, a thirty-three-year-old bodybuilder, liked to wear an Afrika Korps hat around his home town of New Rochelle, New York. His burly eighteen-stone body was covered in Nazi tattoos – a death's head, an iron cross and the double lightning bolts of the SS. Behind the lace curtains of his attic bedroom was a collection of World War Two German guns. On the wall was a poster of Hitler.

Cowan's *Götterdämmerung* fell on St Valentine's Day. Three weeks before, his supervisor at Neptune World Wide Moving Company, where Cowan worked as a trucker's assistant, had sacked him for refusing to move a refrigerator for a customer. The supervisor happened to be Jewish. Cowan woke early on 14 February and donned a pair of brown slacks and a khaki soldier's shirt. Under it, he wore a T-shirt with the words 'White Power' printed across the front. He took his arsenal down to his car and loaded the trunk of his red Pontiac with a rifle, four pistols and a hunting knife.

Cowan drove into the Neptune parking lot at 7.45 a.m., just as the morning shift was clocking in. He armed himself for his own personal blitzkrieg, then started looking for thirty-one-year-old Norman Bing, the supervisor who had fired him.

Fifty-nine-year-old packer Joseph Hicks and drivers James Green, forty-four, and Frederick Holmes, fifty-four, were all standing near the entrance when Cowan came barging in. All three were black. Cowan shot Hicks and Holmes in the chest with his .308 rifle.

Green ran off down the hall. Cowan downed him with a bullet in the back. Terrified employees sprinted for cover as Cowan began to prowl the corridors looking for Bing.

'Where's Norman?' he bellowed. 'I'm gonna blow him away.'

Bing ran from his office and hid under a wooden desk, where Cowan failed to spot him.

At 7.55 a.m. the first patrol car came speeding into the depot. Officer Allen McLeod, a thirty-three-year-old father of two, leapt out and yelled: 'Drop that rifle!' Cowan dropped McLeod instead, with a bullet in the head. Then, in blind fury, Cowan sprayed the company's cafeteria with bullets, killing thirty-two-year-old Indian immigrant electrician Pariyarathu Itty Varghese.

Soon more than 300 local policemen and FBI agents had surrounded the warehouse. Cowan's parents and brothers were contacted. They tried, unsuccessfully, to talk him from his lair. 'Pray for Freddie,' a distraught Mrs Cowan cried. 'He's gone crazy.'

Shortly after noon Cowan phoned the local police station and apologised for the 'inconvenience' he was causing. Then he ordered up some lunch. 'I get very mean when I'm hungry,' he explained. Then, at 2.23 p.m., there was a muffled shot from inside the building. At dusk the police edged forward into the plant. They found Cowan lying face down in the executive suite. He had a .45 pistol in each hand and had joined his idol Adolf Hitler in suicide. The force of the last shot had blown off the black beret he had been wearing. Glinting among the blood on the floor was its cap badge – the skull and crossbones of the SS Panzer Division.

In Cowan's room the police found seven boxes full of guns, shells, knives, pictures and posters of Hitler and Himmler and a belt buckle enscribed, prophetically: 'I will give up my gun when they pry my cold dead fingers from around it.' In the margins of a Nazi propaganda book, Cowan had scrawled: 'Nothing is lower than black and Jewish people except the police who protect them.'

Police also turned up Cowan's membership card to the anti-Semitic, anti-black National States Rights Party. It's leader, J. B. Stoner, also blamed the police. 'The FBI caused niggers to start harassing Cowan on the job,' he told *Newsweek* magazine. 'Apparently, the FBI's to blame for the whole thing.'

According to friends and relatives Cowan had been a bright boy and a good student at the local Catholic parochial school. He only went bad after a hitch in the US Army, when he was stationed in Germany.

'I don't remember him collecting the Nazi propaganda until then,' said his brother James. 'We never expected this. We thought it was just a hobby.'

Some of his drinking buddies at the Galway Bay bar had more sinister memories of Cowan, whom they called 'Fritz' or 'Reinhardt'. Collecting Nazi memorabilia seemed to be a vocation to him. After a few beers he would curse: 'Fuck the Jews, fuck the niggers.'

'I should have been born forty years ago, so I could have been in the SS,' he told one regular.

The Neptune World Wide Moving Company seems to have been blissfully unaware of Cowan's spare-time activities. Under 'psychiatric disorders' in his company medical report, it simply says: 'No'.

But Cowan's spree was just one of a spate of racist attacks, usually directed at young black men. In 1981 US Army Private Joseph Christopher was sentenced to sixty years to life in prison for the racially motivated slayings of three black people in Buffalo, upstate New York, during a twenty-six-hour spree in September 1980. New York State Supreme Court Justice Frederick M. Marshall handed down the sentence. Christopher had stalked the streets with a sawn-off 7.62 mm rifle and terrorised Buffalo's black community. At a preliminary sanity hearing, Christopher was ruled mentally unfit to stand trial. But after two months of psychiatric care, he was declared competent and the trial proceeded. He was found guilty on three counts of second degree murder.

Avowed racist Joseph Paul Franklin was convicted on federal charges in the sniper slayings of two young black men and sentenced to serve two consecutive terms of life imprisonment – the maximum penalty under federal law. Thirty-year-old drifter Franklin, a former Ku Klux Klansman and a member of the American Nazi Party, was convicted by an all-white jury of violating the civil rights of two black men by shooting them to death on 20 August 1980 as they jogged in a Salt Lake park. The victims were eighteen-year-old David Martin and twenty-year-old Ted Fields, who had been jogging with two white women.

There was an uproar at his sentencing when Franklin tried to physically attack the federal prosecutor – a black man – and had to be restrained by ten federal marshals. Franklin screamed that his conviction was a 'farce' and called the judge 'nothing but an agent of this Communist government'. Throughout his trial, Franklin had maintained that the charges were 'trumped up because of my racist views'.

Franklin had been brought up in Mobile, Alabama, the heart of the Deep South. As a boy he had been beaten by his mother. He dropped out of school at seventeen and began getting into frequent scrapes with the police. His juvenile rap sheet included arrests for assault, carrying concealed weapons and disorderly conduct.

He became an evangelical Christian, then a Nazi then a Ku Klux Klansman. At one time he told friends that he was going to join Ian Smith's Rhodesian Army. Instead he started drifting from state to state, driven seemingly by his twin passions – a love of guns and a hatred of black people. In 1976 he was charged with throwing the chemical Mace over a black man and white woman in Maryland, but jumped bail before he could stand trial. He also sent a threatening letter to President Carter and was arrested in Tampa, Florida shortly before the president was scheduled to arrive on his election campaign.

Franklin passionately disapproved of 'race mixing' and, according to prosecution witnesses, had boasted of the killings, though the prosecution could not produce an eyewitness or the murder weapon at the trial. Franklin was caught in possession of a rifle similar to the one used in the sniper attack, and owned a small arsenal of weapons. A car matching the description of Franklin's souped-up Camaro was seen in the area at the time of the killings and the police matched tyre treads. However, the defence maintained that Franklin had a visual impairment and could not have fired the six rapid shots that killed the two victims.

After a three-week trial, the jury deliberated for less than two hours. Franklin was also wanted in connection with the sniper slaying of a black man and a white woman in a parking lot in Oklahoma City in 1979 and the shooting of the publisher of *Hustler* magazine, Larry Flynt, the year before, after the soft-porn magazine published a photo spread showing a white woman with a black man. Flynt's spine had been severed and he was confined to a wheelchair.

Then, on 2 June 1981, while in jail, Franklin was arraigned in South Bend, Indiana on charges of shooting Vernon Jordan, a black civil rights leader, on 12 June 1980. Jordan was shot at while he was getting out of a white woman's car at a motel parking lot after addressing the local chapter of the Urban League in Fort Wayne, Indiana. He was critically wounded. Franklin had checked into a nearby motel a week before and left town immediately after the incident. At the time of the arraignment Franklin was in the prison hospital, recovering from stab wounds inflicted in February 1982 in a racially motivated attack by fellow inmates of the federal penitentiary at Marion, Illinois.

After the Vietnam War, a large number of Asian refugees settled in America. They too became an object of hate. In 1989 Patrick Purdy walked into a schoolyard in Stockton, California and opened fire on Asian children, killing five and wounding seven.

But James Huberty claimed the biggest race-related death toll at that time – twenty-one – when he took out the fact that he had lost his job on the Mexicans who were eating at a McDonald's in San Ysidro in 1984.

It was just another McDonald's along a busy highway in southern California, and a day like any other day. Kids showed up for free ice cream, a Wednesday special. Mexicans stopped by for fast food American style on their way to or from Tijuana, just over the border. Mario Yepez Lopez and his wife, April, finished eating and took their two-year-old daughter Griselda out to romp in the McDonald's playground. Her father heard a popping noise – and then another pop, like 'a soda can exploding,' he said. He turned to see a man inside put a pistol on the counter, then a rifle – a semi-automatic Uzi. Then the man took a shotgun and fired into the body of a woman who already lay sprawled on the floor.

Lopez pushed his family behind the playground's brick wall. As they huddled there in the thirty-six degree heat, the shooting went on quite methodically. Eventually the screams, and the cries of the children, died away.

The bullets kept flying – smashing through plate glass, burrowing into cars, ricocheting off the pavement, plunking into homes. The heavy shooting was over in five minutes. But the pops and staccato bursts continued sporadically for more than an hour, and, Lopez recalled: 'It seemed like it would never end.' When silence finally fell and it was safe to stand up, Lopez said, he felt as if he had been given a new life.

The Lopez family had escaped what was then the worst mass murder by one gunman in one day in US history. Rescue workers found the bodies of twenty victims and nineteen wounded people, one of whom died a day later. Of the twenty-one killed, five were teenagers and five even younger. One baby was carried from the carnage still alive, but critically wounded in the abdomen and pancreas. Other victims were slumped, dead, over their food. One still clutched his baseball cap. Others were prostrate on the floor. Sprawled in their midst was their killer, forty-one-year-old James Oliver Huberty. He had been dropped by a SWAT team marksman seventy-five minutes after the shooting started. Now he was in no position to tell anybody why.

Huberty launched his attack on McDonald's from his apartment just 200 yards away in a shabby area of San Ysidro, a dusty San Diego suburb about a mile north of the Mexican border. He was from Ohio. His parents divorced when he was at grade school. He graduated with a degree in sociology from Malone College, a Quaker institution, in Canton, Ohio. Then he worked as an apprentice embalmer, dropped that, and became a welder.

Although Huberty pulled the trigger in San Ysidro on 25 July 1984, the hammer was cocked more than a year before, when he lost his welder job and subsequently his home in Massillon, a northern Ohio industrial town. His wife recalled that he had put a gun to his head.

Later he said: 'You should have let me kill myself.' After the massacre, she wished she had. Long before he lost his job, his neighbours had come to know him as a man to avoid. He was sullen, full of unfocused anger, a gun-nut always ready to get even with someone. Huberty had left with his wife, Etna, and his two daughters, aged fourteen and ten, to build a new life in California seven months before the massacre. Then just two weeks before his rampage, Huberty lost his job as a condominium security guard.

The day before the massacre, at Etna's urging, Huberty called a mental health clinic to seek counselling, but his call was not returned. The clinic said later that there was no record of such a call. Huberty began his last morning at 9 a.m. in court for a minor traffic violation. He behaved reasonably enough and was pleased when the judge sent him away without a fine. After he left court, at about noon, he took Etna and his teenage daughter, Zelia, to lunch across the street at another McDonald's. Then the family spent the afternoon at San Diego Zoo. As Huberty looked at the animals, his widow said later that he had seemed to reach his terrible decision. He had turned to Etna and said: 'Society had their chance.'

Back home, Etna washed dishes and lay down in the bedroom for a nap. Her husband came in, wearing a dark maroon shirt and camouflage trousers, for a kiss goodbye. Did he need money? she asked. He said no. Then he muttered: 'I'm going hunting – hunting for humans.'

Huberty's wife dismissed this. Her husband had been saying wild things for a long time. Huberty climbed into his battered black Mercury Marquis. Its bumper sticker read 'I'm Not Deaf, I'm Just Ignoring You.' And he drove the half block to McDonald's.

At about 4 p.m. the diners looked up from their Big Macs as the tall, bespectacled man strode in. He had a 9 mm Browning automatic pistol in his belt, a twelve-bore pump-action shotgun in his hand and a 9 mm Uzi semi-automatic rifle slung over one shoulder. 'Everybody get down on the floor or I'll kill somebody,' he shouted. The forty-five customers complied immediately. Then he killed them anyway.

In the first ten minutes, while Huberty sprayed the inside of the restaurant with bullets, twenty people died, including four who had tried to run out of the building when the shooting started. One of them, eleven-year-old Omar Hernandez, made it as far as the bike rack before he was shot in the back. Another eleven-year-old, David Flores, was also killed. Joshua Coleman fell to the ground wounded. He lay still, singing quietly to himself, and survived.

In panic, Maria Diaz fled with her daughter out of a side door when the shooting started, then realised that she had left her two-year-old son inside. She crept back to the window and saw him sitting obediently in a booth. She motioned him towards the door, nudged it open, and the boy toddled to safety.

The miracle was that anybody escaped at all – and that ten people came out of the restaurant alive. Five had hidden in a storage area. One woman played dead beside her murdered husband. A Mexican couple hid behind chair backs while Huberty made his first killing circuit, then slipped out of the door.

Huberty also fired into the first patrol car arriving at the McDonald's. Officers cordoned off San Ysidro Boulevard and Interstate 5, and quickly issued a Code 10 call for a SWAT team. The gunfire was so heavy that the police thought there was more than one gunman inside. One fireman was hit, but the bullet had passed through his fire truck and, slowed, hitting him softly on the head.

The police marksmen held their fire for more than an hour, worried that the gunman had hostages. They did not attempt to contact Huberty by telephone, bullhorn or any other means.

'Our interest in negotiation was gone,' said Police Commander Larry Gore. 'We wanted to take him out as soon as we could.'

At 5 p.m. the gunfire slackened. A McDonald's employee crept from the basement with vital information. Huberty held no hostages. The SWAT team got a green light. 'Fix him in your sights and take him out,' they were ordered.

Officer Chuck Foster took aim with his .308 calibre rifle from the roof of the post office next door. Two other officers fired four rounds, but only Foster's single bullet struck Huberty, in the chest, killing him instantly.

'He dropped like a stone,' one cop recalled.

In the aftermath, the few people who had been close to Huberty over the years could only understand his last assault as the explosion at the end of a long, sputtering fuse. 'He had a gripe against society,' said a friend from Ohio. 'Something's been building up inside of Jim for years. I just don't know what set it off.'

Why had Huberty chosen a McDonald's for his massacre? Neighbours suggested that his dislike of Mexicans and children – the restaurant's regular customers – might have had something to do with it.

The McDonald's Corporation contributed one million dollars to a welfare fund for the massacre's survivors. Within two days of the carnage, workmen had replaced windows and scrubbed the blood from the interior. And they had cleaned the pavement outside where the young boys had fallen. The golden arches were shining again on San Ysidro boulevard, ready to reopen for business

– and hopefully to become once more just another McDonald's. It failed. The restaurant in San Ysidro was razed to the ground on 28 July 1984. The site is now a memorial to Huberty's victims.

Chapter 11

The Political Dimension

Some murder campaigns take on a political character. At 5.20 p.m. on Wednesday 2 October 2002, a shot was fired through the window of the Michaels craft store in Wheaton, Maryland, a wealthy suburb of Washington, DC. It passed over the head of cashier Ann Chapman, ripped through an advertising sign and ricocheted off a metal book rack.

About forty minutes later, James Martin, a fifty-five-year-old program analyst at the National Oceanic and Atmospheric Administration, stopped to buy groceries for his church at Shoppers Food Warehouse in Glenmont Village, some two miles from Wheaton. He was killed by a single shot as he walked across the parking lot.

At 7.41 the following morning, thirty-nine-year-old James 'Sonny' Buchanan was mowing the lawn of a nearby car dealership in White Flint, Maryland when he was killed by a single bullet to the chest. Half an hour later, Premkumar Walekar, a fifty-three-year-old cab driver from India, was killed while filling up the tank of his minivan in Aspen Hill, Maryland. He had quit early that day and was heading home because it was his twenty-fifth wedding anniversary.

Less than an hour after that, thirty-four-year-old Sarah Ramos was shot while sitting on a bench in front of the Crisp & Juicy charbroiled chicken restaurant near the Leisure World retirement community in Silver Spring, Maryland. Just before 10 a.m., Lori Ann Lewis-Rivera, a twenty-five-year-old nanny, was gunned down while vacuuming her employers' maroon Dodge van at a service station in Kensington, Maryland. She was married with a three-year-old daughter.

That evening at 9.15 p.m., Pascal Charlot, a seventy-two-year-old retired carpenter, was shot while crossing the street in Washington, DC. Again the victim had been killed by a single bullet. This time an eyewitness said they had seen two men in a white van similar to a white Mitsubishi or Isuzu truck seen near Leisure World in Silver Spring. The police have no doubt the killings were related. In every case, the victim was killed by a single shot from a distance, taken down by an expert marksman.

As news of the shootings spread, people began to panic. Schools kept their children indoors and parents went to collect them, rather than let them take the school bus. It seemed particularly scary that these killings were taking place within ten miles of the White House – around the Capital Beltway, the expressway that rings Washington, DC. It seemed as if the sniper was using the Beltway to travel between killings, and the newspapers dubbed the phantom sniper the 'Beltway Killer'.

The following day, forty-three-year-old Caroline Seawell was shot and wounded at 2.30 p.m. in the parking lot of another Michaels craft store at Spotsylvania Mall in Virginia, just outside the city of Fredericksburg, while she was loading purchases into her minivan. She was critically injured but later recovered.

Again the police tied this killing to the ones the previous day. They believed that the murders were the work of a single killer using a high-powered .223 calibre gun – probably an assault rifle.

There were no killings over the weekend. Then on Monday 7 October at 8.08 a.m., thirteen-year-old Iran Brown was shot in the chest as he arrived at Benjamin Tasker Middle School in Bowie, Maryland. His aunt, who had witnessed the attack, rushed him to the local hospital. He was then airlifted to a Washington hospital where doctors removed his spleen, pancreas and parts of his stomach in a three-hour operation.

Searching the area, the police found spent cartridges some 150 yards from the school gate, along with a tarot card. Scrawled on it were the words 'Dear Policeman: I am God.' The police then realised that the killer was monitoring the media reports. The day before, the early morning *Today* show had featured a guest who talked about the sniper's apparent 'God complex'.

'This person thinks he's in total control,' he had said. 'He thinks he is God.'

FBI profilers had believed that the sniper had left the message on the tarot card to open a dialogue with the police. It later came out that the police had found tarot cards at other crime scenes. The killer, it seemed, enjoyed basking in the limelight.

Two days later, on 9 October, Dean Myers, a fifty-three-year-old civil engineer and Vietnam veteran, was shot with a single bullet in the chest at 8.18 a.m., after filling his gas tank at a Sunco gas station near Manassas, Virginia. A white minivan was stopped in the area and the occupants questioned but there was no indication that they were connected to the murders.

Another two days passed and, on Friday 11 October, the killer returned to Spotsylvania County. At 9.30 a.m., fifty-three-year-old Kenneth Bridges stopped at an Exxon gas station off Interstate 95 on his way home to Philadelphia to fill up his car. He was shot dead in front of a number of people including a state trooper. A white Chevy van was seen by several witnesses, including the state trooper, but he did not give chase as he was attending to Kenneth Bridges until medical assistance arrived.

The following Monday, Linda Franklin, a forty-seven-year-old FBI analyst, went shopping with her husband to buy items for their new home. At 9.15 p.m., they were loading their purchases into their car in the parking garage of a Home Depot store in Falls Church, Virginia, when a single shot hit her in the chest and killed her.

Matthew Dowdy claimed to have witnessed the incident. He said he had seen a man step out of a van, aim an AK-47 at the victim and fire a single shot. For a moment, the police thought they had a breakthrough. But it turned out that Dowdy was inside the store at the time. He had a criminal record and, under questioning, admitted that he was lying. He was charged with making a false statement to a police officer.

Up until that point, the sniper had never struck on a weekend. Then he changed his modus operandi. On Saturday 19 October, thirty-seven-year-old Jeffery Hopper was shot as he and his wife walked across the dimly lit parking lot of the Ponderosa Steakhouse in Ashland, Virginia at around 8 p.m. Police quickly surmised that the single shot had been fired from a wooded tree line behind the restaurant.

The couple were from out of town and had only stopped to get a bite to eat and fill the car. Hopper was rushed to MCV Hospital where doctors removed his pancreas, spleen and part of his stomach. Ballistic details could not be obtained at first because the bullet remained lodged in Jeffery Hopper's body. When the bullet was removed in a second operation, ballistic tests confirmed that this shooting was linked with the others. It seemed that the sniper had also extended his geographic reach. Ashland is some ninety miles south of Washington, though it is on I-95 that runs through Fredericksburg to the capital. The road had already been associated with other killings.

As FBI profilers had surmised, the killer was trying to communicate with them. Immediately after the attack, the police had received a phone call, which was later traced to an area near Richmond, Virginia. It was from a man using a machine to disguise his voice. He told them that a note could be found at the scene of the crime. Searching the woods behind the restaurant, the police found a four-page letter wrapped in plastic taped to a tree. It was poorly worded, but the specific contents were not immediately released to the public. However, there were soon leaks which said that the note contained specific threats against children and hinted at a demand for money. It was also said that the note contained a timetable for more attacks. Schools now began to close their doors.

Despite the semi-literate letter, it was plain that the killer was a clever man. It was also plain that he had been following the media coverage. He knew that the profilers had spotted that he never killed on a weekend, so he had attacked on a Saturday. Detectives also began to doubt that he used a white van as a getaway vehicle. They were common enough and he could just have waited until a white van was in the vicinity before he loosed off a shot. All they knew for certain was that he used a .223.

The letter rendered little in the way of forensic clues. However, it did give the police the number of an unsubscribed phone line he said he would call on. The police took the phone line, but received no call. On 20 October, they put out an appeal, saying: 'To the person who left us a message at the Ponderosa last night, you gave us a telephone number. We do want to talk to you. Call us at the number you provided.'

The following day they received a call, which was traced to an Exxon station in Richmond. It did not come from the sniper directly. It was a tape recording. The voice had been altered electronically, making parts of the message unintelligible. No accent or any other identifying clue could be discerned, so the police put out another appeal, saying: 'The person you called could not hear everything you said. The audio was unclear and we want to get it right. Call us back so that we can clearly understand.'

An answer came the following day.

At 5.56 a.m. on Tuesday 22 October, there was another attack less than half a mile from the location of the first shooting. Thirty-five-year-old bus driver, Conrad Johnson, was standing on the top step of a commuter bus when he was shot in the chest. He was airlifted to Suburban Hospital in Bethesda where he died, leaving a wife and two children. Police brought in bloodhounds to comb the wooded area near the scene of the attack. Montgomery County schools were ordered to close and staff positioned at all entrances and exits while they were evacuated.

The police then released more details from the note found behind the Ponderosa restaurant. It said: 'Your children are not safe, anywhere, at any time.'

They revealed that another note had been found near the scene of the shooting of bus driver Conrad Johnson. In it, the sniper was critical of the police investigation and had complained that on six occasions he had tried to talk to the FBI over their tip-off phone line only to be cut short. He had also asked for money, but the authorities had replied: 'We have researched the option you stated and found it is not possible electronically to comply in the manner that you requested.'

The sniper called other police lines to boast of his cleverness. He got angry with one startled employee of the Montgomery County police who failed to take him seriously.

'I am God!' he yelled. 'Don't you know who you're dealing with? Just check out the murder-robbery in Montgomery if you don't believe me!'

This puzzled the police. All the Maryland killings had taken place in Montgomery County, but when they checked they could not find a murder-robbery that fitted the killer's profile. It was only the next night that they discovered their mistake. A priest received what he initially took to be a crank call from a man boasting of a murder in Montgomery – Montgomery, Alabama.

On 21 September 2002, Claudine Parker, a clerk at the ABC Beverages liquor store in Montgomery, Alabama, was shot and killed during a robbery. Another assistant, Kellie Adams, had been injured. Their assailant had then stolen their belongings. One of the items taken was a credit card. This was the account that the sniper had wanted the money he had demanded credited to electronically.

A fingerprint had been found at the crime scene. An extensive computer search found it on file with the Immigration and Naturalization Service. It belonged to Lee Malvo, a seventeen-year-old Jamaican citizen. They were also in the juvenile-crime records in Washington State. Further researches revealed Malvo's mother had a boyfriend who Malvo thought of as his surrogate father. His named was John Allen Williams. He was a Gulf War veteran who had converted to Islam and called himself John Allen Muhammad. He was also an expert marksman.

On 8 October – the day after thirteen-year-old Iran Brown had been shot – a police officer had found Muhammad sleeping in his car. This put Muhammad in the general location of the killings. The police now had a description of his car. It was a 1990 Chevrolet Caprice with New Jersey licence plates. The officer had even logged his licence number, NDA 21Z. Checking back, it was discovered that a Caprice had been seen near another shooting on 3 October.

Muhammad was under a restraining order from his ex-wife after reportedly threatened her. The FBI searched a house where he had lived in Tacoma. They found a tree stump he had used for target practice and neighbours said, while he had lived there, they had heard the sound of a high-powered rifle.

On 23 October, details of the car were released to the media. Almost immediately, it was spotted by truck driver Ron Lantz at a rest stop on Interstate 70 near Frederick, Maryland, some fifty miles northwest of Washington, DC.

As they approached the car, the police were expecting a shoot-out. Instead, they found Muhammad and Malvo asleep inside. The Bushmaster rifle that the police believed was used in the snipings lay on the back seat behind them.

A sniper's telescopic sight, a tripod and a sniper's perch were found in the trunk of the car. It had some interesting modifications. The lid of the trunk had two holes drilled in it – one for the barrel of the rifle; the other for the scope. When the back seat was folded down, the sniper could crawl into the trunk and take a shot without leaving the car.

Ballistics tests linked the gun with eight of the ten Beltway killings, along with two other murders. The police also found a laptop computer in the car. It belonged to Paul LaRuffa, a fifty-five-year-old pizzeria owner who had been shot six times at close range while locking up his restaurant in Clinton, Maryland on 5 September 2002.

The prosecution of Muhammad and Malvo was complicated by the fact that they faced Federal charges as well as charges in Maryland,

Virginia and Alabama for murder and terrorism. Nevertheless the couple were convicted. As Malvo was a juvenile at the time of the offences, he escaped the death penalty and has been sentenced to seven consecutive life sentences without possibility of parole. Muhammad has been sentenced to death. Appeals are ongoing.

A civil law suit was also taken against them by those they wounded and the families of the murdered. Though Muhammad and Malvo were penniless, their co-defendants, the gunshop Bull's Eye Shooter Supply, who sold the guns, and gunmaker Bushmaster Firearms, makers of the murder weapon, made a landmark $2.5 million out-of-court settlement in late 2004.

Malvo also told the authorities that he and Muhammad were guilty of five additional shootings. In February or March 2002, they killed a man in Los Angeles during a robbery. They shot and killed sixty-year-old Jerry Taylor while he was practising chip shots on a golf course in Tucson, Arizona, on 19 March. A seventy-six-year-old man was shot at a golf course in Clearwater, Florida, on 18 May but survived. On 27 May, a man doing work in his yard in Denton, Texas, was shot and killed. And a fifty-four-year-old man was shot during a robbery outside a shopping mall near Baton Rouge, Louisiana, on 1 August. He also survived.

The Beltway killings, Malvo said, were part of a sinister plan to stir up racial violence. When they had first met in Antigua in May 2000, Malvo told a court in May 2006, Muhammad had introduced him to the radical doctrines of Nation of Islam. He had then sneaked Malvo into the country and taught him how to fire a gun. Muhammad's plan in the DC area was, he said, to kill six white people a day for thirty days. The liquor store shooting in Alabama was a trial to see if the converted trunk of the Caprice worked as a sniper hide. Afterwards they had move on to white suburbs of Washington in an effort to terrorise the city. Once they had killed 180 white people, they intended to move on to Baltimore, where they were going to kill a pregnant woman by shooting her in the stomach. Then they were going to kill a policeman and set off improvised explosive devices filled with shrapnel at his funeral.

After extorting several millions dollars from the government, they planned to pick up some 140 abandoned or orphaned black boys, set up their own separate African-American country somewhere in Canada where they would give the boys weapons training, then send them back to terrorise American cities as part of a jihad.

Their terrorist intentions were confirmed by a series of exhibits introduced in evidence at Muhammad's trial. These included:

- Exhibit 65-006: A self-portrait of Malvo in the crosshair of a gun scope shouting, 'ALLAH AKBAR!' The word 'SALAAM' scrawled vertically. A lyric from Bob Marley's 'Natural Mystic': 'Many more will have to suffer. Many more will have to die. Don't ask me why.'
- Exhibit 65-016: A portrait of Saddam Hussein with the words 'INSHALLAH' and 'The Protector', surrounded by rockets.
- Exhibit 65-043: Father and son portrait of Malvo and Muhammad, captioned: 'We will kill them all. Jihad.'
- Exhibit 65-056: A self-portrait of Malvo as a sniper, lying in wait, with his rifle and 'JIHAD' written in bold letters.
- Exhibit 65-067: A suicide bomber labelled 'Hamas' walking into a McDonald's restaurant. Another drawing of the Twin Towers burning captioned: 'American did this. You were warned.'
- Exhibit 65-109: Portrait of Osama bin Laden, captioned 'Servant of Allah.'

- Exhibit 65-117: The White House drawn in a crosshair, surrounded by missiles, with a warning: 'Sep. 11 we will ensure will look like a picnic to you' and 'you will bleed to death little by little.'

In the aftermath of 9/11 this did not go down well with the jury.

Pastor Jim Powell of the First Baptist Church in the small town of Daingerfield, Texas, was a charismatic preacher. To dramatise his sermon against the evils of Communism, he had several uniformed men come rushing into the Sunday service. So it was no surprise to the 350 worshippers when, on 22 June 1980, forty-six-year-old Alvin Lee King came bursting in while they were singing the hymn 'More About Jesus'. He was wearing Army fatigues, a flak jacket and helmet, and carrying an arsenal. This included an AR-15 rifle with bayonet fix, an M1 carbine, a pearl-handled .22 calibre pistol revolver and a .38 calibre pistol. Slung over his shoulder was a pack stuffed with 250 rounds of ammunition.

'This is war!' he announced and opened fire with the AR-15. He loosed off five rounds in ten seconds into the stunned congregation. The skull of seven-year-old Gina Linam was smashed, killing her instantly. Seventy-eight-year-old Thelme Robinson also fell dead. And forty-nine-year-old Gene Gandy was fatally wounded just below the heart. She survived until that night.

Chris Hall, the sound recordist who broadcast Pastor Powell's sermon, leapt on King and pushed the gunman, who outweighed him by more than five stone, out into the church vestibule. King dropped his automatic and lost his helmet and his glasses. Without them, he could see no more than six feet. King unholstered his .38 and blasted blindly down the steps into the crypt as Hall made his escape.

Then fifty-three-year-old James 'Red' McDaniel charged at the gunman. He ran him out through the front door, which broke, and down the church steps. But King's .38 went off, and Red McDaniel rolled off him dead.

Forty-nine-year-old councillor Kenneth Truitt tried to run the gunman down. He was shot and killed.

Inside the church Larry Cowan picked up the M1 that King had dropped and fired at the gunman. King dropped his .38 and ran to a nearby fire station. There he shot himself in the head with his .22, but failed to kill himself. At the church, five were dead and eleven wounded.

When policemen went out to King's isolated farmhouse eight miles from Daingerfield, they found his wife, Gretchen, tied to a chair with rope and a telephone cord. On a table was a note. It read: Jeremiah says the King is the King of Kings.' In the basement the officers found a letter from the Soviet embassy in Washington, DC, informing King that he could not become a Soviet citizen. They also found records of a Swiss bank account, where he had deposited $3,000 that spring, and passports for King and his wife. 'He definitely had something planned,' said Deputy Sheriff Emit Kennedy. But no one could say what.

King was born in 1934 and raised in Corpus Christi, Texas by his parents, who owned a pawnshop, a liquor store and a jukebox leasing company. He majored in education at North Texas State University, where he met his wife Gretchen Gains. The couple were married in 1956. Ten years later the Kings, along with their daughter Cynthia and son Alvin Lee King IV, moved to Daingerfield, Texas, where King taught maths at the local high school. 1966 was also the year a terrible accident took place. While examining a loaded twelve-bore shotgun in his parents' home in Corpus Christi, King dropped the gun. It went off, killing his father. The coroner ruled it was accidental death.

At Daingerfield High, his colleagues thought that King was a great teacher, if somewhat eccentric. Local teachers were required to sign the oath saying they believed in God. King refused. And his teaching methods were viewed as radical. Borderline students could pick whether they were moved up or down a grade. Then in 1972, King was asked to teach children with learning difficulties. He refused, and became a truck driver.

Five years later the Kings' house burned down under rather mysterious circumstances. He then moved with his family to a farm where they raised cucumbers and peas. They kept themselves to themselves. Meanwhile, in his leisure moments, King was practising judo and collecting guns. As far as most people in Daingerfield were concerned, King had disappeared.

Then in October 1979 nineteen-year-old Cynthia King turned up at Daingerfield Police Station. She claimed that her father had been forcing her to have sex with him for the last ten years. A friend, twenty-year-old Stanley Sinclair, the son of a Methodist minister, had urged her to file charges of incest against King. The following month, Sinclair was found in Houston. He had been stabbed to death.

After a change of venue, King was due to face trial in Silver Spring. He asked several members of the First Baptist Church to testify as character witnesses. All refused. The trial was set for 23 June 1980, the Monday after the massacre. King did not attend. Instead he faced five counts of murder and ten counts of assault with intent to kill. On 28 July 1980 a jury found him incompetent to stand trial and sent him to Ruskin State Hospital for the Criminally Insane. There it was determined that his IQ was 151, but he was not found competent to plead until November 1981. King was moved back to Daingerfield jail, ready to stand trial. The proceedings were scheduled to start on 25 January 1982, but on 19 January King tore a towel into strips, tied the strips together, made a noose and hanged himself from a crossbar in his jail cell.

Political spree killing spread over the border into Canada in 1984. The attack took place at Quebec's National Assembly, whose debating chamber had long been a battlefield between English-speaking Canadians and the French-speaking Quebecois. Just a month after security guards had been replaced by more appealing hostesses who ushered visitors through the hushed Renaissance-style halls, a man with a beret rushed into the building, spraying the crowds with sub-machine-gun fire. School children fled for cover. One of the hostesses fell to the ground. The gunman ran on up to the second floor where he killed three government employees and wounded thirteen others. But when he barged into the chamber of the Assembly, the politicians were not there. He was too early. The morning session had not yet started.

'I came to kill,' he yelled at staff members as he sprayed the chamber with bullets. 'I must have made a mistake about the time.'

That was as far as Corporal Denis Lortie got in his attempt to destroy the province's ruling Parti Québéçois. The only person who did not flee from the Assembly chamber was René Jalbert, the sixty-three-year-old sergeant at arms. He approached Lortie and offered him a cigarette. Then Jalbert discovered that Lortie served in his old army regiment. He insisted that Corporal Lortie address him as major. After the police surrounded the building, he persuaded the gunman to surrender.

'He just wasn't rational,' Jalbert told reporters after his five-hour ordeal. 'He just kept talking about how he wanted to impress people.'

Lortie, a twenty-five-year-old supply technician from the Carp military base near Ottawa, had started the day by delivering a pre-recorded tape to a local radio station in Quebec City. When station employees played the tape, they heard a frightening message. Ranting about the 1977 legislation that established French as Quebec's pre-eminent language, Lortie said that he planned to eliminate the Parti Québéçois – and kill anyone else who got in his way.

Lortie's attack stirred strong emotions across Canada. Quebeckers had grown increasingly disenchanted with the Parti Québéçois. A few locals even expressed sympathy for Lortie's rampage. One French speaker was unnerved by it. The next day thirty-nine-year-old Quebec City resident Jean-Claude Nadeau opened fire with a twenty-bore shotgun in a city street. Two people were injured, but not seriously. Nadeau barricaded himself in his home, which was quickly surrounded by the police. He surrendered twenty-four hours later.

Most Canadians were, however, horrified. They still believed that spree killing was largely confined to the US. Lortie's attack on one of their seats of government helped convince them that no one was safe.

Chapter 12

The Menace Spreads

In 1987, even a sleepy, peaceful English village found it was vulnerable to a killer with a gun, a grudge and no reason to live.

On 20 August, thirty-three-year-old Susan Godfrey took her two children for a picnic in Savernake Forest, ten miles from Hungerford in Berkshire. It was around 12.30 p.m. They had finished eating and Mrs Godfrey was strapping four-year-old Hannah and two-year-old James into the back of the family car when a man dressed in black appeared.

Incongruously for the Berkshire countryside, he was carrying a Chinese-made AK-47 – a Kalashnikov assault rifle more usually seen in the hands of Third World guerrillas. He took the car keys from the dashboard of the black Nissan and forced Mrs Godfrey to come with him. Less than a hundred yards from the car he emptied the entire magazine of the Kalashnikov – fifteen high-velocity rounds – into her back at point-blank range. The children were later found wandering the forest.

There seems to have been no motive for this savage murder. Mrs Godfrey was not sexually assaulted and there seems to have been no connection between her and her murderer – twenty-seven-year-old Michael Ryan – before her death. There is no evidence that Ryan had trailed the family. He had been in the forest, armed, since the mid-morning. The police could only speculate that she had surprised him during target practice. A local boy had heard a burst of semi-automatic fire from the forest at around 10.30 that morning.

But one senseless act of violence was not enough for the lonely and deluded Ryan. He drove his D-registered Vauxhall Astra back down the A4 towards his home in Hungerford.

Hungerford is an ancient market town with a population of less than 5,000. The broad main street is dominated by the Bear Hotel and the redbrick clock tower that tolls out the hours with a long, flat note. Hungerford was granted a charter by John of Gaunt, whose name is commemorated by a pub in the town and the secondary school Michael Ryan attended.

The summer in Hungerford is quiet and still, though in August the sky is occasionally darkened by smoke from the burning stubble. The redbrick villas of the old town are a symbol of stability in the unchanging English countryside. The only lurking sense of fear emanates from the dark Victorian mental asylum that stands across the cattle grid on the Common. But on the back road from Hungerford to Lambourn there is a monument half-buried in the hedgerow. It commemorates the death of two policemen who were murdered there by a gang of robbers in 1870. It was Hungerford's only previous experience of public slaughter.

On the way back to Hungerford, Ryan stopped at the Golden Arrow filling station in Froxfield, Wiltshire. It was 12.40 p.m. The cashier mother-of-three Kabaub Dean recognised Ryan. He stopped there for petrol every other day, normally paying by credit card but never passing the time of day.

Today was somehow different. Mrs Dean noticed Ryan was hanging around nervously. He appeared to be waiting for another customer to leave. Then she saw him fiddling about with something in the boot of his car. Suddenly he pulled a gun out and started shooting at her. The glass window of her booth shattered and she was showered with glass. She dived for cover.

Ryan approached as she lay helpless under the counter. She begged for her life as he stood over her. Coldly he took aim and – at point-blank range – he pulled the trigger.

Mrs Dean heard the click of an empty gun chamber. Ryan had run out of ammunition. He pulled the trigger again and again. Mrs Dean heard four or five clicks. Then Ryan walked back to his car and drove away.

His next stop was his mother's house at 4 South View in Hungerford where he also lived. There he had built up a fearsome arsenal. In a steel cabinet bolted to the wall of the house he kept at least one shotgun, two rifles, the 7.92 mm Kalashnikov, three handguns including a 9 mm pistol and an American-made M1 carbine and fifty rounds of ammunition which he had bought for £150 at the Wiltshire Shooting Centre just eight days before the incident.

Ryan had joined the shooting centre a month before the incident. There he was known as 'polite' and 'unremarkable'. Those who got to know him better found him articulate, especially about his favourite subject – guns. He could reel off a detailed history of the M1 and its use in World War Two and the Korean War. He had been practising with the M1 on the club's shooting range the day before the shootings.

Little is known about what occurred between Ryan and his mother when he got home. But less than twenty minutes after the shooting at the petrol station, Ryan shot his mother. Her body was found lying in the road outside the house. Ryan then set the house on fire. The blaze quickly spread to the three adjoining houses in the terrace.

A neighbour, Jack Gibbs, was the next to die. He was in the kitchen of his home when Ryan began his murderous assault. Sixty-six-year-old Mr Gibbs threw himself across his sixty-three-year-old, wheelchair-bound wife, Myrtle Gibbs, to protect her from the burst of semi-automatic fire from Ryan's Kalashnikov. Four high-powered bullets passed through his body, fatally wounding his wife. She died in Princess Margaret Hospital, Swindon, the next day.

Then Ryan shot neighbours Sheila Mason and her seventy-year-old father Roland as they rushed from their home at Number 6. He gunned down eighty-four-year-old retired shop-keeper Abdur Khan who used to wander the streets of Hungerford from his home in Fairview Road, talking to anyone he met.

He shot at passing cars, killing George White from Newbury who happened to be driving through Hungerford. Ian Playle, the thirty-four-year-old chief clerk of West Berkshire Magistrates Court, was driving down the A338 through the village with his wife Elizabeth, his six-year-old son Mark and their eighteen-month-old baby daughter Elizabeth when Ryan sprayed their car. Mr Playle was hit several times and died later at the John Radcliffe Hospital in Oxford.

As Ryan roamed the village where he had lived his entire life the death toll mounted. Kenneth Clements was killed as he walked down a footpath at the end of South View. Douglas Wainwright was shot in his car on Priory Avenue. Cab driver Marcus Barnard was on his way home to his wife and month-old baby when he was shot. Eric Vardy was also found dead in his car in Priory Road.

Ryan's last victim was Sandra Hill. She too was shot in her car on Priory Road. She was rushed to the local doctor's surgery, but it was too late. She died shortly after arrival.

In less than an hour and a half, Ryan's murderous rampage left fourteen dead and fifteen wounded. But there was nowhere to run to – and the police would soon be closing in on the quiet Berkshire village whose name would soon be synonymous with mindless murder.

At 12.45 p.m. Mrs Kabaub Dean, the cashier at the Golden Arrow service station, called the police. But she thought the shooting incident was just a robbery until much later when she heard about the bloodletting in Hungerford on the radio. Five minutes after her call the Wiltshire police alerted the neighbouring Thames Valley force assuming that Ryan would have moved into their jurisdiction.

At 12.47 p.m. the Thames Valley police got their first 999 call from Hungerford. The caller reported a shooting in South View, the street where Ryan lived with his mother. Shortly after 1 p.m. Police Constable Roger Brereton arrived in South View. At 1.05 p.m. he radioed the message: '18. 109. 109.' It was the code for 'urgent assistance required, I have been shot.' No more was heard from him. His body was later recovered from his police car near Ryan's house. He had been shot in the back. He left a wife and two teenage sons.

By 2 p.m. the killing seemed to have stopped. The caretaker at John O'Gaunt Secondary School reported seeing a man enter the school building at around 1.52 p.m.

Michael Ryan had attended the school ten years before. It had made little academic impression on him. He had been in the C-stream for pupils of below average achievement. The headmaster David Lee could not recall him. Lyn Rowlands, who had been classmates with Ryan at Hungerford County Primary School and John O'Gaunt Secondary School, said that he never seemed a very happy child. He was always on his own, always on the sidelines. Other children would try to include him in their games but he would be moody and sulky. Eventually people left him to his own devices. But she did not remember him ever being nasty in any way. He was not the kind of boy who got involved in fights. He was very introverted and 'a bit of a mystery'.

Another of his schoolmates, Andy Purfitt, told much the same story – that Ryan was a loner. He never mixed with anyone and did not play football with the other boys. But Purfitt remembered that Ryan was picked on by the other children a lot. As if to compensate for this bullying, Ryan developed an interest in guns. Even at the age of twelve, he used to fire a .177 airgun at the cows in the fields behind the house, a neighbour recalled. Later he went out at nights shooting rabbits. One night he met a man who was much bigger than him. The man got a bit stroppy, so Michael pulled a gun out of his pocket and pointed it at the man. The man turned on his heels and ran.

'That just goes to prove the power of the gun,' Ryan used to boast.

He collected ceremonial swords, military badges and medals, and military magazines. School friends say he preferred guns to girls. When he left school, one of the first things he did was get a small-arms licence.

During his last year at school, Ryan hardly ever turned up for classes. He left with no qualifications and drifted through a number of labouring jobs. He worked at a local nursery and Peter de Savary's theme park at Littlecote. Ryan lived for guns and seemed to disappear into a fantasy existence. He often boasted to neighbours of the latest gun he had purchased and the sound of him firing nearby was quite common.

Now, after his murderous rampage through his home town, Hungerford, Michael Ryan was back at school and – as ever – alone. Chief Constable of the Thames Valley Police Colin Smith claimed that prompt action by armed police officers prevented Ryan from killing more people than he did. But it was not until 5 p.m. that the police confirmed that Ryan was in the school. They surrounded it.

The local police admitted that they did know Ryan, but only in the way that most of the inhabitants of a quiet friendly market town knew each other. He had no criminal record. A local constable had visited Ryan's home in South View in June, just two months before the massacre, when Ryan had applied to have his firearms licence extended to cover the 7.62 mm automatic rifle. Ryan already had a firearms licence and, when he registered his new Kalashnikov, the police had checked on the house to make sure that the gun was stored securely. The officer they sent was Police Constable Trevor Wainwright, the son of Douglas Wainwright who was later to become one of Ryan's victims. Trevor Wainwright's sixty-three-year-old mother was also injured when Ryan opened fire on their car. They were on their way to visit their son.

Wainwright said of Ryan: 'From local knowledge I knew he was not a yob or mixed with yobs. He was not a villain and I knew he did not have a criminal record. He was a loner but you could not hold that against him. The checks were very thorough.'

The young police officer had checked that the cabinet where Ryan kept the weapons was secure, then approved the extension of his licence and forwarded it to the headquarters of Thames Valley Police.

While Michael Ryan was holed up in his old school, the children of his first victim, James and Hannah Godfrey, had been found. Apparently, despite witnessing the horrific murder of their mother, they had been tired and had had a little sleep. When they awoke, they had gone to look for help.

They met Mrs Myra Rose, herself a grandmother, who was taking a stroll in the forest. She saw the two children coming down a hill towards her. The little boy was wearing a Thomas the Tank Engine T-shirt and his sister had her hair tied back with a pink headband.

Two-year-old James grabbed Mrs Rose's hand and refused to let go. Hannah, who was four, acted as spokesman.

'A man in black shot my mummy,' she said. 'He has taken the car keys. James and me cannot drive a car and we are going home. We are tired.'

Seventy-five-year-old Mrs Rose lived in Bournemouth and was visiting friends in nearby Marlborough when she decided to go for a walk alone in the Savernake Forest. She found what the children were telling her hard to believe.

'It was such a horrific story for a little girl to tell,' Mrs Rose said, 'I did not know whether to believe it. The children were not crying.'

She was confused about what to do, but then she bumped into another family in the forest and told them what the children had said. One of them went to call the police and Mrs Rose sat down with the children to tell them stories.

'I don't think the youngsters really understood what had happened to their mother,' she told the newspapers later. 'James would not leave my side and I wanted to stay with the children.'

When the police came, they quickly found the bullet-riddled body of Susan Godfrey. Soon they were mounting a huge search of the 4,500-acre forest with teams of tracker dogs in case its glades contained the bodies of any further victims of Michael Ryan.

Talking to the police at John O'Gaunt School, Ryan appeared lucid and reasonable. He expressed no regret for killing Mrs Godfrey, nor any other of his victims. Only the murder of his mother seemed to trouble him.

Michael Ryan was thought of as a mummy's boy. Born when his mother Dorothy, a canteen lady, was thirty-three, he received the usual over-attention of an only child. He spent most of his time with his mother and was jealously guarded by his father. A friend of the family described Ryan as a 'spoilt little wimp'. It was said: 'He got everything he wanted from his mother.' She would buy him a new car every year.

Ryan's father, Alfred, was a council building inspector. Michael was devoted to him. When he died in 1985, two years before his son made the name Ryan notorious, Michael seemed to go to pieces. 'He was his life, you see,' said Michael's uncle Leslie Ryan. 'When he went, Michael seemed to go.'

He became violent and unpredictable, and he focused more of his attention on his collection of guns. The family were relieved when they heard that Michael was about to get married. The date was set, then the wedding was called off. 'He doesn't know whether he wants to be married or not,' his mother told relatives. 'First of all it's on and then it's off.'

Many doubt that there was a girl at all. He had certainly never been seen with one. Next-door neighbour Linda Lepetit said that Ryan and his mother had been close.

'It's unbelievable that he shot her,' she said. 'They got on so well. We could often hear them laughing and joking together. He had a natter to me and my children several times, but he was a bit of a loner.'

But others report a different story. Dennis Morley, a friend of the family, claims that Ryan used to beat his mother up.

'He used to hit his mother a lot,' said Morley. 'But he would not pick on a man.'

During his long conversations with the police from John O'Gaunt school, Ryan claimed to have been a member of the Parachute Regiment. He was not. But he was an avid reader of military and survivalist magazines, and he had fantasies about being a paratrooper.

Along with his usual attire of a brown jacket and slacks, he wore a pair of Dutch parachuting boots. He also wore sunglasses in all weather and was self-conscious about going prematurely bald. Even his only drinking buddy described Ryan as 'extremely quiet, he never gave anything away about himself'.

Apart from walking his Labrador, Ryan's only recreation had been shooting. He belonged to two shooting clubs where he spent an hour twice a week. Andrew White, partner in the Wiltshire Shooting Centre in Devizes, said: 'He'd come in for a chat, pick up his targets, go down to the range for an hour's shooting, come back, have another chat, and then go.'

But White did notice that, unlike some of the other 600 riflemen at the club, Ryan would not use targets that showed a human figure or a soldier's head. He would insist on the standard circular accuracy targets.

During his negotiations with the police, he confessed to the murders he had committed. Although he could shoot other people, he could not kill himself, he mused. But at about 6.30 p.m. a muffled shot was heard from inside the school. Ryan did not answer any more.

The armed police still held back though. There were fears that Ryan had been holding hostages and they could not be sure what had happened inside the school. It was only at 8.10 p.m. that armed officers finally burst into the classroom to find Ryan shot with his own gun – and the Hungerford massacre was over.

Britain was so shocked by Michael Ryan's murderous outburst that the BBC quickly dropped several films they had scheduled which depicted undue violence or gun play. The first was an American movie called *Black Christmas* which was due to go out on BBC1 at

11.50 on the night of the massacre. It depicted a psychopath killing college girls and was replaced with the Dick Emery comedy *Ooh... You Are Awful!*

The BBC's own film *Body Contact*, described as a 'stylish pastiche with echoes of Bonnie and Clyde', was also dropped. The ITV company Anglia dropped the western *Nevada Smith* and switched an episode of *The Professionals* for a less violent one.

The day after the Hungerford massacre a fund was set up to provide support to the injured and the families of the dead.

Local millionaire Peter de Savary gave £10,000. He had employed Ryan as a labourer when he was building his medieval theme park at nearby Littlecote House and about eighty per cent of the people who worked at his theme park lived in Hungerford. Another anonymous donor gave £10,000 and Newbury District Council gave £5,000. Local radio stations GWR Radio and Radio 210 launched appeals. Soon smaller donations poured in and within a couple of days, the fund topped £50,000. Ryan's victims would also be eligible for compensation from the Criminal Injuries Compensation board. Murder victims' spouses and children under eighteen would also be eligible for a bereavement award of £3,500 and a 'dependency' award.

Hardly a single person among Hungerford's 5,000 population was unaffected. In a community of that size everyone knew someone who had been killed. Quickly the Hungerford Family Unit was set up, giving ninety-minute grief therapy sessions. It was staffed by social workers who had counselled victims' families from the Zeebrugge ferry disaster and the Bradford tragedy where football fans had been burnt to death in a football stand.

The local church also played a role, offering prayers for the victims and flying its flag at half-mast. They also offered prayers for the soul of Michael Ryan. However, the church soon found itself in an awkward position. While Michael Ryan's mother Dorothy had asked to be buried at Coine in Wiltshire, close to the village of Cherhill where she was born, Ryan himself was to be buried in Hungerford alongside his victims. Some residents of Hungerford muttered darkly that, if he was buried there, his body would be dug up and thrown out.

Prime Minister Margaret Thatcher was on the streets of Hungerford two days after Michael Ryan. She visited the area where fourteen people had been gunned down and the four houses that had been gutted when Ryan set his mother's house on fire. At the local vicarage she met some of the relatives of Ryan's victims and was soon close to tears. After visiting the wounded in the Princess Margaret Hospital in Swindon, Mrs Thatcher described the incident as 'not an accident in which we get a terrible tragedy, it is a crime, an evil crime'.

She pledged to tighten up the gun laws so that such a thing could never happen again. But it did. In April 1989, twenty-two-year-old Robert Sartin committed a 'copycat shooting' similar to Ryan's at Monkseaton, near Newcastle upon Tyne, killing one and injuring fourteen.

Australia already had some experience of spree killing in 1963. On a summer Saturday night in a comfortable Perth suburb, a gunman started picking off people, seemingly at random. Nicholas August, a poultry dealer and a married man, was out with Ocean beach barmaid Rowena Reeves. They were sharing a drink in the car around 2 a.m. on 27 January 1963 when Rowena saw a man. Thinking he was a peeping Tom, August told him to 'bugger off'. The silent figure did not move, so August threw the empty bottle at him.

'Look out,' screamed Rowena to her companion. 'He's got a gun.'

The man raised a rifle and took careful aim at August's head. At the last moment, Rowena pushed August's head down and the bullet nicked his neck. It bled profusely. Rowena yelled at him to start the car and run the gunman down. August sped off, with bullets singing past them. By the time he reached the hospital, Rowena was unconscious. The bullet emerging from his neck had lodged in Rowena's forearm. Both August and Rowena survived the incident.

Just over an hour later and a couple of miles away, fifty-four-year-old George Walmsley answered the door bell. He was shot immediately as he opened the front door. The bullet hit him in the forehead and he was dead by the time his wife and daughter, woken by the shot, got downstairs.

Around the corner at Mrs Allen's boarding house, nineteen-year-old agricultural student from the University of Western Australia John Sturkey was sleeping on the veranda. At around 4 a.m. fellow student Scott McWilliam was awoken by Mrs Allen's niece Pauline. 'There's something wrong with John,' she said. McWilliam went out on to the veranda. A strange noise was coming from Sturkey's throat. McWilliam raised Sturkey's head. There was a bullet hole between his eyes.

Next morning Brian Weir, who lived nearby in Broome Street, did not show up for training at the Surf Lifesaving Club. One of the crew went round to get him out of bed. Brian was found with a bullet wound in his forehead and serious brain damage. He died from his wounds three years later.

The police had little to go on and the press offered a £1,000 reward for the capture of the 'Maniac Slayer'. Local homeowners slept with loaded guns next to their beds. Nothing happened for three weeks. Then the killer struck again.

Joy Noble was up early making breakfast one Saturday morning when she glanced out of the kitchen window of her West Perth home. Outside she saw the naked body of a young woman spread-eagled on the back lawn. At first she thought it was her daughter and she ran through the house shouting: 'Carline.' In fact, it was the body of Constance Lucy Madrill, a twenty-four-year-old social worker who lived in nearby Thomas Street. She had been raped, strangled and dumped on the Nobles' lawn. The attack had taken place in the girl's own apartment, while her flatmate, Jennifer Hurse, slept. No one could explain why the attacker had dragged her all the way to the Nobles' lawn, then abandoned her. An Aborigine had probably done it, the police concluded – even though there were no records of Aborigines in Western Australia attacking white girls. And it certainly had nothing to do with the shootings three weeks before.

Six months passed uneventfully. Then on the thundery night of 10 August, Shirley McLeod, an eighteen-year-old science student at the University of Western Australia, was baby-sitting Carl and Wendy Dowds' eight-month-old son, Mitchell. When the Dowdses returned from their party they found Shirley slumped on the sofa with a peaceful look on her face like she had just fallen asleep. She had been shot by a .22 rifle and was quite dead. Baby Mitchell was unharmed. There could be no doubt that this killing was linked with the murders in January.

Perth experienced mass panic. *The West Australian* advised people to lock their doors at night – unheard of in Perth before that time. Baby-sitters were warned not to sit near windows, and there were proposals to close the old alleyways that ran down the back of people's houses. The police began to fingerprint every male over twelve in the city, at a rate of 8,000 a week.

Then on Saturday 17 August an elderly couple were out picking flowers in Mount Pleasant when they spotted a rifle hidden in some bushes. It was a Winchester .22. The police believed that it had not been discarded but hidden there so it could be used again. They staked out the area for two weeks before a truck driver named Eric Edgar Cooke turned up, looking for the gun.

Cooke had been born in Perth in 1931 with a hare lip and a cleft palate. Early operations improved his condition, but his speech remained blurred and indistinct and his appearance was mocked by others. From an early age he suffered severe headaches and blackouts. These were aggravated by a fall from a bicycle and a dive into shallow water at fourteen. Doctors suspected brain damage, but X-rays and an exploratory operation revealed nothing.

At home, his father beat him regularly. At sixteen he spent three weeks in hospital after trying to protect his mother from one of his father's onslaughts. He told the doctors he had been fighting with other boys.

Expelled from several schools, Cooke quit completely at the age of fourteen. He took a series of manual jobs, none of which lasted long, before being called up for National Service. In the army, he was taught how to handle a rifle.

In November 1953 he married an eighteen-year-old immigrant from England called Sally. The couple had seven children – four boys and three girls. Their first child was born mentally handicapped and their eldest daughter, one of twins, was born without a right arm. Nevertheless it was a happy household. Cooke was a faithful husband and a loving father. Other children from all over the neighbourhood came to play in the Cookes' house.

However, behind it all was what Sally Cooke described as her husband's 'restlessness'. She could not keep him at home. He constantly went out on sprees of petty thieving. He had burgled some 250 houses and spent three short terms in prison before the police picked him up as a murder suspect.

At the police station Cooke claimed to have been home on the night Shirley McLeod was killed. His wife said he was not. Then Cooke confessed.

On the way home from bowling that day, he had started looking for somewhere to burgle. He found a house in Pearse Street with its back door open and went in. There was a couple sitting in the lounge, so Cooke crept through into the bedroom to look for money. Instead he found a Winchester .22. He took it, and some cartridges, thinking he could probably sell it later.

He said he remembered parking his car again on the way home, then – later – finding the rifle in his hand with a spent cartridge in the breach. It was only the next day, when he saw a report about the baby-sitter's murder on the television, that he realised what he had done.

The next day he was taken to the scene of Lucy Madrill's murder and confessed to that killing as well. He said he had been robbing the girl's flat when he had knocked over a framed photograph. Lucy had woken up and he had hit her. She tried to scream but he throttled her. He dragged her through into the next bedroom, strangled her with a lamp flex, then raped her. He had intended to hide the body.

He dragged it outside and left it on the Nobles' lawn while he looked for a car to steal. But he could not find one, stole a bicycle instead and rode home.

Later he confessed to the spree on 26 January. He had shot five people that night because he 'wanted to hurt somebody', he said. Out on his usual Saturday night prowl, he had stolen a Lithgow single-shot .22 and a tan-coloured Holden sedan.

He had been driving aimlessly when he saw a man and a woman in a parked car. The interior light went out, so Cooke thought he would stop and spy on the couple. He took the rifle with him. And when they spotted him and threw a bottle at him, he shot back.

In Broome Street he stopped again, intent on doing a bit more burglary. He clambered over some railings and climbed up on to a balcony. Inside some French windows a man lay sleeping. The bed barred Cooke's way into the room, so he shot from the hip at the sleeping body. The result was Brian Weir's irreversible brain damage.

Prowling around the block, Cooke saw a man sleeping on the veranda. Another shot from the hip ended John Sturkey's young life. The next killing was even more deliberate. He leant the rifle against the garage of a house he had picked randomly in Louise Street and went to ring the front door bell. Then he ran back to the gun and aimed at the doorway. When a man answered the door, Cooke shot him. Then he threw the rifle off the Narrows Bridge into the Swan River and returned the Holden to the house where he had stolen it. In the morning the owner noticed that the bulb of the interior light had been removed, but the matter was too petty to report to the police.

Only the death of John Sturkey upset Cooke. 'He was so young,' he told the police. 'He never had a chance. I will never meet him because he is up there and I'll be down there. I'm just a cold-blooded killer.'

With that last sentence, Cooke ruled out the possibility of being found not guilty by reason of insanity.

Cooke also confessed to the murder of thirty-three-year-old divorcee Patricia Vinico Berkman in 1959. Her lover, local radio personality Fotis Hountas, found her body in bed in her flat in South

Perth. She had been stabbed repeatedly in the head and chest. She left a nine-year-old son. And Cooke said that he had killed wealthy society beauty Jillian Brewer later that year. Aged twenty-two, she had been viciously murdered in her own flat. The killer had used a hatchet and a pair of scissors. There were no fingerprints. The doors were locked from the inside and there was no sign of any windows being forced. The police were mystified.

Four months later, twenty-year-old deaf-mute Darryl Beamish, arrested for molesting four little girls, confessed to the Brewer murder through a sign language interpreter. At his trial, Beamish claimed the confession had been forced out of him. The prosecutor produced no other evidence. Nevertheless, Beamish was found guilty and sentenced to death.

Cooke's confession was extraordinarily detailed. His description of the flat on the night of the murder fitted exactly with the photographs taken by the scene-of-crime photographer. He even explained the locked doors – he had stolen the key to the flat on a previous raid.

On 17 March 1964, Beamish appeared before the appeal court with Cooke's statement. However, the three appeal court judges – one was the original trial judge, the other two had dismissed Beamish's appeals on two previous occasions – did not believe Cooke's confession. But they did commute Beamish's sentence from death to life imprisonment. He was exonerated in 2005. Cooke was hanged in Fremantle Prison on 26 October 1964.

Cooke's January night rampage is peculiar, but he otherwise exhibited the profile of a serial, rather than a spree, killer. But in 1987 a lone gunman loosed off a hail of bullets in a more typical, random, mindless spree killing.

At 9.30 p.m. on Sunday, 9 August 1987, young Alan Jury was driving along Hoddle Street near the suburb of Clifton Hill, Melbourne, when he heard a noise like a firecracker. His windscreen shattered. Quickly realising that someone was shooting at him, he stamped down on the accelerator and roared away from the danger. At the next service station he reported that a gunman was firing at passing cars.

In the car behind him, Rita Vitcos also heard a bang and saw sparks fly off the surface of the road. She too accelerated away. Later, when she got out of the car, she found two bullet-holes in the driver's door and realised how lucky she had been.

Twenty-three-year-old Vesna Markonsky's windscreen exploded as she drove down Hoddle Street. She jammed on the brakes. When the car came to a halt she discovered that a bullet had hit her in the left arm. She got out and a second bullet hit her, then a third. Her boyfriend Zoran, who was following her, stopped too. So did a young doctor. More bullets filled the air as the two men ran towards the wounded girl. The doctor collapsed, hit.

Another driver pulled up behind Zoran's car. A bullet hit him in the right temple. He died instantly. A girl student stopped to help. She too was gunned down. When Zoran reached Vesna, he cradled her in his arms. She spoke a few words then lost consciousness.

Constable Belinda Bourchier arrived in a police car shortly afterwards. Zoran ran to her and tried to pull her revolver out of its holster. Covered in blood and in a state of shock, he wanted to kill the bastard who had just murdered his girlfriend, he yelled. More shots screamed past them. 'Let's get out of here,' said Constable Bourchier, and they ran for cover behind some trees at the edge of the road.

The gunman continued firing with deadly accuracy. More windscreens shattered and cars careered across the road. A motorcyclist swerved and crashed. He lay in the road trapped under his bike and two more bullets slammed into his body.

After ten minutes of shooting the police turned up in force. The shots were coming from the 'nature strip', a grass verge alongside Clifton Hill railway station. The police set up road-blocks and closed off the area.

A police helicopter was called in. It flew in low over the nature strip. Its search light swept the ground. But the gunman had vanished.

A few minutes later a police car, turning into Hoddle Street from the north, came under fire. A policeman on a road-block there was also winged by a bullet. Another shot struck the helicopter flying overhead, but bounced off its armoured underside.

Seeing the gunman near the track, a signalman managed to stop an oncoming train. He ran up the line, expecting to be shot in the back. But the gunman now seemed to be firing into the ground. The signalman reached the train and told the driver to reverse. When he looked back, the gunman had disappeared.

In a street close by, two constables in a police car spotted a man with a rifle running along the road. They pursued him. The gunman turned in to a lane and they stopped the car, closing off the end. Out of the darkness of the lane came a hail of bullets. One shot hit Constable John Delahunty in the head. He flung himself to the ground and managed to crawl towards the gunman. His partner, Constable Lockman, crawled after him. They got within a few yards of the gunman when the wounded Delahunty saw his head rise above some bushes. Delahunty leapt to his feet and fired his revolver.

The gunman ducked back down behind the bushes. A moment later a voice called out 'Don't shoot me, don't shoot me.'

'Put your gun down and come out with your arms up,' Delahunty shouted back.

A dark silhouette rose from behind the bushes. 'Don't shoot me,' said the gunman again as he walked forward with his arms high above his head. He had a small moustache, a military haircut and identified himself as nineteen-year-old Julian Knight.

Knight was an illegitimate child who had been adopted when he was a baby. His adoptive father was a career army officer, whom he greatly admired, and it was an emotional shock when his parents divorced when he was twelve.

Although he was generally regarded as bright, his schoolwork soon began to deteriorate. His reports said he was lazy, too easily distracted and too complacent about his abilities. He always had difficulty accepting authority. Unlike other spree killers, Knight was not shy. He had girlfriends and something of a reputation as the 'class clown' at Fitzroy High School. But from an early age he was preoccupied with Charles Whitman and other lone snipers. Eventually he was expelled from school for his violent outbursts. Then he was accepted by the Royal Military College at Duntroon. He was almost nineteen when he went to their in January 1987. An army assessor described him as immature, over-confident and stubborn. He could not knuckle down to army discipline. In May he was charged with eight offences, including four counts of being absent without leave. Then, on 31 May, after a weekend confined to barracks, he slipped out and got drunk in a nightclub near Duntroon. A sergeant caught him and ordered him out. Knight stabbed him twice in the face with a penknife. He was charged with assault and discharged from Duntroon in July 1987, after only seven months.

Back at the police station, Knight seemed calm and subdued. He described how he had started the evening by drinking twelve glasses of beer in a local pub to alleviate a terrible feeling of depression. Since his discharge, his whole life had been turned upside down. His mother had changed his bedroom into a living room, so he was forced to camp in his own home. It was just a few yards from Hoddle Street, on the other side of the railway tracks. His girlfriend had broken up with him. He owed the bank thousands of dollars. A car he had hoped to sell had broken down that afternoon, and something had snapped.

He had decided it was time to die – but to commit suicide offended his sense of military honour. Since his schooldays, he had fantasised about wars, particularly heroic 'last stands'. He decided to go down fighting.

He left home that evening at 9.25 p.m., carrying a shotgun and two rifles. He crossed the railway line to the nature strip. He knelt down, took careful aim and started to shoot at the cars coming down Hoddle Street.

He kept on shooting until he had used up all his ammunition. He claimed to have hoped that a 'battle' might develop, but no one shot at him until Constable Delahunty fired his revolver. However, by then Knight had no ammunition let. He groped in his pocket for the last bullet he said he had saved for himself. It had gone. So he surrendered, like a soldier who was surrounded and had run out of ammunition.

In the space of forty-five minutes Knight had fired at more than fifty cars, hitting twenty-six people. Seven of his victims were dead, or dying in the nearest hospital. Two days later, when what he had done had sunk in, Julian Knight had a nervous breakdown and had to be confined to a padded cell. In November 1988 he was sentenced to life imprisonment. Julian Knight will not be eligible for parole until the year 2013.

At around 1 p.m. on Saturday 17 August 1991, thirty-three-year-old Wade Frankum went to the Strathfield Plaza, a shopping mall in an upper-middle-class suburb west of Sydney, Australia. The two-storey complex of shops, boutiques and small restaurants was filled with customers that afternoon. Frankum took a seat in a cafe called The Coffee Pot where he drank a number of cups of coffee and bided his time.

At approximately 3.30 p.m., apparently without provocation, Frankum pulled a machete from the army surplus duffel bag he had with him and repeatedly slashed one of two teenage girls who were sitting behind him, killing the fifteen-year-old.

Leaving the machete stuck in her body, he pulled an AK-47 out of his duffel bag and loosed off shots around the cafe, killing four more people. As the cafe owner George Mavis walked out of the kitchen, Frankum shot him in the chest. He then moved out into the main area of the mall, where he killed again. Witnesses said the gunman appeared to be calm while screaming shopkeepers and shoppers ducked for cover or fled.

'I grabbed a lady's baby and we jumped over the railings,' said thirty-eight-year-old Carolyn Healey, who was in a nearby grocery store when the rampage began. 'We were running, but we could still hear the shooting as if he was coming after us.'

Frankum made his way to the rooftop car park. Donning a stocking mask, he continued firing indiscriminately from the roof, wounding passers-by below. One person was hit at a railway station about a hundred yards away. Mall workers found sixty spent shells.

Frankum was still firing when the police arrived at the mall. Then he tried to make his escape. He held up a car owner at gunpoint and demanded that she take him to Enfield, a nearby suburb. Before the woman could start her car, police arrived. As sirens wailed below, Frankum apologised, got out of the car, knelt on the ground and shot himself in the head. In just ten minutes, he had killed seven people and injured six, none of them personally known to him.

'Blood was everywhere,' said Constable George Kohahila. 'People were running frantically around. It was total chaos.'

Frankum himself was dead, so he could offer no explanation. He had no criminal record.

'There doesn't appear to be any rhyme or reason for it,' said Doug Kelly, chief superintendent of the Blacktown District Police. 'It was a horrendous killing.'

There were few clues in his background. Frankum's parents were reportedly very strict. They sent him to the exclusive Wesleyan single-sex private school Newington College, where he was bullied for being overweight. He would often skip lessons and sit in the library, reading books, or just not bother to show up for school at all. He was expelled at sixteen for poor attendance, completing his education at Homebush Boys High School, a local comprehensive. Eventually he got a job at a clothing store and was, by most accounts, a good worker, although not particularly sociable.

Franklin lived alone. In his apartment, the police found a large collection of violent videos and literature. Among his books was a copy of the controversial novel *American Psycho* by Bret Easton Ellis. Some have blamed the misogynist violence in the book for his actions – five of the seven people he killed were women. However, Frankum also owned a copy of Dostoevsky's *Crime and Punishment* and Germaine Greer's *The Female Eunuch*.

When he purchased his rifle, he was quoted as saying that he was going to use the firearm to protect himself and, more chillingly, 'wipe people out'.

Psychiatrist Dr Rod Milton postulated that four factors motivated Frankum's mass murder: 'Anger, because he was a failure, chronically unassertive and could not tolerate intimacy; guilt, over his mother's suicide; conflict, over his grandmother's estate and certain trivial disputes with the neighbours, and finally; impecuniosity, his money had run out, depriving him of the outlet for his loneliness and sexual needs with prostitutes.'

Chapter 13

Going Postal

Patrick Henry Sherrill was a postman. He was known as 'Fat Pat', 'Crazy Pat' – but never, ever, 'Postman Pat'. He just wasn't that nice, or that efficient. After sixteen months as a part-time postman in Edmond, Oklahoma, Sherrill was still receiving complaints over slow performance and misdirected mail.

The summer sun was just over the horizon on 20 August 1986 when Sherrill reported for work as usual. He was wearing his blue US Postal Service uniform, with his mailbag slung over his shoulder. But instead of carrying letters, it contained instruments of death: three pistols and several boxes of ammunition. One survivor described what followed this way: 'Imagine your worst nightmare; then scream as loud as you can.'

Without a word, Sherrill gunned down Richard Esser, one of the supervisors who had criticised his work record, and fellow postman Michael Rockne at point-blank range. The gunman then chased a group of fleeing employees through a side exit, shooting one man who died later in the parking lot.

Sherrill pursued his quarry through the labyrinthine corridors of the sorting office. He bolted several doors to prevent their escape, then he sought out co-workers who were hiding under tables and in cubicles. Three were shot at one work station, five at another.

Debbie Smith was sorting letters when the shooting started. 'I froze, I couldn't run,' she said. 'He came to shoot clerks in the box section next to mine.'

She hid. And Sherrill passed her by and opened fire in the next section. As she ran for the door, she said she could hear all the clerks screaming as they were shot. Two employees escaped by hiding in broom cupboards. Another survivor locked herself in a vault where the stamps were kept.

The police arrived just minutes after the shooting had started. For forty-five minutes they tried to communicate with Sherrill by telephone and bullhorn. There was no reply. A SWAT team went in. They found Sherrill's body among the carnage. After killing fourteen people and wounding another six, he had put a bullet into his own head.

Sherrill's motive was thought to have been revenge. The day before, he had been reprimanded by supervisor Bill Bland with Esser present. Bland had threatened to fire him. But, on the morning of the massacre, Bland had overslept. Esser was both Sherrill's first victim and final companion. Their bodies were found less than eighteen inches apart.

Forty-four-year-old Sherrill had lived on the same street in Oklahoma City for twenty years. He was notorious in the area for mowing his lawn at midnight, tying up dogs with baling wire or cycling alone on a bicycle made for two. He could often be seen staring blankly out of his window wearing combat fatigues. He was also an avid reader of *Soldier of Fortune* and *Soviet Life* magazines. An ex-Marine sharpshooter, he often talked about his time in Vietnam. He in fact never got further than Camp Lejeune, North Carolina, before he was discharged in 1966.

After his mother, who shared the house, died, most of Sherrill's social contact was via his ham radio set. He remained a reservist though, and in 1984 he joined the Oklahoma National Guard's marksmanship team. This allowed him to sign out of the armoury his two deadly accurate .45s, as well as a supply of 'woodcutters' – flat-nosed bullets that mushroom out inside their victims. These were used against his co-workers.

One of Sherrill's neighbours pointed out that whoever Crazy Pat was, he was no Rambo, but a shy, gentle little man who said 'please' and 'thank you'. However, in his room, the police found ten sets of camouflage fatigues, limbless human silhouettes and dozens of bull's-eye targets nailed to boxes and walls.

Melbourne had scarcely recovered from the shock of the Hoddle Street rampage when four months later another mad gunman claimed a further eight victims.

On 8 December 1987, twenty-two-year-old Frank Vitkovic went to the post office, ostensibly to kill an old school friend against whom he harboured a grudge. He was suffering from depression and severe headaches. But the gun misfired and his friend escaped. Vitkovic then began to shoot at random.

The night before, twenty-year-old Judy Morris photographed the last sunset of her life from the roof of her father's funeral parlour.

'It's beautiful,' said Judy, a Telecom Credit Union teller, as she pointed her camera at the horizon. 'I want it on film so I can always remember.'

She was speaking to her fiancé, nineteen-year-old Jason Miles, an apprentice chef she had met just a year before. According to Judy's father, it was Jason who had coaxed his shy daughter out of her shell.

Shortly before sunset that night Judy told her fiancé that something was worrying her. Her Credit Union workmates on the fifth floor of the Australia Post building, at 191 Queen Street, had met about security that morning. The tellers had complained that the bullet-proof screens they had asked for a year before had still not been installed.

'She was horrified at not having any security at work,' Jason said. 'Not for herself, but for everyone else.'

As Jason moved to leave that night, Judy said: 'Don't go.' They lay in each other's arms for a long time. It was as if she knew her time was up, Jason said.

Next morning Judy Morris waved to her mother, Nola, as she walked to the train station and called out that she would see her that night. Six-and-a-half hours later Frank Vitkovic caught another train to Queen Street and entered the blue-tiled foyer of the Australia Post building.

As Judy and Jason had the previous evening contemplated the happy course of their own lives it is likely that Vitkovic had already decided the course of his. Vitkovic came from the West Preston area of North Melbourne, home to many European immigrants of the late 1950s and 1960s. Yugoslav house painter Drago Vitkovic and his wife lived in a small white-painted weatherboard house on May Street, the very picture of respectability. The front lawn had been covered with concrete to give more off-street space for Mr Vitkovic's brown Valiant station wagon and the family's two other small vehicles.

In these affluent surroundings, their son Frank grew into a good-looking, big-framed youth who was over six foot tall. At high school he was placed in the top five per cent of students. Vitkovic also had a passion for playing tennis, becoming something of a legend on the twin clay courts of St Raphael's tennis club. A strong backhand drive floored many opponents and scared others. Margaret O'Leary, a former club secretary, recalled that Vitkovic sometimes aimed his returns at an opponent's body. It was enough to help him win the club championship in 1983.

The young sons of immigrant families in the club quickly identified with Vitkovic. They became known in the clubhouse as 'the ethnics'. Mrs O'Cleary recalled that some of the young men idolised Vitkovic and his confidence blossomed.

'The topic of conversation was always Frank Vitkovic,' she said. 'He found it very hard to lose.'

Everyone agreed that Vitkovic was destined for bigger things. Nobody was surprised when, in 1984, he won a place at Melbourne University's Law School. To start with everything went fine. Vitkovic told tennis-club friends he was 'breezing through'. But in early 1986 things began to go wrong. Midway through his last year, Vitkovic abandoned his studies and helped his father paint houses.

Those who knew him still detected no hint that Vitkovic was having problems. His family were good people. Nobody ever expected anything bad to happen to Frank.

Vitkovic returned to Law School at the beginning of 1987, but it was a brief and unhappy experience. He left his studies again soon after because of 'unsatisfactory progress'. He also sought help from Melbourne University's counselling service during this period. He did not work after leaving university.

Vitkovic kept a file of Melbourne newspaper clippings of Julian Knight's massacre on Hoddle Street. Vitkovic underlined sections of the clippings in red. He also kept *Rambo* videos in his bedroom.

In mid-September he obtained a gun permit from the Central Firearms Registry in Melbourne after failing just one of fourteen questions. It was: 'Should firearms be unloaded before you enter a house or building?' He had answered: 'No'.

In mid-September, a salesman from Precision Guns and Ammo in Victoria Street, West Melbourne, sold Vitkovic an M1 semi-automatic rifle for £275, on a two-week lay-by. Vitkovic sawed the stock and barrel off the 75 cm weapon to make it easy to conceal.

The night before he went into the Australia Post building, he wrote in his diary: 'The anger in my head has got too much for me. I've got to get rid of my violent impulses. The time has come to die. There is no other way out.'

Judy Morris returned to her office from her 1 p.m. lunch-break on top of the world. Not only had she had the spectacular picture of the sunset developed, but she had bought a new outfit – white slacks with braces and a matching pink blouse. She showed them to her closest friend, a young Credit Union supervisor.

Judy also passed the pictures of the sunset around to her Credit Union colleagues. Twenty-two-year-old Con Margellis, one of the regular staff, may have seen them.

Margellis is the only apparent link between Vitkovic and the 1,000 people working that day in the Queen Street offices. He lived just a few streets from the Vitkovics in West Preston. He and Vitkovic had been at school together and had been friends for a number of years.

At 4.10 p.m. that Tuesday Vitkovic emerged from the lift and greeted Mr Margellis inside the fifth-floor Credit Union office with the word 'G'day'.

Vitkovic brought out the carbine from under his green top. He began firing shots in the direction of his friend. Police ruled out any homosexual relationship between them. Nor was there any dispute over a woman. Nevertheless Vitkovic was now shooting with murderous intent at his former classmate.

The Telecom Credit Union staff scattered in fear. Someone pressed the alarm button. Judy and her best friend ran towards the glass exit doors. A shot rang out. Both women fell. Vitkovic finished shooting and disappeared out of the exit to the lift wells. Margellis was safe. He had hidden in the women's toilets. But Judy Morris was dead.

The security doors shut tight behind Vitkovic, trapping him outside. He kicked the doors, trying to get back in. He went to the elevators and waited until one of the pink arrows flashed up. Then he rode to the twelfth floor.

The Philatelic Bureau was quiet when Vitkovic burst in. In the customer sales section he let rip with automatic rifle-fire. The bureau's twenty-nine-year-old supervisor Warren Spencer was killed while trying to take cover behind the office photocopier. His wife, Susan, mother of their two children, who also worked at the bureau, watched in horror as her husband died. Twenty-year-old Julie McBean and eighteen-year-old Nancy Avignone were shot dead at their desks.

Below, Melbourne became aware of the shootings. As crowds began to stare from the street, Vitkovic took a sniper's perch from a broken twelfth-floor window. He fired several bullets at the first motorcycle police officers who arrived at 4.15 p.m.

Vitkovic ran down the stairs to the eleventh floor, which housed the Australian Post accounts department. In the stairwell Vitkovic fired one volley that blew a fist-sized hole in the office window to his right. Turning left he confronted Michael McGuire in the data-processing room, where McGuire trained staff and fixed machines. Vitkovic fired at point-blank range into the young father of three.

One bullet passed through the partition McGuire sheltered against and punched a crater in the corridor wall. McGuire had been hoping to be home early that night. His youngest daughter was celebrating her fifth birthday.

The staff in the accounts department now found their escape path blocked by the killer. The shots rang out as Vitkovic entered the room, his fire concentrated to the far corners of desks. Thirty-two-year-old Rodney Brown was shot beside the desk he had worked at for seven years. He died in the arms of an ambulanceman. Thirty-eight-year-old Marianne Van Ewyk and Catherine Dowling, twenty-eight, died as they cowered under their desks.

Van Ewyk, who had emigrated from Holland as a child, had worked with at Australia Post since she was a teenager. Next to her desk was a school-term calendar to keep track of holidays she could spend with her only son. At 4.30 p.m. Marianne's husband, Bernie Sharp, rang her to warn her of a rail strike. At the same time Frank Vitkovic was downstairs, waiting for the elevator.

The accounts department assistant manager Tony Gloria then put an end to the massacre. A quiet man who was never known to lose his temper, he tackled the gunman.

A head shorter than Vitkovic, he grabbed the killer around the waist. Another of the office workers, who had been shot in the shoulder, helped to drag Vitkovic down. A third man grabbed the rifle and hid it in the fridge.

Vitkovic, who was now bent on taking his own life, struggled to make his way through to the broken window. Gloria fought to save him. Office workers in nearby buildings saw the struggle and the shower of glass that preceded the killer as he fell to the pavement sixty metres below, where he died.

Chapter 14

The Body Count Climbs

In the 1980s, the whole of Europe was experiencing a spate of spree killings. In April 1983, twenty-seven-year-old Sevdet Yilmaz shot and killed six people and wounded another five in Delft, South Holland. In June that year, thirty-four-year-old Karel Charva shot dead five people and wounded fourteen others in Eppstein, near Frankfurt. In November, thirty-four-year-old Miloud Amrani shot and killed five people, wounding three others, in Lyon. In January 1984, Russian teenager Anatoly Markov went on a drunken spree with his father's rifle. He shot at anything he could see – birds, squirrels, the tops of trees. When a helicopter flew over he shot at that too, fatally wounding the flight mechanic. Markov was jailed and his father was punished for buying the rifle illegally and failing to keep it in a secure place. In June 1985, Guy Martell rampaged through a series of towns in Brittany, killing seven and wounding five. In 1987, a Belgian gunman shot and killed seven.

Also in 1987, twenty-six-year-old Josef Schwab slaughtered five people in the remote 'Top End' region of New South Wales, Australia, and an unknown intruder killed four teenage girls who were watching TV in a plush Sydney suburb. Joseph Wesbecker, forty-seven, blamed the drug Prozac for the spree in which he killed eight fellow workers at a printing plant and wounded nineteen others.

In 1988, an army corporal shot and killed four people, wounding twelve others, and a military policeman in Italy killed four. Then in July 1989, thirty-one-year-old Christian Dornier committed the worst spree killing on mainland Europe – killing fourteen and wounding nine others. After a few pastis, he shot his sister, mother, father and a guest at the lunch table. Then he got in his car and drove around the small French village of Luxiol, shooting anyone he could find – including children, one as young as five, and a brother and sister in their eighties. He shot the first gendarme who came to their rescue. The rampage ended when he drove into an ambush set up by gendarmes on the road to the next village. No one knew what set off the rampage, but his brother said that Christian had never been the same since his military service eight years before.

In 1990 three Red Army soldiers went on a shooting spree, killing eight of their comrades, including a lieutenant colonel, at a military depot in the Ukraine. After spraying the depot with machine-gun fire, they escaped on a truck but were captured when it broke down.

That same year, a gunman with a high-powered rifle went on a shooting spree in New Zealand, killing eight people including a toddler and a policeman. The bodies were strewn on the street of Aramoana, a seaside village with a population of only about fifty. The community there will never fully recover.

Spree killing continued to spread throughout America as former history teacher Carl Brown, fifty-one, rode his bike into a welding shop in Miami after buying two shotguns, an automatic rifle and some ammunition from a gun shop. He killed eight and wounded three, before himself being killed by a passing motorist. After the massacre, Miami thought it might be wise to introduce a 'cooling off' period, rather than let people buy guns over the counter with no delay.

Another casual spree killing was committed by Wayne Lee Crossley. A thirty-one-year-old unemployed carpenter from Hot Springs, Arkansas, Crossley would boast during his regular drinking binges: 'I'm going to die in a gun battle with the police.' He was nearly right.

Crossley was a Rambo-style survivalist who rambled on about 'living wild with nature'. He had a skull tattooed on his arms, loved guns and camouflage clothing, allegedly pistol-whipped his elderly parents, and twice pulled guns on bar-owners who had tried to eject him for rowdiness.

Crossley's last rampage began when a police officer stopped his car near the Hot Springs city hall. Crossley shot him three times with a .45 calibre pistol, wounding him seriously. The officer shot back with his .357 Magnum, hitting Crossley and a passenger in his car. But Crossley, bleeding profusely, drove the car to the Grand Central Motor Lodge. He had been thrown out of the motel a few weeks earlier. Now he had vengeance on his mind. He wounded a bartender with his pistol, then, grabbing a shotgun from his car, he fatally wounded Helen Frazee, the bar's owner. He went on to kill two customers and a truck driver who had stopped to make a phone call. When the police closed in, they found Crossley's body in the lobby. He had shot himself in the head.

In March 1993, an Adelaide schoolboy wounded two schoolmates and three passers-by with a semi-automatic rifle. He surrendered to the police after barricading himself in his school.

You can never tell who might go berserk. Sixty-one-year-old retired librarian William Cruse snapped one day, killing six – including two policemen – and attempting to kill another twenty-four in a shopping centre in Palm Bay, Florida. The jury recommended death. Now in his eighties, he is still alive in prison.

Michael Hayes of Winston-Salem, North Carolina shot nine people, killing four of them, because he wanted to be famous. And California winery worker Ramon Salcido killed seven people with knives and bullets, and slashed the throats of his three little daughters. One, two-year-old Carmina, survived. She identified her father as the killer.

And the killing continues. At 2.19 p.m. on Tuesday 2 September 2008, a 911 call was received from Dennise Zamora, a resident of the small town of Alger in North Skagit County, Washington state. Deputy Anne Jackson was sent to investigate. At 2.50 she arrived the 19300 block of Bridle Place in the Alger. When she did not check in with her dispatchers, other deputies were sent. They found Jackson dead. There was also the body of a dead man.

At 4.10 p.m. the police received a call saying that the deputies were 'under fire' in the 19300 block. Next a motorcyclist was shot in the arm at a Shell gas station. Officers identified the perpetrator and started a sixteen-mile car chase south down Interstate 5. Shots were exchanged and forty-two-year-old Washington State Trooper Troy Giddings was shot in the arm, but he was able to drive himself to hospital in Sedro Woolley, six miles from the interstate, where he was treated and released.

The police then received word of a fatal collision at mile post 238 near the Bow Hill Creek Road exit of I-5. They found an SUV on the central reserve. The driver had been shot and killed.

Then, at 4.30 p.m., twenty-eight-year-old Isaac Zamora drove up to the sheriff's office in Mount Vernon, Washington, and turned

THE BODY COUNT CLIMBS

himself in. He was the killer, he said and his spree, it seemed, had come to an end. But there was more to come.

At 5 p.m., one of Zamora's neighbours came home to find two workmen dead in her house in the 1950 block of Silver Creek Road. Zamora had also stabbed a sixty-one-year-old man, who had escaped and run for help. While the wounded man was being treated in hospital, the police found the dead body of a woman in his house. In all, six people were dead and four wounded.

Zamora had only been released from jail on 6 August, less than four weeks before. The custodial sentence was to be followed by one year's community supervision. Zamora had been checking in to the Department of Corrections regularly and had passed drug and alcohol tests on 21 August.

Now, he was charge with twenty felony counts, including six counts of aggravated first degree murder that could bring the death sentence. At his first hearing, Zamora mumbled 'guilty, guilty, guilty, guilty' as he entered. 'Can you hear me? I'm guilty,' he told Skagit County Superior Court.

The public defender Keith Tyne said that it was clear that Zamora had significant mental health issues and he would defend him on that basis. But Zamora's mother, Dennise, did not want to hear any excuses made for her son.

'I'm not one of those people who say he's not guilty by reason of insanity,' she said. 'He is guilty by reason of insanity.'

Friends said that, on good days, Zamora could be charming, warm, creative. He could be strange, too. He would walk aimlessly around the streets alone at all hours or cause trouble by grabbing a fistful of paper towels from the gas station and let them trail out of the window of his car as he drove off. More recently though, they said, he had become increasingly scary.

For ten years, he had shown signs of serious mental illness. Meanwhile, he racked up dozens of criminal charges. While none of them were for particularly violent offences, the state Department of Corrections had put him on a programme for offenders with mental illness. However, Zamora would not continue his mental health treatment, despite his family's urgings, and the law prevented them from forcing a twenty-eight-year-old to do so.

After he had been released from jail, his parents threw him out and he began sleeping in the woods, then on neighbours' lawns. The week before his murder spree, he told neighbour Shirley Wenrick: 'I am going to get even with them.'

However, that Saturday, he had agreed to the first of two evaluations he needed to qualify for state mental health programmes.

There was little in Isaac Zamora's early life that indicated that he would become a spree killer.

'I remember a sweet, sweet, sensitive mama's boy,' said Rachel Brown who grew up with him.

His mother cosseted him. She taught him at home, rather than sending him to school, while his father took him to Boy Scouts. Neighbour Christie Howard remembered him as a quiet, unremarkable kid. At worst, she recalls, he 'was one of the kids who rode his obnoxious motorcycle through the property'.

Then, when Zamora was about 14, the family home burned down and they lost everything. They struggled to cope both emotionally and financially.

'It's all we can do to keep the electricity on,' his mother wrote in the family's bankruptcy petition.

Zamora was deeply affected. A doctor diagnosed he was suffering from post-traumatic stress disorder and said that his problems would subside after puberty. But they did not.

The family stayed in the neighbourhood, putting a large mobile home on the lot. Around the same time, Zamora stole his mother's gun to sell it to another teenager. He was later charged with filing a false report after telling police that a stranger had stolen it.

But there was hope. Around 2000, he met Connie Hickman when they were both working at a healthcare facility.

'He was kind,' she said. 'He was easy to talk to, easy to get along with.'

They began going out, but he had trouble holding down jobs. He would make threats and start fights over 'things that never happened', Hickman said. Initially, she attributed this to Zamora's drinking and drug use. He was arrested for the possession of marijuana and cocaine.

In 2001, Zamora and a friend were accused of stealing an outboard motor. Zamora refused to cooperate with the Mount Vernon Police Department who were investigating the theft. But his mother got into his room by climbing through the window of the trailer, found the outboard motor and turned it over to police. Zamora pleaded guilty to second degree theft and served three days in jail plus seventeen days community service.

After several suicides attempts, Zamora told Connie Hickman that he was hearing voices. In 2003, Hickman and Dennise Zamora took him to a Whatcom County hospital, saying they feared for their safety. He was diagnosed with both bipolar disorder and schizophrenia, and was held there for several weeks before being discharged.

'The night after he was released, he called me and said, "I want to go back",' Hickman said. But when he returned to the hospital, they refused to admit him.

Eventually, Zamora was admitted to another hospital. During that stay, court records show he bit an orderly who was trying to restrain him. Criminal charges were filed, then dropped.

'The next day, they discharged him,' Hickman recalled. 'How could they put him out on the streets when it was obvious the man had some issues?'

After being released, he stopped taking his medication. He did not have a job and could not afford to pay for it. His behaviour became increasingly volatile. Hickman dropped him, changed her phone number and took out a protection order. But he was able to track her down through friends. One night, after she bumped into him on the street, a wine bottle came flying through her apartment window. On another occasion, the windscreen of her roommate's car was smashed.

Eventually, Hickman fled the state, but he tracked her down, leaving rambling messages on relatives' answering machines. She managed to elude him. Meanwhile, his family tried to get him back into treatment. But his trouble with the law continued.

In May 2007, he flew into a rage when a friend refused to go hiking with him. Zamora was charged with second degree malicious mischief after he hurled a concrete block through a friend's car, damaging it. In a statement to Skagit County Court, the friend described Zamora as 'devious and vengeful'.

On 15 May, he pled guilty. As part of his sentencing, he agreed not to possess firearms, although neighbours said he had a collection of six or seven guns. On his release, he was supposed to undergo a mental health evaluation, but he did not have the money to pay for one. The Department of Corrections had to go to the state's Department of Social for the money. All this took time and by the time the first of his evaluations was scheduled, it was too later for Zamora and his victims.

Although he still had enough sense to hand himself in after the spree, by the time he got to court his condition had deteriorated further. At a second hearing on 5 September, he said: 'I kill for God. I listen to God.'

He was charged with the fatal shooting of Skagit County Sheriff's Deputy Anne Jackson, forty; neighbours Chester Rose, fifty-eight, and Julie Binschus, forty-eight; carpenters David Radcliffe, fifty-eight, and Greg Gillum, thirty-eight; and motorist Leroy Lange, sixty-four, who was driving on I-5. He was also accused of stabbing his sixty-one-year-old neighbour and of shooting Binschus' husband and two other motorists. Those victims survived.

Chapter 15

School's Out

At 11.10 a.m. on 20 April 1999, nineteen-year-old Eric Harris drove into the student car park at Columbine High School in Littleton, a suburb of Denver, Colorado and parked his 1986 grey Honda Civic in a space assigned to another student. Harris, who avowedly hated Jews, gays and blacks, together with his co-conspirator seventeen-year-old Dylan Klebold, had chosen that day deliberately because 20 April was Hitler's birthday.

Soon after, Klebold arrived in his 1982 black BMW and parked in a space assigned to another student in the south-west senior car park. Their two cars flanked the lower level of the school cafeteria. This was their target.

Harris got out of his car and spoke to a fellow student, telling him to flee the school because he liked him. The student took his advice. He was the only person they would willingly spare that day.

A few minutes later Harris and Klebold walked into the school cafeteria, carrying two large duffel bags containing enough explosives to kill most of the students who would be arriving for lunch. They put the bags on the floor beside two lunch tables where they did not look out of place among the hundreds of other backpacks and bags scattered around the cafeteria. Each of the duffel bags contained a 20 lb propane bomb timed to explode at 11.17 a.m. At that time there would be 488 students in the cafeteria.

The two would-be assassins then returned to their cars to watch the explosion. According to their home-made videotapes, they planned to shoot down anyone who escaped the blast. Their cars were also fitted with bombs and timers set to explode when, afterwards, the two had gone back into the school on a further killing spree.

Around the same time, there was a small explosion in a field on the east side of Wadsworth Boulevard three miles from the school. Harris and Klebold had left two backpacks there, filled with pipe bombs, aerosol canisters and small propane tanks. These were diversionary devices, aimed to keep the police and the fire department from tending the devastation at the school. However, only the pipe bombs and one of the aerosol canisters exploded, but this had set the grass on fire. The pair, it seems, were inexpert bomb-makers and, fortunately, the devices in the cafeteria failed to go off. But that did not mean that those at Columbine High School would get off scot-free.

At 11.19 a.m. Harris and Klebold were seen standing together at the top of the west steps, the highest point on the campus. Both were wearing black trench coats, which hid 9 mm semi-automatics, and were carrying a duffel bag and a backpack. A witness heard one of them say: 'Go! Go!'

Then they pulled shotguns out of their bags and began shooting at the other students around them. The first shots killed Rachel Scott and injured Richard Castaldo who were eating their lunch on the grass outside the school library. Lance Kirklin, Sean Graves and Daniel Rohrbough were hit by gunfire as they came out of the side door of the cafeteria. Five other students, who had been sitting on the grass to the west of the stairs, tried to run and were shot at. They made for the outdoor athletic storage shed. Michael Johnson suffered gunshots wounds, but managed to take cover there with the others. Mark Taylor was gunned down.

Klebold then descended the stairs to the cafeteria and shot Daniel Rohrbough again at close range, killing him instantly. He also shot Lance Kirklin a second time, again at close range, but Kirklin miraculously survived.

After entering the cafeteria briefly, perhaps to ascertain why the bombs had not gone off, Klebold rejoined Harris at the top of the stairs. Meanwhile Harris shot at Anne-Marie Hochhalter, hitting her numerous times as she sought cover in the cafeteria. Then the two gunmen were seen lighting explosive devices and throwing them into the car park, onto the school's roof and onto the grassy slope outside.

Witnesses then heard one of the gunmen shout: 'This is what we always wanted to do. This is awesome!'

By then, the police had begun to get calls. The cafeteria supervisor called Jefferson County Sheriff's Deputy Neil Gardner – the community resource officer at Columbine High School – on the school's radio, saying he was needed in the rear car park of the school. And a student called 911, reporting that a girl was injured in the lower south car park of the high school.

'I think she's paralysed,' the caller said.

This message was conveyed to Deputy Paul Magor, who was on his way to the grass fire on Wadsworth. Deputy Gardner was pulling onto Pierce Street and heading south to the student car park when he heard the call 'Female down in the south lot of Columbine High School' and switched on his siren. Motorcycle patrolman, Deputy Paul Smoker also heard the call and radioed in that he was on his way.

At 11.24 teacher William 'Dave' Sanders and staff members Jon Curtis and Jay Gallatine went into the cafeteria and told the students to get down under the lunch tables. Meanwhile teacher Patricia 'Patti' Nielson saw two male students outside the west entrance of the school carrying what she thought were toy guns. She assumed that they were being filmed as part of a school video production. They were making a bit of a commotion and she was on her way to tell them to knock it off when Harris fired into the doorway. Nielson was showered with shards of glass and metal fragments, cutting her knee, forearm and shoulder. Student Brian Anderson was also injured by flying glass when he was caught between the inner and outer doors and Harris fired at the doors in front of him. Although injured, Nielson and Anderson managed to flee into the school library. At the time Harris and Klebold were distracted by the arrival of Deputy Gardner, who pulled up in the lower south car parks with his lights flashing and siren wailing.

As Gardner stepped out of his patrol car, Harris fired about ten shots at him before his rifle jammed. Gardner returned fire. For a moment, Gardner thought he had hit Harris. But seconds later Harris was firing again, spraying bullets around the car park, before he retreated into the school through the west doors.

In the cafeteria, the students were painfully aware that they were involved in something much more serious than a school prank. They fled up the stairs to the second level with Sanders directing them to safety down the hallway to the eastern exits. Hiding under the counter in the library, Nielson made a 911 call to report that shots were being fired. Smoke began wafting in through the doorway and she yelled at students to take cover under the tables.

At 11.25 Jefferson County Sheriff's Office put out a general alert: 'Attention, south units. Possible shots fired at Columbine High School, 6201 South Pierce, possibly in the south lower lot towards the east end. One female is down.'

Gardner also called for backup.

'Shots in the building,' he radioed. 'I need someone in the south lot with me.'

Then he sent a 'Code 33'. This means 'officer needs emergency assistance.'

Jefferson County Deputies Scott Taborsky and Paul Smoker soon arrived at the west side of the school and began to attend to two wounded students lying on the ground near the sports fields. Then Smoker saw Gardner down the hill to his right, brandishing his service revolver. A gunman carrying a semi-automatic rifle appeared inside of the double doors and Smoker yelled a warning to Gardner. Harris then leant out of a broken window and began shooting. Smoker returned fire and Harris disappeared, but Smoker could still hear gunfire from inside the building.

By this time, Harris and Klebold were in the main north hallway and began firing at students there. They were laughing.

Student Stephanie Munson and another student walked out of a classroom into the hallway. A teacher yelled at them: 'Run! Get out of the building!' They fled towards the eastern exit. Stephanie was hit in the ankle, but both managed to escape, finding safety across the street in Leawood Park.

Klebold chased some other students down the hallway, stopping near the phone booth in the main lobby. A student on the phone with her mother looked to see the sleeve of a black trench coat and a 9 mm pistol shooting towards the main entrance. She dropped the phone and hid in a nearby restroom. Klebold then ran back towards the library. When she could hear no more commotion from the hallway, the girl went back to the phone. She whispered to her mother, telling her to come pick her up, then escaped through the east doorway.

Dave Sanders was on the second level outside the library when he saw a gunman coming down the hallway. He had turned to run away when he was shot. However, he managed to crawl to the science block where teacher Richard Long helped him into classroom SCI-3. There, two Eagle Scouts, Kevin Starkey and Aaron Hancey, gave him first aid. Despite their efforts, Sanders died.

Outside Deputy Magor set up a road-block on Pierce Street where a teacher and students told him that someone was patrolling the school with a gun. Then he received a report that hand-grenades had gone off at the school. These were, in fact, pipe bombs which Harris and Klebold had set off in the hallway. They threw two more down the stairwell into the cafeteria and shot up the hallway outside the library.

Students were now running from the school, seeking safety behind Taborsky's patrol car on the west side. They told the police that gunmen were inside the school randomly shooting at people with UZIs or shotguns and throwing hand-grenades. The younger of the two gunmen was of high-school age. The other was 'taller, a little older'. Both were wearing black trench coats.

By this time, deputies were ringing the school and more reports of injuries were coming in. Deputy Gardner was requesting emergency medical help to the west side when he came under fire from a large calibre weapon.

Harris and Klebold then walked into the school library and told the students to get up. When Harris shot up the front counter, one student, who was hiding behind the photocopier, was injured by flying splinters of wood. Another student was killed before Harris and Klebold began a gunfight out of the windows with the police. Then they turned their attention back on the students in the west section of the library, killing four and injuring four more. They shot out the display cabinet near the front door before firing their guns into the east section of the library, injuring five and killing three. Reloading, they went into the centre section where they killed two more students and injured another two. One gunman yelled: 'Yahoo!'

In the seven-and-a-half minutes the gunmen were in the library they killed ten people and wounded 12 more. Those who survived did so only because they hid until they were evacuated later by a SWAT team: Patti Nielson managed to hide in a cupboard; another teacher hid in the periodicals rooms; and two of the library staff sought refuge in the library's TV studio. At 11.30 Jefferson County Patrol Deputy Rick Searle began evacuating the students, some of them wounded, who had taken cover behind Taborsky's patrol car. He moved them to a safe location at Caley Avenue and Yukon Street south-west of the school where a triage point was set up. At the south end of the student car park Deputy Kevin Walker provided cover for the students fleeing from the cafeteria. Through the windows on the upper level, he saw one of the gunmen wearing a 'white T-shirt with some kind of holster vest', leading to speculation that there were three gunmen. They didn't know that by this time, Harris had discarded his black trench coat.

Fearing that the situation was escalating, Deputy Magor radioed the Sheriff's Office that more help was needed. However, the Denver Police Department was already on its way as one of its officers had a son who was a student at Columbine and had called his father.

Minutes later, the Jefferson County SWAT team, led by Lieutenant Terry Manwaring, was on its way to the high school, and they quickly established a command post at the corner of Pierce Street and Littlewood. Jefferson County Sheriff's Office also requested assistance from other agencies. Soon after the Colorado State Patrol turned up and took up positions on the north-east side of the school by the tennis courts. Firemen from Littleton's fire department also arrived on the scene.

At 11.35, the gunmen shot their last victim. Then they made their way down the hallway to the science block. On the way, they peered in through the windows of the classrooms, making eye contact with some of the students. Several students saw Harris and Klebold shooting into empty rooms. Then they taped an explosive device to the door of a storage room. But they did not appear to be particularly eager to get into any of the locked classrooms or harm anyone. They could easily have shot the locks off. The gunmen seemed to have run out of steam. Their killing spree was over. Now their behaviour appeared directionless.

They rained down more pipe bombs into the cafeteria from the library hallway above – but everyone there had already either been killed, escaped or taken cover.

As explosions blew out windows of the cafeteria, several students ran out and took cover behind cars, while Deputy Walker covered them with his gun. He radioed in that he had students with him, but he did not have any safe route to get them out of the car park. Meanwhile a 911 call was received from seventeen students hiding in the kitchen who feared that the gunmen were closing in on them.

Around thirty students who had been in the library made their escape out of the west doors and took cover behind patrol cars. Deputy Taborsky, who was with them, reported that he had been told the gunmen were wearing bullet-proof armour and that one of them was probably 'Ned Harris'. His informant had more than likely said 'Reb', which was Harris' nickname.

Harris and Klebold went down into the cafeteria. On the stairs, Harris knelt down with his rifle resting on the banister and loosed off several shots into one of the large 20 lb propane bombs hidden in a duffel bag in an attempt to set it off. He failed. Klebold then walked over to the bomb and fiddled with it.

The two of them took swigs from the water bottles on the school lunch tables. A witness who was hiding then heard one of the gunmen say: 'Today the world's going to come to an end. Today's the day we die.'

Klebold threw something at the propane bomb. The cylinder failed to detonate, but there was a small explosion. This started a fire which set the sprinklers off.

Denver Metro SWAT arrived and Jefferson County Undersheriff John Dunaway authorised the SWAT teams to enter the school. A live bomb was found nearby at Wadsworth and Chatfield, and at 11.55 the command post received a description of one of the suspects. He was, informants said, 'Eric Harris, five foot ten inches, thin build, shaved blonde hair, black pants and white T-shirt, light blue gym backpack.'

Ambulances turned up to evacuate the wounded. Meanwhile Harris and Klebold wandered around the cafeteria, inspecting the damage they had done. They looked in the kitchen then went back upstairs to the library.

The media had already picked up on the story and the command post asked Channel Seven's news helicopter to pick up a deputy so he could make an aerial survey of the school. Meanwhile fire department paramedics attempted to rescue Lance Kirklin, Sean Graves and Anne Marie Hochhalter who were lying wounded outside the cafeteria, but the gunmen fired on them from a second-storey library window. Deputy Walker spotted the muzzle flashes and returned fire, and Deputy Gardner joined in the firefight. With the Denver police officers providing cover fire, the paramedics managed to retrieve the three wounded teenagers from in front of the cafeteria. The gunfire from the library window then stopped and Deputy Gardner seized the opportunity to evacuate the fifteen students who were taking cover behind his patrol car. More students made their escape through the side door of the cafeteria.

At 12.06, the first SWAT team arrived at the east main entrance to the school. Manwaring then ordered Deputy Allen Simmons to take his Jefferson County SWAT team into the school through the southeast doors. Using the fire truck as a shield, Manwaring led the second team around to the west side where students had reported gunfire. However, by this time, Harris and Klebold were already dead. They shot themselves shortly after that last gunshot was fired from the library window.

The triage point at Caley and Yukon began dispatching the wounded to hospital by ambulance and helicopter. Bomb squads from Jefferson County, Denver and Arapahoe County were soon supplemented by bomb experts from Littleton Fire Department, the Bureau of Alcohol, Tobacco and Firearms (ATF) and the FBI. They began examining the diversionary device found at Wadsworth and Chatfield, while others were sent to the homes of the suspects.

At the command post on Pierce, there was a report that a gunman and hostages were at the front door of the school. Moments later a lone student came out of the main door and ran to the fire truck. The teenager was quickly checked for weapons. It was soon ascertained that he was not one of the gunmen.

On board Channel Seven's news helicopter Sergeant Phil Domenico conducted a survey of the school's roof. Meanwhile extra staff were called into Jefferson County Sheriff's Office which was now inundated with calls from the world's media. Parents and students were gathered at Columbine Public Library and Leawood Elementary School, where counselling was provided.

An officer from the Salvation Army called in a mobile kitchen, which was set up near the command post. Then the Red Cross moved into

Clement Park to provide food and water for the media, students and their families.

At 12.17, a young man wearing a white shirt and black pants and carrying a .22 rifle and a knife was seen walking along the west side of the school. He was arrested at gunpoint. The rifle was found not to be loaded. The young man said he had heard of the shooting on the TV and came to 'help the police'.

At 12.20, a student being interviewed on TV said that the gunmen shot one of his friends. He said that there were two or three gunmen and they were armed with automatic weapons, sawn-off shotguns and pipe bombs. He did not know their names but said they were part of Columbine's 'Trench Coat Mafia'.

The Trench Coat Mafia was a loose association of disaffected youths who complained that they were harassed by the school's athletes – the 'jocks'. There were some twenty-one members. Some worked at Blackjack Pizza with Harris and Klebold. Others knew them from school. They identified themselves by wearing black trench coats or dusters. In the senior class photograph of 1999 several members – including Harris and Klebold – posed as if pointing weapons at the camera. Some had actually seen the pipe bombs and CO_2 cartridge devices Harris and Klebold had made, but none of them knew that they were planning the Columbine killings.

By 12.35 Manwaring's SWAT team was at the back entrance of the school on the west side's upper level. Their first objective was to rescue two students lying in front of the west doors. The fire truck inched up to the west doors and two Denver SWAT members grabbed Richard Castaldo. They laid him on the bumper of the fire truck then Deputy Taborsky transferred him to his patrol car and rushed off to seek medical assistance. Next the SWAT team tried to retrieve the bodies of Rachel Scott and Daniel Rohrbough.

The situation remained chaotic as, at this point, no one knew the gunmen were dead. Students inside the school continued calling 911, their parents and the media with reports of hostage taking, explosions and as many as eight roaming gunmen as well as the sound of gunshots coming from the auditorium, the gymnasium, the music rooms, the science block, the business wing and the school's offices. The firing they heard probably came from SWAT team during their rescue of Richard Castaldo at the school's upper west entrance. Meanwhile other schools in the area were 'locked down' with no one being allowed to enter or leave.

Manwaring's SWAT team then asked for a floor plan of the school. Soon after, another ten-man SWAT team from Jefferson County, under the command of Sergeant Barry Williams, arrived at the command post on Pierce Street.

Deputy Simmons, leader of the first SWAT team that entered the school on the east side, called for back up. The school covered 250,000-square-feet and had numerous rooms and hallways that had to be searched. It was full of students hiding, some injured and in need of assistance.

Two SWAT marksmen positioned themselves on the rooftops of houses on West Polk Avenue, the first street south of the school. From there, they had a clear view over the south car park, the cafeteria and the library windows.

Williams' team moved into position at the north-west corner of the school, directly opposite the point where Simmons' team had entered the building. They planned to make their way to the cafeteria and the library. But a bomb blocked the outside west doors to the upper level and the library and instead they had to enter by breaking the window of the teachers' lounge, situated next to the cafeteria.

Inside they were met with the deafening noise of fire alarms and the flash of strobe lights from the burglar-alarm system. Tiles were hanging from the ceiling and water was pouring under the door to the cafeteria. Along with the noise of the sprinklers, there was a hissing sound, which Williams feared might be coming from a broken gas pipe. Quickly his team cleared the kitchen and back storage areas, evacuating the staff and students hiding there through the teacher's lounge window. They evacuated another sixty students from the school's music area on the second floor, and continued to work from west to east on the lower level while Simmons' team worked from east to west on the upper.

Simmons' team evacuated thirty students and faculty from south-facing classrooms on the upper level before meeting up with Williams' team who had, by then, cleared the stairs to that level. The teams continued to receive warnings from the squads inspecting the diversionary bombs placed on Wadsworth that there could be similar devices planted throughout the school, and also received messages from the marksmen that there were more injured students on the upper levels, including one student who had hung a banner out of the window with 'I bleeding to death' scrawled across it. A little later three males dressed in black clothing and matching the general description of the gunmen were arrested in a field north of the high school. They were not Columbine students and identified themselves as the 'Splatter Punks'. They insisted they had shown up at Columbine High School out of curiosity. Cleared of any involvement in the shooting, they were released.

At 2.30, President Clinton was scheduled to make an announcement about the American economy. Instead he talked about Columbine.

Ladies and gentlemen, we all know there has been a terrible shooting at a high school in Littleton, Colorado. Because the situation, as I left to come out here, apparently is ongoing, I think it would be inappropriate for me to say anything other than I hope the American people will be praying for the students, the parents and the teachers and we'll wait for events to unfold and there will be more to say.

In the library, Patrick Ireland, who had been shot, slipped in and out of consciousness. Nevertheless, he slowly made his way to the west window. Sergeant Domenico in the news helicopter spotted him trying to climb out of a broken window on the second floor. Below him was a concrete sidewalk. Deputies sent in an armoured vehicle with members of the Lakewood SWAT team, caught the young man as he fell.

Williams' team eventually reached the library where there were numerous bombs among the survivors. Among the twelve dead they found there were two males who had self-inflicted gunshot wounds to the head. They matched the description of the gunmen.

By 4.45, the SWAT teams had finished their search of Columbine High School. The building had been cleared and the two suspects were dead. The massacre at Columbine was over. Between them Harris and Klebold had killed twelve of their schoolmates and one teacher, and injured twenty-three others. More fatalities followed. Greg Barnes, a seventeen-year-old school basketball star who saw his best friend killed in the shootings hanged himself the following year and Carla Hochhalter, the forty-eight-year-old mother of a girl injured in the shootings, shot herself.

But Columbine, it seemed, had got off lightly. According to their video-taped testimony, Harris and Klebold had planned to blow up a sizeable part of the school with hundreds of students in it. As it was, it took several days for the authorities to find and defuse all the bombs they had left behind them. The bomb-making factory in Harris's garage had turned out over thirty pipe bombs as well as the two larger propane devices. Examining their diaries and websites, the police learned that the two had originally conceived a larger plan to reduce the school to rubble, and then blow up a plane over New York City. They wanted a film made of their story and discussed who should direct, Steven Spielberg or Quentin Tarantino.

The couple left videotapes to assist with the production. In one, Harris appeared with a sawn-off shotgun he called Arlene, after his favourite character in the video game *Doom*.

'It's going to be like fucking *Doom*,' he said. 'Tick, tick, tick… Ha! That fucking shotgun is straight out of *Doom*.'

They also idolised Hitler. But the motivation for the killings was not clear. One survivor recalled that Harris and Klebold ordered all the jocks who had harassed them to stand up.

'We're going to kill every one of you,' they said.

But in the end the killings were blindly indiscriminate.

'They shot at everybody,' said one survivor, 'including the preps, the jocks and the people who wore Abercrombie and Fitch clothes. But it would be hard to say they singled them out, because everybody here looks like that. I mean, we're in white suburbia. Our school's wealthy. Go into the parking lot and see the cars. These kids have money. But I never thought they'd do this.'

In another tape, Harris and Klebold also thanked Mark Manes and Phillip Duran for supplying them with the weapons they needed.

Manes was later charged, under a Colorado state law forbidding the sale of handguns to a juvenile, with selling an Intrac TEC-9, 9 mm pistol to Klebold for $500. He was also charged with possession of a dangerous or illegal weapon as he had gone shooting with Harris and Klebold in March 1999 and had fired one of their sawn-off shotguns. He supplied one hundred rounds of 9 mm bullets to Harris on the night of 19 April. Pleading guilty, he was sentenced to six years in a state penitentiary.

Phillip Duran, who worked with Harris and Klebold at Blackjack Pizza, was charged with brokering the deal with Manes and handling a sawn-off shotgun during target practice. He was sentenced to four-and-a-half years in jail. Both Duran and Manes denied any knowledge of Harris and Klebold's plans.

Eighteen-year-old Robyn Anderson, a friend of Harris and Klebold, also admitted accompanying Harris and Klebold to a gun show in late 1998 and buying two shotguns and one rifle, which were later used in the killings. But as the purchase had been made from a private individual rather than a licensed gun dealer, no law had been broken.

Some attempt was made to blame their parents, but both the Harrises and Klebolds seem to have provided an exemplary family life. Both boys felt remorse for their parents.

'It fucking sucks to do this to them,' said Harris on one of the tapes they left behind. 'They're going to be put through hell once we do this.' Speaking directly to them, he added: 'There's nothing you guys could've done to prevent this.'

Klebold told his mother and father that they had been 'great parents' who had taught him 'self-awareness, self-reliance... I always appreciated that.' He added: 'I am sorry I have so much rage.'

In an attempt to explain what they were about to do, Harris quoted Shakespeare's *The Tempest*, saying: 'Good wombs hath borne bad sons.'

On the morning of the shootings, just before they set off for Columbine High School, Harris and Klebold made one final videotape, saying goodbye to their parents. Klebold said: 'It's a half hour before Judgement Day… I didn't like life very much… I just know I'm going to a better place than here.'

Harris concluded: 'I know my mom and dad will be in shock and disbelief… I can't help it… That's it. Sorry. Goodbye.'

Chapter 16

Copycats

The massacre at Virginia Tech in 2007 claimed thirty-three lives, the highest death toll of any shooting incident by a single gunman in America. The perpetrator was Seung-Hui Cho, a South Korean student. He had already been accused of stalking two female students and, in late 2005, a judge declared him to be mentally ill and a danger to himself, and ordered him to seek outpatient treatment. But still he was allowed to buy a gun. Cho had two semi-automatic handguns – a 9 mm Glock 19 and a .22 calibre Walther P22.

At around 6.45 a.m. on 16 April, Cho was seen near the entrance to West Ambler Johnston Hall, a co-ed residence hall at the college that housed 894 students. His student pass should have allowed him entry only after 7.30 a.m., but somehow he got in. He went to the room of nineteen-year-old freshman Emily Hilscher on the fourth floor. Hilscher was not one of the women Cho had been stalking. She had just returned home after a night out with her boyfriend. Not long after 7.15, shots were heard. The police could find no motive for her slaying.

Resident assistant, Ryan Clark, a twenty-two-year-old senior, heard the shots and went to investigate. He too was shot and killed. Cho left the scene, leaving bloody footprints, and went back to his dorm room in Harper Hall two minutes walk away. Meanwhile a student in a room nearby called the Virginia Tech Police Department.

While the emergency medical services units rushed to the scene of the killing, Cho changed out of his bloodstained clothes and logged on to his computer to delete his email and wipe out his account. He then removed the hard drive and disposed of it, along with his mobile phone. The police thought he had thrown them in the campus duck pond – an Asian male was seen there between 8.10 and 8.20 – but they were never found. It appears that he also planned to dispose of the guns as the serial numbers had been filed down.

The police were told that Hilscher's boyfriend owned a gun. The boyfriend immediately became a 'person of interest', but it was ascertained that he had left the campus. Consequently they were not prepared for what happened next. The authorities later concluded that, if Cho had stopped after the first two killings, he might never have been caught. But he didn't.

Less than two hours after the murder of Hilscher and Clark, Cho was seen at a post office off campus where he mailed a package of writings and video recordings to NBC News in New York. The package was postmarked 9.01 a.m. and signed 'A. Ishmael'. A Virginia Tech professor in the post office said that Cho looked frightened.

Inside the package were videos of Cho outlining his extreme complaints about the world. The videos appear to have been shot at various times in a motel, a rented van and possibly his dorm room over the previous weeks. He could be seen adjusting the camera, so it is thought he was alone. There were also pictures of Cho wielding weapons and two rambling, single-spaced letters reiterating the complaints in the videos. He railed against society and how it had ill-treated him, and he posed as the 'avenger', even claiming to be a 'saviour'. His diatribe was filled with biblical and literary references, and allusions to international figures. Although delivered in a largely stream of consciousness manner, it was clearly scripted. No one he knew was mentioned in the videos. Rather, he outlined a grandiose fantasy of becoming a significant figure through the mass killing, the way notoriety clings to the assassin of a president and public figure. He also mentioned the Columbine High School killers by name. They also came up in his high-school writings.

After posting the package, Cho headed for Norris Hall, which housed the Engineering, Science and Mechanics faculties. He was carrying a backpack that contained several heavy chains, locks, a hammer, a knife, two handguns, nineteen ten- and fifteen-round rapid-loading magazines, and almost 400 rounds of ammunition.

At Norris Hall, Cho chained the three main entrance doors shut. An Asian male wearing a hooded garment had been seen practising this two days before. Cho placed a note on one of the chained doors, warning that a bomb would go off if anyone tried to remove the chains. The note was found by a faculty member who took it to the dean's office on the third floor. Over the previous three weeks, other bomb threats had been found. They had all proved to be false alarms. Nevertheless, the dean was about to call the police when the shooting started.

Students on the second floor saw Cho poke around several classroom doors, in some cases more than once. Survivor Erin Sheehan said: 'It was strange that someone at this point in the semester would be lost, looking for a class.' Then at around 9.40 a.m., Cho walked into room 206 where Professor G. V. Loganathan was teaching a class in advanced hydrology and shot and killed the professor. Saying nothing, he turned his gun on the students, killing nine of the thirteen students in the room and injuring two others. Only two survived unharmed. Hearing the shots, Jocelyne Couture-Nowak, who was teaching French in room 211, asked student Colin Goddard to call the police on his mobile phone.

Next, Cho moved across the hall to room 207, where Christopher Bishop was teaching German. Cho shot Bishop and several students near the doorway, then moved down the aisle of the classroom, shooting others. Bishop and four others died, six were wounded.

In room 211, the students tried to barricade the door, but Cho pushed his way in, shot Jocelyne Couture-Nowak and moved down the aisle, shooting the students. Again Cho said nothing. Colin Goddard was among the first to be shot, but another student, Emily Haas, picked up Goddard's mobile phone and stayed on the line while the shooting went on. Even though she was wounded twice in the head, she spoke quietly to the dispatcher, then closed her eyes and played dead.

Students attending a class in computing in room 205 heard the commotion, lay on the floor to avoid gunshots and held the door closed with their feet. Cho tried to force his way in and fired through the door several times, but no one was injured.

Cho then returned to room 207, but four survivors managed to hold the door closed. Cho beat on the door. He forced it open an inch and fired about five shots around the door, then gave up and left. He returned to room 211 and walked up one aisle and down another, shooting students, often at point-blank range. There were few places for the students to hide, except behind their desks which afforded little cover. Colin Goddard who was playing dead was shot twice more. Nevertheless, he survived. But the teacher and eleven students lay dead. Another six were wounded. The entire class had fallen victim to Cho's bullets.

A janitor saw Cho reloading his gun in the hall on the second floor and fled downstairs. Cho then tried to enter room 204 where

Professor Liviu Librescu was teaching mechanics. Librescu braced his body against the door and yelled for the students to escape through the windows. They pushed out the screens and jumped onto bushes or the grassy ground below. Ten of the sixteen students escaped this way. Librescu was then shot fatally through the door. Two students were shot trying to jump from the window. In all, four students in the mechanics class were shot, one fatally.

The massacre continued for about ten to twelve minutes. The police took nearly five minutes to gain entry to the barricaded building. When they could not break the chains, an officer shot out the deadbolt lock on a door leading into a laboratory. As police reached the second floor, they heard Cho fire his final shot. They found him dead from a self-inflicted gunshot wound to the head in room 211, where Jocelyne Couture-Nowak had been teaching French.

Cho had murdered twenty-five students and five faculty members. Another seventeen were shot and survived, and six were injured when they jumped from the windows of room 204. Cho expended at least 174 bullets. The police found seventeen empty magazines and recovered 203 live cartridges, 122 for the Glock and eighty-one for the Walther, including two fully loaded 9 mm magazines containing fifteen cartridges each. The ammunition was hollow-point, inflicting terrible injuries on those who survived. If Cho had not committed suicide it seems clear that he would have gone on shooting and the death toll would have been even higher.

Twenty-three-year-old Seung-Hui Cho was a South Korean citizen with a US green card living in Virginia. He had a troubled history. At nine months, Cho developed whooping cough, then pneumonia and was hospitalised. Doctors diagnosed a heart problem. When Cho was three, they carried out exploratory surgery. After that,

Cho did not like to be touched. Throughout his childhood, he was frail. He was extremely quiet and sweet natured, but had few friends.

In 1992, his parents moved to the US in the hope of improving their children's educational opportunities. Financial necessity forced them to work long hours. None of the family spoke English and Cho and his older sister naturally felt isolated. They were made fun of by other children, but within two years the children learnt to understand, read and write English. But Cho could not read and write Korean, which was spoken at home.

In fact, he spoke very little at home. When called on to address visitors, he would grow pale, sweat and sometimes cry. Cho grew more withdrawn and the only person he would communicate with was his sister. While his mother was sympathetic, his introspection was a constant source of friction with his father.

At elementary school, Cho would not interact with other children or participate in group activities. At break, he played alone. Despite the best efforts of his teachers, parents and the local church, Cho still refused to communicate. Eventually, his parents decided to let him be the way he was. There were, after all, no disciplinary problems and everyone saw him as a very gentle, tender and good person. Nevertheless, the school encouraged them to put Cho into therapy and he was diagnosed with severe social anxiety disorder. It was also noted that his IQ was above average.

He continued to isolate himself at middle school. Then in March 1999, when he was in the eighth grade, he grew more anxious. His therapist even feared that he might be suicidal. In April, the Columbine High School massacre occurred and Cho wrote an essay expressing 'generalised thoughts of suicide and homicide'. According to someone who knew him then, there were fears that 'he wanted to repeat Columbine'. His therapist recommended a psychiatric evaluation. This was at a key juncture in his life as his older sister – the only person he would communicate with – was about to leave home to go to college.

A psychiatrist diagnosed 'selective mutism' and prescribed an anti-depressant. Cho reacted well and the anti-depressant was stopped. But when he went to high school that autumn, his teachers found him unwilling, if not unable, to speak. Nevertheless he got good grades and he was put on a special programme for what was seen as his chronic shyness. He fought against this.

'There is nothing wrong with me,' he protested. 'Why do I have to go?'

Cho was particularly gifted in science and mathematics, and it was clear that he should go to college. A school counsellor urged that he be sent to a small college close to home, but Cho was determined to go to Virginia Tech.

His grades assured him a place, but no one had passed on his mental health records. His parents, who visited him regularly, felt that he settled in well. In his second year, he switched courses from business information technology to English and contacted a professor about having a novel published. Despite having his proposal rejected by a New York publishing house, writing became a passion. Then in the autumn of 2005, he began to write less, but what he did write was dark and violent.

The two students who shared his dorm would take him to parties, but Cho would always end up sitting in a corner on his own. Once they took him to a female student's room, where he started stabbing the carpet with a knife. After that, they did not take him out any more. Others invited him out, but he would not talk and they dropped him.

He ate, played basketball or worked out alone. Otherwise he watched videos on his laptop and played computer games, always alone. He got into heavy metal and stuck lyrics up on the walls around the dorm. Sometimes, roommates would find him burning papers.

In poetry classes, he would appear wearing reflective sunglasses and a hat pulled down over his face. When he read, his voice was inaudible. What he wrote was dark and he accused his classmates who ate meat of being complicit in the massacre of animals.

'If you despicable human beings who are all disgraces to the human race keep this up, before you know it you will turn into cannibals – eating little babies, your friends,' he wrote. 'I hope y'all burn in hell for mass murdering and eating all those little animals.'

His fellow students grew afraid of him and fewer attended poetry classes. His teacher threatened to resign if Cho was not removed from her class. Again he became more withdrawn. The college recommended him for counselling. Then the stalking started.

After the police warned him to stop, he began communicating with female students via text message, emails and Facebook. When one recipient grew fearful, the police were called and Cho was warned to stop. He became suicidal and was sent for a psychiatric evaluation. He was found to be mentally ill, but a further screening on 14 December 2005 found that, as he did not present an imminent danger to himself or others, he should not be hospitalised. However, a judge disagreed with the diagnosis and ordered outpatient treatment. This did not begin until January 2006.

In class, he did not participate and his attendance flagged. His written work continued in its dark vein. In one story, the protagonist, clearly based on himself, tells a 'gothic girl': 'I'm nothing. I'm a loser. I can't do anything. I was going to kill every goddamn person in this damn school, swear to God I was, but I... couldn't. I just couldn't. Damn it I hate myself!'

That autumn, he took a class called 'Contemporary Horror'. In the final exam, he had to analyse a horror film. He got a B. Though he continued to get good grades, he was urged, once again, to go for counselling. Cho dropped all his classes and, in the spring of 2007, began buying guns and ammunition. On 15 April, the night before the massacre, Cho made his regular Sunday call to his parents. They suspected nothing.

In the ensuing investigation, police found a suicide note in Cho's dorm room that included deprecatory comments about 'rich kids', 'debauchery', and 'deceitful charlatans'. In the material he sent to NBC, he said: 'You forced me into a corner and gave me only one option... You just loved to crucify me. You loved inducing cancer in my head, terror in my heart and ripping my soul all this time.'

A review panel at Virginia Tech concluded that Cho chose to engage in a fantasy where 'he would be remembered as the saviour of the oppressed, the downtrodden, the poor, and the rejected' because of his inability to handle stress and the 'frightening prospect' of being 'turned out into the world of work, finances, responsibilities, and a family'.

'His thought processes were so distorted that he began arguing to himself that his evil plan was actually doing good,' the panel said. 'His destructive fantasy was now becoming an obsession.'

In 2007, spree killing moved on to – of all places – Finland. At about 11.40 a.m. on 7 November, eighteen-year-old Pekka-Eric Auvinen walked into Jokela High School in Tuusula, southern Finland, and opened fire, cutting down his fellow pupils in the entrance way. The headmistress, sixty-one-year-old Helena Kalmi, called the police then ordered all students and teachers to barricade themselves in their classrooms.

Instead of seeking safety herself, she went out to confront the assailant. Auvinen forced her to her knees in the schoolyard, then shot her seven times in full view of pupils watching from a classroom window. The forty-three-year-old school nurse who went to the aid of injured students was shot and killed too.

Auvinen then began walking around the school, firing through classroom doors and shooting people at random. The victims sustained multiple injuries to head and upper body. Some had been shot up to twenty times. But Auvinen also pointed his gun at some people without shooting them. Shouting orders at students, he proclaimed that he was starting a revolution, and urged the students to destroy school property. He doused the walls and floor of the main corridor with two-stroke fuel – a mixture of petrol and oil – but he was unable to set it alight.

The police arrived at 11.55, but when they tried to start negotiations, they were answered by a hail of bullets. Soon the school was surrounded by one hundred officers, including a special operations unit. Even off-duty police officers turned up. In just twenty minutes, Auvinen had loosed off sixty-nine rounds.

The attack ended at 12.24, when Auvinen turned the gun on himself. However, the police held off storming until 1.53 p.m., more than two hours after they had first been called. Auvinen was found in a school toilet still alive but unconscious. He was taken to Helsinki University Central Hospital, but died from his injuries that evening.

In their investigation, the police confirmed that Auvinen had been a victim of school bullying for years. Born locally, he described himself on his YouTube user page as 'a cynical existentialist, antihuman humanist, antisocial social Darwinist, realistic idealist and godlike atheist'.

He had a conventional two-parent family. His father was a musician; his mother was deputy member on Tuusula municipal council. He also had an eleven-year-old brother.

One of his teachers said he was above average academically and took an interest in history, philosophy and politics – particularly extreme left- and right-wing movements. However, he had been on anti-depressants since he was seventeen. These sometimes induce suicidal tendencies as a side-effect in adolescents.

The massacre had not been long in the planning. Auvinen had only received his gun licence three weeks before the school shootings. He was a registered member of the Helsinki Shooting Club, but had only attended a single one-hour training session.

His weapon, a SIG Mosquito .22 calibre handgun, had been obtained legally and was registered to Auvinen on 19 October. Auvinen himself wanted to buy a more powerful Beretta 9 mm pistol, but his application was rejected by police. In Finland the police usually require a hobby shooter to begin with a .22 calibre weapon.

An hour before the shooting, Auvinen uploaded a home-made video called the 'Jokela High School Massacre – 11/7/2007' to YouTube. KMFDM's song 'Stray Bullet' was used as background music. This German rock metal band's track was also used on the website of Columbine shooter Eric Harris.

There were earlier indications of what he had in mind. Weeks before the shootings, he had uploaded videos of himself shooting his new gun. Many of his other YouTube videos were about other shootings and violent incidents, including the Columbine High School massacre, the Waco siege, the Tokyo sarin gas attack, and bombings during the Iraq invasion. He also fleshed out his personal profile:

Occupation: Unemployed Philosopher, Outcast
Companies: Human Race (evolved one step above though)
Interests and Hobbies: Existentialism, Freedom, Truth,
Misanthropy, Social/Personality Psychology, Evolution Science,
Political Incorrectness, Women, BDSM, Guns (I love you
Catherine), Shooting, Computer Games, Sarcasm, Irony, Mass/
Serial Killers, Macabre Art, Black Comedy, Absurdism
Movies and Shows: *The Matrix*, *A View to a Kill*, *Falling Down*,
Natural Born Killers, *Reservoir Dogs*, *Last Man Standing*, *Full
Metal Jacket*, *Doctor Butcher M.D.* (aka *Zombie Holocaust*),
Saw, Saw II, Saw III, Lord of War, *The Deer Hunter*, *True
Romance*, *The Untouchables*, *28 Days Later*, *28 Weeks Later*,
Idiocracy, *They Live*, *Apocalypse Now*, *End of Days*, *The
Shining*, *The Dead Zone*, *Dr. Strangelove*, *House M.D.* (TV),
Monty Python (TV) Documentaries Relating To History
Music: KMFDM, Rammstein, Eisbrecher, Nine Inch Nails,
Grendel, Impaled Nazarene, Macabre, Deathstars, The
Prodigy, Combichrist, Godsmack, Slayer, Children of Bodom,
Alice Cooper, Sturmgeist, Suicide Commando, Hatebreed,
Suffocation, Terrorizer
Books: *Fahrenheit 451* (Bradbury), *1984* (Orwell), *Brave New
World* (Huxley), *The Republic* (Plato), all works of Nietzsche

And he posted a rant where he tried to explain himself:

*I am prepared to fight and die for my cause. I, as a natural selector,
will eliminate all who I see unfit, disgraces of human race and
failures of natural selection.*

*You might ask yourselves, why did I do this and what do I
want. Well, most of you are too arrogant and closed-minded to*

understand... You will probably say me that I am 'insane', 'crazy', 'psychopath', 'criminal' or crap like that. No, the truth is that I am just an animal, a human, an individual, a dissident.

I have had enough. I don't want to be part of this fucked up society. Like some other wise people have said in the past, human race is not worth fighting for or saving... only worth killing. But when my enemies will run and hide in fear when mentioning my name... when the gangsters of the corrupted governments have been shot in the streets... when the rule of idiocracy and the democratic system has been replaced with justice... when intelligent people are finally free and rule the society instead of the idiocratic rule of majority... in that great day of deliverance, you will know what I want.

Long live the revolution... revolution against the system, which enslaves not only the majority of weak-minded masses but also the small minority of strong-minded and intelligent individuals! If we want to live in a different world, we must act. We must rise against the enslaving, corrupted and totalitarian regimes and overthrow the tyrants, gangsters and the rule of idiocracy. I can't alone change much but hopefully my actions will inspire all the intelligent people of the world and start some sort of revolution against the current systems. The system discriminating again nature and justice is my enemy. The people living in the world of delusion and supporting this system are my enemies.

I am ready to die for a cause I know is right, just and true... even if I would lose or the battle would be only remembered as evil... I will rather fight and die than live a long and unhappy life.

And remember that this is my war, my ideas and my plans. Don't blame anyone else for my actions than myself. Don't blame my parents or my friends. I told nobody about my plans and I *always kept them inside my mind only. Don't blame the movies I see, the music I hear, the games I play or the books I read. No, they had nothing to do with this. This is my war: one man war against humanity, governments and weak-minded masses of the world! No mercy for the scum of the earth! HUMANITY IS OVERRATED! It's time to put NATURAL SELECTION & SURVIVAL OF THE FITTEST back on tracks!*

Justice renders to everyone his due.

A spokesman for the cyber crime department of Helsinki police said that 'it's highly probable that there was some form of contact between Pekka-Eric Auvinen and Dillon Cosey', a fourteen-year-old boy arrested the month before on suspicion of planning an attack on his school in a suburb of Philadelphia. Acting on a tip-off, the police found a 9 mm semi-automatic rifle, handmade grenades, a .22 pistol and a .22 single-shot rifle at his home. Less than two weeks later Auvinen, already a member of a shooting club, was buying his first gun – a .22 pistol – and expressing interest in a 9 mm semi-automatic. The police do not believe this to have been a coincidence. The two youths are thought to have made contact over two MySpace groups, 'RIP Eric and Dylan' – a reference to Eric Harris and Dylan Klebold, who killed twelve fellow pupils at Columbine – and 'Natural Selection'.

Ten months later, the police were also investigating whether there had been any communication between Auvinen and Matti Juhani Saari, the twenty-two-year-old catering student who killed ten in the Kauhajoki school shooting in western Finland.

At about 10.40 a.m. on 23 September 2008, a man wearing a ski mask appeared in a classroom in the middle of an exam and started shooting. Then he threw a petrol bomb, setting the classroom on fire.

Apparently, Saari had entered through the school buildings via the basement and concealed himself until roughly two hundred people were assembled inside the college. Armed with a .22 calibre Walther P22 semi-automatic pistol, he walked calmly around the classroom, approaching his victims individually before shooting them. He seemed to be revelling in his actions. Some students escaped by jumping from windows. They were hindered by a river that ran behind the school and took to rowing boats to make their getaway.

After around five minutes Saari ran down a corridor and threw a petrol bomb into a language laboratory. He then shot out all of the windows in the school's main corridor and took aim at the janitor Jukka Forsberg, who escaped, ducking and weaving to avoid the shots.

At around 11 a.m., the police arrived. As they entered the yard of the college Saari shot at them and they were forced to retreat. Forty-five minutes later more police units turned up in armoured vehicles. They attempted to enter the building through the main corridor, but were forced back by black smoke.

When they finally gained entry at around 12.30, they found Saari in the main corridor with a gunshot wound to the head. They rushed him to Tampere University Hospital, where he died at 4.46 that afternoon.

Nine bodies were found in the exam room, some so badly burnt that they could only be identified from DNA and dental records. Another was found in the nearby corridor, shot down after fleeing the burning classroom. Most victims suffered multiple gunshot wounds; one as many as twenty. Eight of the victims were female students. One was a male student. All were in their twenties and were classmates of Saari's. The tenth was a teacher in his fifties. Another twenty-one-year-old woman was shot in the head but recovered after two operations. A further ten students were treated for minor injuries including sprains and cuts from broken glass. With ten dead, Saari had clocked up the highest death toll of any peacetime attack in Finnish history. But it could have been so much worse. Saari had fired a total of nearly two hundred shots, some aimed harmlessly in the air.

The male student who died was thought to be a close friend of Saari's. The pair had spent an evening out together in February 2008. A photo of them together has been circulating on the Internet, where Saari was jokingly pointing at his friend's head with his forefinger.

Two days after the killings, a friend of Saari's, named Rauno, told a magazine that he received a call from Saari at 11.53 a.m. on the day of the massacre where he confessed to having killed ten people. He calmly told Rauno that he was calling to say goodbye.

On the day of the shooting Saari uploaded a photograph of himself to the Internet. He left behind two handwritten notes in his school dormitory, saying that he had been planning the massacre for six years. His motive for the shooting was, he said: 'I hate the human race... The solution is Walther 22.'

But that is not how people remembered him. Former classmate, Susanna Keronen, said: 'He was happy, a sociable guy – there was nothing exceptional – and he got along with people well and he was not lonely. He had friends.'

The police noted the similarities between the Auvinen and Saari massacres. They had bought their guns from the same store. Both had taken photographs of themselves in similar poses. They both had been part of an Internet group, who used YouTube and Finnish social networking site IRC-Galleria. Users of this site, which included people from Finland, Germany and the US, exchanged videos related to school shootings. Jari Neulaniemi, the detective leading the Kauhajoki investigation, said that it was 'very likely' that the two men had been in contact at some point.

Although most of Saari's victims were female, the motive did not seem to be a hatred of women. Rauno said Saari had opted for a catering course so that he would be surrounded by female students. However, Saari also had told Rauno that he had been the victim of bullying in secondary school. Saari's behaviour had begun to worry Rauno over two years before the shootings. He had begun expressing a fondness for guns and an interest in the school shootings in the US. Around eighteen months before the massacre, Saari had sent Rauno a message saying that he was going to carry out a school shooting the next day. It seems that he had been seeing a psychologist in the months before the shooting.

He had bought his handgun only in August 2008. In the weeks leading up to the massacre, Saari had posted several videos on YouTube, showing him firing a handgun at a local shooting range. It was accompanied by the quote 'Whole life is war and whole life is pain. And you will fight alone in your personal war.' These are lyrics from the song 'War' by the Bavarian band :wumpscut:. Among his video favourites he included footage of the Columbine High School massacre and he listed his interests as 'horror movies, guns, sex, beer and computers'.

The police had received an anonymous tip-off about his website on the Friday before the shooting. They talked to Saari and searched his home on the day before the incident, but found no reason to arrest him as he had a temporary weapons permit. But the police did not know about another video Saari had posted on a Finnish social networking site, where he pointed a gun at the camera and said, in English, 'You will die next.' Then he fired four shots in the direction of the camera. The police said that they would have been detained Saari if they had known about this second video when they had questioned him. They also believed Saari's videos were shot by someone else, most probably the male friend Saari had murdered in the massacre.

Epilogue

We are all in danger. When we go to school or work, go out shopping or just walk down the street, a bullet aimed at random might cut us down. Nowhere is safe from the mad gunman who simply wants to kill a large number of people without rhyme or reason, before killing themselves.

There is no way we can protect ourselves against these madmen. As long as guns are available, there is no stopping them. Even in countries such as the UK where the possession of guns is strictly controlled, a large number circulate illicitly. There are few clues to why people suddenly snap and start killing. Few killers survive to tell the tale. Those who do are less than forthcoming. Sixteen-year-old Brenda Spencer, one of the few females to take to spree killing, said simply: 'I don't like Mondays.' Bob Geldof and The Boomtown Rats gave her fifteen minutes of fame in 1979.

There are some who are plainly insane – and those who claim they were told by God to kill. The Beltway killers in 2002 hoped their murderous spree would spark a race war in the United States, but one cannot impute a political motive to other random killings. Tensions in families can sometimes spark a massacre and, at one time, it seems that middle-aged employees of the US Postal Service had a particular penchant for shooting their colleagues.

Now, though, spree killing seems to be the province of young men. The massacre at Columbine High School in Colorado in 1999 has sparked a number of copycat killings. Adolescent followers ghoulishly communicate via the Internet. They dictate personal statements and offer profiles, though these juvenile ramblings do little to explain why these specific individuals turned to violence, while others survive adolescence to become ordinary citizens or simply channel their teenage angst in other ways such as heavy metal music.

The classic example of a spree killer is the sniper in the tower who killed fifteen people and wounded thirty-one in Austin, Texas on 1 August 1966. At the time, such mindless killing was associated with the Vietnam War – American ground troops had been sent into Vietnam the previous year. But although the perpetrator Charles Whitman had been a Marine, he had been honourably discharged in 1964 and had never served in a war zone. And spree killing had started long before 1965. A World War Two veteran named Howard Unruh killed thirteen in Camden, New Jersey in 1949.

Spree killing was also thought to be a uniquely American phenomenon because of the gun worship there. However, in August 1987, Michael Ryan stalked Hungerford in Berkshire, killing at random, bringing spree killing to the peace of the English countryside. Since then Canada, Australia, Finland and many other countries have witnessed spree killings on home soil.

These killers present us with a challenge. For them, it seems that life – other people's or their own – is meaningless. It does not matter how many they kill – the more the better – as they do not expect to survive. They know that their killing spree will end with either their suicide, being shot down by police marksmen or being incarcerated for the rest of their lives in a high security prison or a mental institution. Effectively, their life in any normal sense is bound to come to an end through their own actions. But this begs the question: if they want to end it all, why don't they commit suicide before they start killing others?

It's true that some have a grudge against the world. They want to kill their family, friends, school mates, work colleagues or simply other human beings for some perceived wrong the world has done them. But others are simply indifferent to their victims. They are uninterested in the lives they destroy. They don't care about the suffering of those they wound or the families they bereave.

We all go through periods where we think that the world has done us wrong, or when we are simply so wrapped up in our own concerns that we are indifferent to the fate of others. But we don't pick up a gun and start shooting anyone we see walking down the street. This book attempts to discover why this is.

This is only a selection of the world's widely differing cases – this book could hardly be comprehensive as there are many more spree killings in the world than you would imagine. By presenting the facts, what the killer did, then given as much background on the perpetrator as possible, it is hoped that these accounts will shed some light on the motive for what seems like a motiveless crime. But we must not forget the victims. They must always be in our minds. Some of these cold-blooded killers seem to crave some vicarious fame – vicarious because they are liable to be dead when their name hits the headlines. But it is the victims, not the killers, who should be memorialised. It is their life and potential that has been snuffed out for no discernable reason, except that they were in the wrong place at the wrong time.

Though it is all too easy to imagine that any one of us could pick up a gun and go on a killing spree, we are far more likely to be victims. At any time, anywhere, you, your friends or loved ones could be shot down or injured at the whim of one of the numerous gunmen who stalk this planet.